THE
NATIONAL
RAILWAY
COLLECTION

THE
NATIONAL
RAILWAY
COLLECTION

Collins
8 Grafton Street, London W1
1988

William Collins Sons & Co Ltd
London · Glasgow · Sydney · Auckland
Toronto · Johannesburg

First published 1988
© National Railway Museum

British Library Cataloguing In Publication Data
The National railway collection.
1. Railroads—Great Britain—Equipment
and supplies
I. National Railway Museum
625.1'00941   TF57

ISBN 0-00-218215-7 Hardback
ISBN 0-00-218256-4 Paperback

Set in Palatino by Ace Filmsetting Ltd, Frome, Somerset
Printed and bound in Spain by Cronion S.A., Barcelona

Contents

Preface

This is a book about Britain's railway heritage as reflected by the collections of the National Railway Museum based at York. It is neither a definitive history of railways in Britain nor a balanced and comprehensive overview; rather, it is a selective dip into the past inspired by the objects and artefacts which the British nation, either by accident or design, has put in the care of its major institution devoted to the preservation and conservation of the British railway story.

It has been written entirely by those who have had these precious objects in their care since the Museum opened in 1975. Consequently, it is something of a personal document, reflecting the opinions and preferences of those who are looking after the collection. I do, nevertheless, apologise to them for having, at times, savaged the size of their contributions; but I hope the book still contains the sort of variety and specialized knowledge which truly reflects the nature of its authorship.

The writers' names appear with their contributions. In thanking them, it would be quite wrong to exclude the names of those 'in the backroom' who also helped to put the book together: the vast picture research was undertaken almost single handed by John Edgington of the library staff; the preparation of the pictures themselves, many dozens of which were taken for the book, was almost wholly under the control and supervision of Christopher Hogg and his Studio staff, Lynn Patrick and Ronnie Hodsdon; and not least, the all-essential typing from preliminary drafts to final copy was tackled by Elizabeth Culyer in the Museum office who, on one incredible occasion, produced no fewer than 24,000 words of final copy in a single working day! My thanks go to them all.

D. Jenkinson
Editor
York, 1988.

Introduction

by Dr J. A. Coiley, Keeper of the National Railway Museum

This book describes and illustrates the National Collection of historical railway relics, the majority of which are kept at the National Railway Museum in York. To appreciate fully the richness of the collection, it is necessary to consider much more than the highlights of the locomotives or the Royal carriages, important and striking as these may be. The collection reflects the broad technical and commercial interests, as well as the character, of the private railway companies at their zenith: signalling, civil engineering, shipping, docks, warehousing, hotels, catering and road distribution. Intense competition encouraged self-promotion and the stamping of the company name or initials on artefacts as diverse as dog tickets, clothes brushes, route guides or even the head of a copper nail.

Although this volume is much more comprehensive than the Museum Guide, it can only describe a selection of the material in the different collections. Without pre-empting the description of them by my colleagues, it is important to explain something of the background to the collections and the operation of the Museum past, present and future.

Historical Background

The story of the development of the British National Collection of railway relics has been well told before.* The first independent actions led to significant acquisitions by the Commissioners of Patents in the 1860s, including *Puffing Billy* (built 1813), *Rocket* (1829) and *Agenoria* (1829), all of which were later acquired by the Science Museum. Some of the private railway companies then took action, initially for the benefit of their own business and staff, and later for more altruistic reasons. The London & North Eastern Railway (one of the 'Big Four' railways created by amalgamation in 1923) opened the first museum in this country devoted exclusively to railways, at York in 1927, following the celebrations to mark the centenary of the Stockton & Darlington Railway in 1925. After nationalization in 1948, the newly created British Transport Commission appointed a Curator for Historical Relics, the late John Scholes. Working with a consultative panel formed from representatives of leading railway societies, he did much to secure a rich collection of material for a new Museum of British Transport, which opened in 1962–3 in a former bus garage at Clapham in south London.

In the mid-1960s the British Railways Board (which succeeded the BTC as the body responsible for the railways of this country) decided that it no longer wished to be responsible for the collection of historical relics displayed in its museums at York, Clapham, Swindon (opened in 1962) and Glasgow (opened in 1964), the last two being operated by local authorities. In consequence the Transport Act of 1968 contained clauses transferring responsibility for railway relics to the Department of Education and Science which meant, in effect, the Science Museum. Since the latter had no

Museum on the Move: a complete train of the Museum's restored catering vehicles was sent on a 2500 mile tour in 1979 to mark the centenary of railway catering. Named the 'Centenary Express' it is seen here leaving Hereford for Shrewsbury on 15 September pulled by one of the Museum's own preserved steam locomotives – former GWR 4-6-0 No 6000 *King George V*, at the time based, on loan, at the Bulmer Steam Centre, Hereford.

Britain's Transport Museums (George Allen and Unwin, 1970), *Dandy Cart to Diesel* (HMSO, 1980).

The original *Rocket*, displayed at the Science Museum, London, in its final configuration.

room at South Kensington for the collection the British Railways Board was also charged with the provision of a new museum building. After much debate about its location – since this was to be a national museum and hitherto all these had been in the capital city – the old motive power depot at York was chosen. The decision was based on a number of factors, including the availability of a suitable site and buildings with rail access, the pre-eminence of York as a large railway centre in its own right, the city's role as a tourist centre and its relative proximity to large centres of population with good rail and road communications. Work started on the building in 1973 and was completed in time for the scheduled opening on 27 September 1975, exactly 150 years since the opening of the pioneering Stockton & Darlington Railway.

The new Museum comprised the refurbished motive power depot with a new roof covering and floor, and along one side a viewing balcony which also doubled as a gallery for small exhibits. The two original turntables were retained in an operational state and directly connected to the British Rail network via sidings across a car park. The outside of the building was clad with blue engineering bricks, giving the appearance of a new building. New construction included an office block with lecture theatre, library and restaurant as well as other services such as workshops and photographic studio.

The large exhibits comprised an amalgamation of those previously displayed at York and Clapham, together with notable examples which had become available since those museums were effectively completed: locomotives such as *Green Arrow*, *Evening Star* and North Eastern Electric No 1 of 1904 and rolling stock such as the Midland six-wheel carriage of 1885 and the Great Northern six-wheel brake-van of 1887. Another significant new exhibit was the sectioned rebuilt 'Merchant Navy' 4-6-2 express locomotive of the Southern Region.

Other revised exhibits included the Weatherhill and Swannington winding engines, both of which could now be demonstrated in motion, and the re-erection of Stephenson's Gaunless Bridge in a more natural position outside but unfortunately not yet over water. While the exhibits in the Main Hall also included representative signalling and civil engineering displays of largely technical content, the new balcony display summarized the impact of railways on the social and economic life of the country by means of an extensive display of small objects and an audio-visual presentation. A new gallery near the Museum entrance afforded space for a display of prints, paintings, posters and photographs.

This was the starting point for the first visitors to the Museum and for its new staff. Still in store at the old railway museum were many smaller items awaiting classification, restoration and conservation. Elsewhere, many locomotives and carriages were in store on British Rail premises or on loan to other museums or the larger private railways. Besides running the Museum – which received over two million visitors in the first

Separated by almost a century of development, Furness Railway 'Coppernob' No 3 and LNER *Mallard* make a striking contrast both in form and colour. In the background can just be distinguished Midland Compound No 1000 and former LMS 4-6-2 *Duchess of Hamilton*.

twelve months compared with the expected half million – an early task for staff was to secure further storage space close to the Museum and to plan the move to York of unrestored material located elsewhere. Fortunately a former railway freight depot very close to the Museum was found and acquired in 1976. This building so resembled a station train shed that future possibilities for exhibition were immediately apparent; but despite this extra accommodation it was still not possible to house many of the larger objects already on loan, and this situation still obtains.

Collecting Policy, Past and Present

The following ten years have seen the continuation of these basic tasks and the development of plans for the future. To help planning, the principal aim of the Museum has been formulated as follows: 'To illustrate the history of railways and railway engineering in the British Isles from the beginning of the Industrial Revolution to the present day and to look at some of the probable future developments'. Secondary objectives include the need to look at the railway industry apart from its links with British Rail, and in the overseas activities in particular; and the case for acquiring, or at least displaying on a temporary basis, modern prototype or experimental equipment from British Rail or the railway industry.

This was a wider remit than that of the former British Rail-owned museums and it has been successfully fulfilled in several ways. The Museum has received on loan from the Ffestiniog Railway the first Beyer Garratt type articulated locomotive, built in Manchester in 1909 for Tasmania. The Chinese government has given the Museum a 4-8-2 locomotive, built in 1935 at the Vulcan Works, Newton-le-Willows, Lancashire for working out of Shanghai. In 1978 the experimental gas-turbine-powered advanced passenger train was acquired. The first unit for the Tyne and Wear rapid transit system was placed on short-term loan in 1979, and in 1985 the prototype High Speed Train power unit became part of the collection.

Whilst slowly developing the Museum to meet these overall aims, consideration has been given to the relationship of the National Railway Museum to the rail transport collection at the Science Museum. Opportunities for change at South Kensington are far more limited, but it has been agreed that where possible the emphasis in London should focus on the important railway technical developments on a worldwide rather than a purely national basis. For this reason the Science Museum is directly responsible for the French Nord 4-6-0 locomotive at present operational, with an appropriate French-built carriage, on the Nene Valley Railway at Peterborough.

Besides broadening the scope of the National Railway Museum, the balance of the collection has been improved by the addition of more modern item, such as

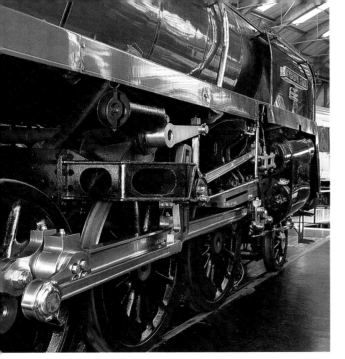

Machinery of motion – the last steam locomotive built for main line service in Britain, 2-10-0 No 92220, *Evening Star*.

The smoothly modern but still very impressive lines of the 1941 built Royal Saloon No 798 for HM King George VI.

diesel-electric and electric locomotives and electric multiple units, with a suitable diesel-mechanical example to follow. Further examples of ordinary rolling stock have been acquired to balance the carriage collection against the already pre-eminent Royal saloons, further examples of which have also been added since 1975. A wider variety of other material has been secured as well, especially signalling and permanent way items, which include two examples of early semi-automated machines for work on the track. It will be some time before even a selection of this material can be displayed. Indeed, because of its specialized nature, some of this material may never be suitable for putting on display and much of it is of little interest or value to private collectors. It will, however, be carefully restored over the years with a view to making it available by appointment as a study collection. Similarly, important flat material such as engineering drawings, photographs, prints, paintings and posters also continue to be acquired. A small selection of this material is on display at any one time.

The need for such an active collecting programme to fill the identifiable gaps prompted the early drafting of an acquisition policy to suit the aims of the Museum.

Although this is quite straightforward for the larger objects, it is less easy to specify an acquisition policy for smaller objects since much depends on what is available. The whole question of acquisition policy raises interesting philosophical issues for any museum, particularly one dealing with such large objects.

Firstly, there is special emphasis on the problem facing all museums – that of finding sufficient space for exhibits *and* storage. This poses a rather more fundamental question: why are the objects being collected and how many locomotives, carriages or signals are needed to meet the aims of the Museum? This in turn focuses attention on what the Museum does with the objects in its collection; how it uses them to tell the story, or 'interprets' them to use the currently more fashionable expression. A public museum needs to relate quality and quantity to its ability to meet its objectives, if not always the enthusiasms of its visitors. So much of a technical museum, especially a transport museum, is taken up with the splendour of its prime objects that the superficial appeal, and indeed the success of the Museum, may be judged mainly on the number of these large objects, the quality of their restoration and the manner of their display. While these factors are undoubtedly important, it would be wrong if they were the only or even the main criterion for assessment. It is surely as important that the visitor grows to appreciate why the objects, especially the prime ones, are in the museum and their relevance to the history of the subject.

Factors which influence collecting policy include when the item was built, its condition and likely cost of renovation, the availability of better alternatives, whether the object is typical or remarkable by being unusual or unique, or whether it has a special history. The object may be under consideration by virtue of the owning railway, the building company, the geographical area of operation, or technical details. These factors make the establishment of an acquisition policy by no means straightforward. The National Railway Museum reaches a decision only after careful consideration and consultation, bearing in mind the holdings

of other museums and private collections. Occasionally the owners of private collections wish to dispose of them; if they contain important items that the National Collection lacks, it is important that the Museum is aware and ready to respond should the situation arise.

Acquisition of items from British Rail was facilitated by the terms of the 1968 Transport Act which granted the NRM the right to claim redundant items without cost. This makes the development of an acquisition policy all the more important because, although the Museum has enjoyed splendid co-operation from the British Railways Board since 1975, it is not practical for the Board to draw our attention to all redundant material in which we may have an interest.

A factor when considering acquisitions may sometimes be the condition of a particular object in relation to the cost of restoration. It may then be necessary to debate the

Children's study coach, water column, a small signal box and snow make an interesting light and shade pattern in the Museum's South East garden and give a valuable pointer to future outdoor display possibilities.

The c. 1965 vintage interior of preserved Pullman kitchen and parlour car *Eagle*, while quite different from those of former days, still presents a very comfortable travelling environment. Since restoration in 1978–9, this car has been regularly used for special trains, often serving food cooked in its own kitchen.

possibility of a similar object being available at some time in the future, perhaps in better condition. Alternatively, another object in better condition and/or smaller in size may present itself and still cover the same historical or technical point. Such deliberations force a realistic appraisal of any object which is being considered for acquisition by the Museum.

Even with stringent collecting policies, the facility to obtain historical items from British Rail has helped the Museum to reach the point at which only part of the entire holding is on display. Many national museums can show only a small proportion of their collections, and even that portion is often too much to assimilate in a day's visit. Nonetheless, it is important that the unseen material is saved on educational and research grounds, and that it is accessible by appointment for study.

The presentation of individual items and their relationship to the principal function of railways – the safe carriage of people and goods – requires careful thought. To take one facet of operation, the control and stopping of trains, a satisfactory explanation may entail focusing the visitor's attention on such varied items as signals, ancient wooden-bodied signalling instruments from signal boxes, a brake-van and a track-maintenance machine. But without their elucidation by diagrams, special lighting and clear prose, the visitor is unlikely to reach a full understanding of their impor-

This large scale model of a 1920s 'cabin de luxe' in the LMS steamer *Duke of Lancaster* gives an evocative impression of a past and more leisured form of travel than most people can now experience. Although intended for no more than an overnight crossing of the Irish Sea, the accommodation matches that of many a luxury liner of the day.

tance and interrelationship. Modern audio-visual techniques and the development of participatory, or 'hands-on', displays have both helped in the interpretation of the more technical aspects of the collection. The successful interpretation of the items on display may mean a reduction in the number of actual objects on exhibition

The use of models to display concepts otherwise difficult to explain is exemplified by this small diorama (1:43 scale) of a breakdown crane at work, recovering a derailed coal wagon.

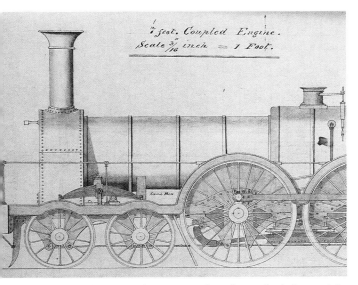

This page from Daniel Gooch's notebook (see Chapter 7) shows an exquisite drawing of a broad gauge Waverley Class 4-4-0 of 1855 – the first British example of this wheel arrangement.

and their replacement by thoughtful combinations of labels, diagrams and particularly models, audio-visual presentations and interactive displays. In this way it is hoped that visitors will be able to discover and understand the full railway story, as well as to continue to enjoy the 'fun' appeal of the locomotive and the footplate or the imagined world of the Royal train of bygone days.

This approach in turn raises the fundamental dilemma of all transport museums: the attempt to present a dynamic subject in an essentially static form. Although new techniques do much to bring the spirit of action into the Museum, there is undoubtedly no substitute for the action itself. For this reason the National Railway Museum has operated a number of its steam locomotives and, to a much lesser extent, its carriages in the past ten years. Such operations are very demanding on staff time and financial resources if they are to be carried out properly. No matter how carefully such operations are conducted, there must always be an element of risk for the locomotive or carriage involved. Some of the various issues are discussed in Chapter 8 but despite the experience acquired over the years it is probably inevitable that such operations will gradually diminish as far as this Museum is concerned. The main priority for the Museum is to ensure that all the objects are conserved indefinitely. We hope, however, that adequate film records, including the skills of operating and maintaining the steam locomotive, will be made available while such operations are possible.

An alternative to the problems of operating unique locomotives which has proved both popular and successful from the instructive point of view, has been to commission the building of accurate working reproduction locomotives. A reproduction *Rocket* was built in 1979 and the Great Western Railway broad gauge *Iron Duke* in 1985; hopefully, one or two more will follow in the years to come. The main drawback, apart from the cost, has been that *Rocket* has been in such demand elsewhere in Britain and worldwide that it has not been in York for visitors to appreciate as much as would have been preferred.

A further solution to the problem is to build accurate models. The fairly substantial $7\frac{1}{4}$ in gauge chosen for the National Railway Museum's working steam models represents a compromise between the desire for impact and authenticity and the constraints of space and cost. Although resources have not yet allowed such locomotives to operate on many days at York, they are probably far more use to the education staff with school parties. They are much more economical and practical than a full-size, main-line locomotive and rather more reassuring for younger visitors encountering a live steam locomotive for the very first time.

Since 1975 attention has also been given to fine-scale, hand-built and commercially manufactured models of many gauges and different ages, as well as the engineering models acquired from the British Railways Board. By popular request, a model railway gallery has been established featuring fine-scale layouts in 4 mm/1 ft scale (the linear equivalent of the popular 00 gauge) and 7mm/1ft (more familiarly known as 0 gauge).

There can be few bigger visual aids than this – the sectioned Merchant Navy class 4-6-2 *Ellerman Lines*, a constant attraction to visitors and a vital 'prop' for the Museum's education service (D. Jenkinson).

Future Development

In conclusion, having reviewed some of the factors affecting the collections at York, it is appropriate to consider how they will influence the future development of the Museum. The major collections have been established so, apart from additions which become redundant after regular or experimental use, there will be only limited acquisition of large objects. Smaller three-dimensional material will continue to flow for some time, as will collections of flat material.

The major developments will involve the interpretation and display of what has already been acquired. In addition to the difficulty of explaining how the railway operates in an overall view, the major omission from the exhibitions at York has been a display which captures the spirit of travel by train – the romance and glamour. A permanent exhibition devoted to this is now possible. Sufficient restoration has been carried out on the reserve collection of rolling stock and other varied objects in the freight depot acquired in 1976,* to allow an extensive development programme to fill the sidings and platforms inside the building. This will comprise a selection of symbolic trains (locomotives coupled to one or more appropriate carriages), mostly standing against platforms. Included in this display will be virtually the whole of the Museum's extensive collection of Royal saloons. On the platforms and in the carriages will be costumed figures of travellers (in some cases the actual historic 'users') and station staff reflecting the period of the appropriate vehicles with examples of platform furniture from the period(s) in question.

It is hoped that such treatment will not only capture the spirit of travel by train of the last one and a half centuries but also introduce the human aspect of railways to the Museum. Existing collections have been displayed, largely of necessity, in a manner designed to concentrate on the technical aspects of the story and, in consequence, are quite comprehensively labelled. However, it is the intention that the new exhibition will require far less conventional labelling. Group labels should, at most, suffice, and an historical and social background will also be provided by means of an optional audio-visual presentation. In due course a smaller display of freight trains will be added, while

*This building is now known as the Peter Allen Building after Sir Peter Allen, first Chairman of the NRM Advisory Committee.

Dinner is Served: the use of correctly costumed character figures can materially enhance the interpretive quality of many exhibits, as demonstrated here in the kitchen of Midland dining car No 3463.

Third class compartment interior of a Southern Railway suburban electric coach. In this case the original upholstery and woodwork was good enough to be retained and 'revived' rather than replaced with new material.

much later, visitors will be able to inspect, outside the building, many more examples of freight wagons, as well as other large objects of a predominantly outdoor nature such as signal boxes and goods cranes.

To achieve trains of the required composition in this new display, it has been necessary to make adjustments within the present exhibitions. Advantage has been taken of these exchanges to rearrange the entrance exhibition to create a 'How it all Began' display, leading into a chronological sequence of locomotives and rolling stock around the larger turntables.

At a later stage it is hoped to open the recently acquired former British Rail diesel depot building which shares a wall with the present Museum. Here, it is expected that some of the more modern large objects concerned with the technical development of railways will be exhibited. At the same time visitors may be able to see something of the restoration workshop. The timetable for this, as with the rest of the Museum's plans, will inevitably depend on the availability of money. Thus, fund raising including direct sponsorship over and above centrally provided allocations, may well prove the determining factor.

A magnificent array of silverware from railway hotels and dining cars. Every piece carries the badge of its owning company. The various styles represent changing contemporary fashion but the railways tend to follow rather than lead in this respect.

Chapter 1

Rolling Stock
by David Jenkinson

While it might be argued that the locomotives in the National Collection are the most important, striking and glamorous single group of objects, there is an equally strong case for saying that the rolling stock collection is the real key to understanding everything else which the visitor might see. For one thing, its ancestry is much older and goes straight to the heart of the railway's main function – that of moving traffic. Secondly, the understanding of the locomotive itself is incomplete without an appreciation of the task it had to perform – the movement of rolling stock. In fact, as years went by, the two areas became ever more closely interlinked and eventually were often combined in the form of self-propelled load-carrying vehicles. Nevertheless, rolling stock can claim *primus inter pares* if only because it really did come first!

Primitives

The real beginning was hundreds of years before Stephenson *et al* came so strikingly on to the scene. No one knows who invented the railway, neither when nor where. The Romans and possibly even earlier civilisations, had a primitive form of wheel guidance system embodying ruts deliberately cut into the road surfaces, but they were not railways in the modern sense because they did not employ a specialized form of matching track/wheel configuration. To search for the origin of this uniquely 'railway' feature, one has to move forward to medieval times and rudimentary mining activities. Con-

temporary historical sources (notably *De Re Metallica* by Agricola, published in 1556) make it quite clear that a form of guided wheel/track system was developing in central Europe between the fourteenth and sixteenth centuries. They were quite widespread and generally made use of a single man-powered truck, most commonly called a *Hund*, which ran on wooden track with suitable restraining methods for keeping it on the rails. This concept was particularly well developed in what is now Germany and the name *Hund*, German for 'dog' or 'hound', arose, apparently, from the noise which these vehicles made underground which reminded the miners of the sound of dogs.

Sadly little hardware from those early years survives. But the first primitive railways are so important that the Museum has commissioned not only a small model of one of the mining complexes, but also a full-size reproduction of a typical *Hund*, both based on Agricola. This is now almost the first object visitors see when they enter the main hall of the Museum.

By the end of the first Elizabethan age, a recognizable form of railway had crossed the Channel, but surviving evidence from this time is very thin on the ground. The most important item of early rolling stock in the National Collection is the Peak Forest truck of 1797 which represents a quantum leap both in size and technology from the *Hund* with which it is displayed. The railway 'truck', which we may now call it, quickly exceeded the size which a man could move so the horse replaced him as the source of motive power during the eighteenth century. The advantages of metal over wood for both wheels and track was soon apparent in

The Peak Forest truck of 1797, the oldest original complete vehicle in the collection, is now displayed against a facsimile quarry setting.

reduced frictional forces, strength and durability. The commercial benefit of railways over conventional road transport may be epitomized by the ability of a horse to shift four to six times the pay load when attached to a railway truck.

This innate efficiency of the railway, allied to its superiority over canal transport, meant that it was singularly well placed to be the means whereby the growing need for transport in the early nineteenth century was satisfied.

The First Moves to Sophistication

Railway rolling stock began to develop its quintessential 'modern' characteristics more or less co-incidentally with the evolution of the locomotive itself and at this point (c. 1830 onwards) one can witness, for the first time, the beginnings of a two-fold nature to the problem, best summarized in two words 'technology' and 'utility'. One cannot entirely separate the two strands but it is helpful to start with the technological side.

The 'primitive' railway vehicle, exemplified by the 'Hund', Peak Forest Truck and several 'chaldron' (coal carrying) wagons displayed at the NRM was a very unsophisticated object. The main objective was to keep it on the rails and most other considera-

tions were a reflection of the power source available (man or horse), combined with the obvious necessity of carrying an (inanimate) load. However, once the locomotive began to come into the equation, two factors became, more or less simultaneously, apparent.

Firstly, the greater speeds and haulage capacity of the steam locomotive began to impose considerable physical strains on the truck's strength and suspension. Secondly, the first human 'cargo' was carried in 1807 between Swansea and Mumbles, though this was a horse-drawn operation. The opening of the Liverpool & Manchester Railway in 1830 vindicated the hopes of people like George Stephenson that the fully mechanized railway could provide the solution to many transport problems probably unperceived hitherto, particularly the conveyance of people in addition to goods. If nothing else, Stephenson was the first real 'ideas' man in that his visionary views of what the railway *could* do proved truly seminal; this was to have a profound effect upon the evolution of railway vehicles as well as the locomotives which hauled them.

In essence, the advent of the locomotive forced upon the railway a need to examine such matters as springing, suspension and couplings. An inanimate cargo was hardly likely to complain on any of these counts, but the human payload was not slow to voice its views. As a result, vehicle evolution during much of the nineteenth century was largely influenced by the ever-increasing demands of the human cargo and relatively little by the requirements of freight haulage. That goods traffic was for many large railways the major source of revenue counted for little in the evolution of vehicle technology. It is therefore not entirely surprising that the residual mid- and late nineteenth-century rolling stock possessed by the National Railway Museum is heavily biased towards passenger vehicles; these were evi-

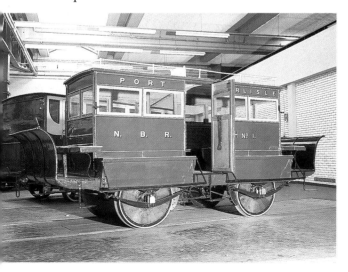

The horse-drawn Port Carlisle 'Dandy' No 1 as restored by the NRM Workshops in 1975. First and second class passengers rode inside the carriage but third class travellers sat on the outside benches.

This full size replica of a medieval German 'Hund' truck and its operator is based on data from Agricola's 'De Re Metallica' and is positioned at the entrance to the museum's main hall to illustrate the 'How it all began' theme.

A typical coal-carrying Chaldron wagon, dating from c. 1850 and originally used at South Hetton Colliery, Co. Durham.

dently seen as the true pioneers in vehicle technology when the first tentative moves were made by some companies in the 1920s towards establishing a railway collection. While it is obviously a source of regret that little in the way of freight vehicles other than chaldrons survive in the National Collection from c. 1826 to 1889 (the BP oil tank), the story of technological evolution has not materially suffered.

Paradoxically, however, the first significant vehicles which the visitor sees at the Museum entrance are freight vehicles in the form of the various chaldron wagons, so named because it carried a 'chaldron' (about $2\frac{1}{2}$ tons) of coal. Together with the dead weight of the vehicle itself, it was well within the capacity of a horse to pull. Indeed, a really strong horse could manage possibly two or three loaded chaldrons and rather more if they were going back empty to the mine.

The classic chaldron was a simple vehicle with no springs and only rudimentary wooden buffers for end protection. Some of them had brakes of sorts and the 'hopper' shape, usually associated with bottom opening doors, was determined by the gravitational unloading process when the vehicle was run on to a coal 'staithe', from which it discharged its load into the waiting canal boat or sea-going ship below. This was a

sophisticated operation, and the modern railway has not come up with any more efficient procedure for the bulk discharge of coal. Present-day hopper wagons – albeit capable of carrying vastly increased quantities of material – still discharge through bottom doors when they arrive at their usual destination, the power station. Even their shape is little more than a chaldron wagon 'writ large'.

So useful were the chaldrons that they continued in manufacture for many decades, well beyond the introduction of more sophisticated vehicles, and remained in use at collieries well into the modern period. They were not, however, well suited to main line work – the longer haulage of commodities at higher speeds between main centres of traffic. This requirement demanded consideration of such matters as brakes, wheel springing, couplings and end-shocks which largely transcended the strict passenger/freight sub-division; both kinds of vehicle received more or less simultaneous treatment, but the Museum's exemplars of the transition are exclusively passenger carrying and date from the 1830s.

Not surprisingly, the influence of the newly opened Liverpool & Manchester Railway was profound, and it is representatives from this system which, chronologically, set the scene. The Museum's L&M coaches are full-size replicas built in 1930 for

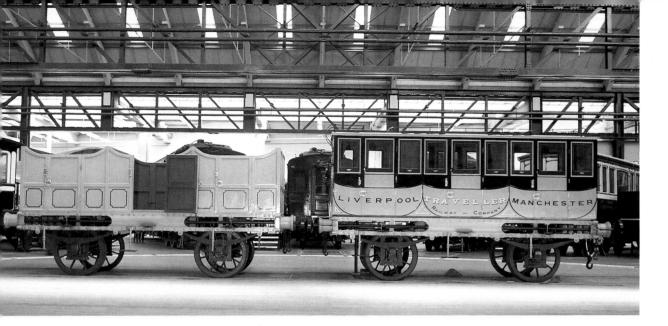

Two of the Liverpool & Manchester replica carriages, third and first class. These vehicles were built in 1930 to mark the centenary of the L&M Railway and are highly accurate representations of the typical early four-wheelers.

End view of the Stockton & Darlington composite (i.e. first *and* second class) carriage No 59 of 1845. The guard sat perched on the roof and amongst the technical developments may be noted the handbrake (lower right corner), the adjustable screw coupling, the safety chains and the sprung buffers.

First class compartment interior of S&DR No 59. Everything on view is entirely original.

the line's centenary. Nevertheless, their historic accuracy is undoubted and, save for the mandatory fitting of 'modern' brakes to allow them to run with the replica *Rocket*, they deserve careful attention for several reasons. Firstly, they show a remarkable degree of technical sophistication. The axleboxes, housing the ends of the axles, are carried in metal frame plates, known as horn-guides, which allow the axle ends to slide up and down under the control of strong leaf springs. This was an adaptation of road coach practice and proved a highly effective way of damping down the vertical movement of the vehicle, particularly when it passed over rail joints. Interestingly, this form of basic wheel suspension is still commonplace on many railway vehicles. Lubrication of the rotating axle within the axlebox was achieved by 'packing' the box with semi-solidified grease or fat. Axle friction melted this grease to provide a film of liquid lubrication which prevented overheating. It has its limitations but, for slower moving freight vehicles, 'fat' boxes were commonplace well into the twentieth century, long after they had been replaced by oil on faster moving passenger vehicles.

End shocks were taken care of by four buffers acting at each corner against a longitudinal spring set behind the bottom side members (solebars) of the carriage chassis (underframe). Once again, this method of shock-absorption became widespread on all manner of vehicles and is still a common form of fitting throughout much of the world's railways. The form of springing against which the buffers act has varied over the years and, nowadays, each buffer is usually independently sprung; but the basic principle remains sound and can be seen on virtually every modern locomotive and wagon, though superseded on some coaching stock.

The L&M vehicles were coupled together by a form of chain linkage, fitted with an adjustable screw thread, which allowed the link to be dropped 'slack' over the hook of the adjoining vehicle and then tightened up by winding in the screw link. This was done so as to bring the adjacent buffers into firm contact with each other, or even slightly compressed, thus minimizing the end movement between vehicles and making the whole train more 'solid' when moved by a locomotive – to the considerable benefit of the passenger. It also improved general ride quality by damping movement between vehicles. While no longer universal, it is still a widespread practice on passenger stock.

Unfortunately, the humble British freight wagon has rarely shared the benefit of screw couplings, even if fitted with springs and buffers. The goods wagon has usually made do with a simple 'three plain links' arrangement which could sometimes allow as much as a foot or more of independent movement between adjacent vehicles. This 'loose' coupling of most freight vehicles remained endemic in Britain until well after the Second World War, and the consequential banging and bumping of freight vehicles

into each other became the standard 'musical accompaniment' of goods train working throughout the land.

The Achilles' heel of the early L&M coaches (and their contemporary freight vehicles) was undoubtedly the braking system. For some reason, the early vehicle builders, while developing several ideas which well stood the test of time, seem to have been at a loss to know how best to stop trains efficiently. Engines often had brakes (of sorts) and this seems generally to have been regarded as sufficient. Primitive handbrakes were sometimes fitted (to secure a stationary vehicle when on a falling gradient or siding), but the idea of braking the whole train automatically from the locomotive was slow to develop and the whole of the early vehicle collection in the National Railway Museum is witness to this fact.

Oddly enough, freight vehicles were more likely to have a form of hand brake at this time than a coach – even the humble chaldron frequently had one. But this seemed to breed a sort of complacency in the mind of the goods vehicle designer, with the result that most freight stock remained hand braked with only loose couplings for well over a century. It was, if nothing else, a cheaper option. Nevertheless, these early L&M vehicles represented highly developed concepts for the time. In two particulars (springs and buffing gear) they established the 'norm' for most railways and had the screw coupling been universally adopted for *all* vehicles, the only serious omission would have been adequate braking.

That they were highly sophisticated can be appreciated by comparing them with the oldest genuine (as opposed to replica) passenger coaches in the collection, the Bodmin & Wadebridge carriages, whose precise date is unknown but which are certainly no later than 1840 and may be earlier than 1836. These are rudimentary things by comparison: axleboxes and springs are a somewhat crude imitation of the L&M type; coupling is by a primitive three-link arrangement (with links at one end only and a hook at the other!); there are no brakes and end-shocks

'Dumb' buffers and primitive couplings on the Bodmin & Wadebridge carriages.

The apparently spartan interior of the Bodmin & Wadebridge third class carriage was in fact, by 1830s standards, quite luxurious – it actually had seats!

are taken care of by 'dumb' buffers of solid wood construction, which must have proved grossly ineffective even if they afforded some sort of protection for the vehicle itself against collision damage. At the same time, however, their survival reveals the less sophisticated approach to vehicle building which was to continue for many years in the *freight* category if not the passenger field; dumb-buffered freight vehicles of a kind not dissimilar to the Bodmin & Wadebridge carriages remained commonplace for several generations.

Both of these early carriage types tell us much about the way in which passenger traffic was first seen in those early steam days and was to continue thereafter – namely the matter of accommodation by class. From the outset of mechanized communication, provision was made for three classes of passenger, differentiated by price and sometimes by service. The Liverpool &

Manchester examples offer us only the first- and third-class extremes; but the Bodmin & Wadebridge trio are fortunately a 'full house' – probably the oldest in the world. Together, they constitute all the basic elements of a train (save for the locomotive, of course) and in this respect are of greater social than technical importance.

The class differentiation of railway travel was a straight throw-back to the inside and outside travel options offered by the stage-coach on the turnpike roads. The difference was that with locomotive haulage, it was clearly dangerous to travel on the roof of a carriage, so an alternative arrangement was sought which was less elaborate for the lower orders than for the first-class passengers. Thus, the typical first-class carriage showed distinct signs of its stage-coach ancestry. Indeed, many erstwhile makers of stage-coaches turned to railway carriage.

building when the railway began to threaten their former livelihood. The typical compartment was, in effect, the inside part of a stage-coach, provided with upholstered seats facing each other and side doors. Normally, three of these often quite luxurious compartments, built as a unit, were considered the right length for mounting on a set of railway wheels. Even terms such as drop light and quarter lights were taken from road vehicles. The second class, formerly the 'outside' passenger, was given something similar but devoid of upholstery (and most windows); while the new third-class carriage was often an open-topped box on wheels with side doors for access and a few holes in the floor to take away the rain water. Third-class passengers could expect to stand all the way; in this respect, the Bodmin & Wadebridge third-class is distinctly luxurious in having seats at all. This was by no means common at the time.

This archive view from the Ransome-Wallis collection shows a train of the last four-wheel carriages built for locomotive haulage in Britain. They were completed by the Caledonian Railway in 1922 just before its absorption into the London Midland & Scottish Railway at the 1923 grouping. The picture shows the vehicles and the engine in early LMS colours during the mid 1920s.

The Evolution of the Passenger-Carrying Vehicle

The ease with which the newly emerging steam railway defeated any competition for business during the 1840s and '50s had some long-lasting and detrimental effects for much of Victoria's reign as far as vehicle design and evolution was concerned. The want of a viable alternative to the railway meant there was little stimulus to improve the vehicles themselves except, occasionally, where rival railways were in direct competition. Gladstone's Act of 1844 forced reluctant railways to put roofs on to third-class carriages and to run at least one third-class service per day to all stations – the famous (or infamous, depending on one's viewpoint) 'Parliamentary' trains. These later became the butt of music hall comedians and demonstrated a distressing tendency on the part of many railways not to do anything unless pressured into action. As usual, there were interrelated technical and social elements to any move towards change.

The four-wheel vehicle had a long innings, and even when it became possible physically to enlarge rolling stock, both by increasing the number of wheels and the

overall body size, the four-wheeler continued to find favour as long as its weight could be borne by no more than two axles. Some railways were quite notorious in this respect, especially if they held a territorial monopoly, and the primitive four-wheeler rattled along on some lines, even in the London suburbs, well into the twentieth century! In time it became tolerable, and was fitted with brakes and some form of heating, but it was no credit to some of the bigger companies that persisted with this obsolete mode. There were alternatives.

The most obvious solution, clearly stimulated by the strictly commercial demand to sell more seats and travel faster, was to enlarge the vehicle and give it more wheels and greater stability. In Britain, this gave rise to a particularly common type, the six-wheeler and the Museum's examples of this configuration are typical of those belonging to many contemporary companies. In its most characteristic form, this type of vehicle was rendered possible only by the high grade civil engineering of most British lines. The six-wheeler is essentially a rigid wheel-base vehicle with an extra pair of wheels to carry the increased weight, and it was only because the curvature of British main lines was usually very gentle that such a long wheelbase could readily negotiate 'corners'. Even then it could often generate jerks and judders because of the small, or even non-existent, lateral movement of the fixed sets of wheels. The Midland six-wheeler in the collection, built in 1883, reveals evidence of this in that its centre axle springs are hung from longer 'J' hangers than the end wheels. This effectively allowed limited lateral movement to the middle axle. This vehicle was, however, a considerable leap forward in most socio-economic respects, as will be revealed later.

The logical solution to the size problem is the one now almost universally adopted – a much longer vehicle fitted at each end with separate swivelling sets of wheels (bogies) to allow it to negotiate bends more readily. The idea was not new. It began in the 1830s in North America in an attempt to cope with

the generally less well engineered and somewhat tighter curvature of their early railways. The bogie did not cross the Atlantic to Britain until the 1870s and was not particularly widespread in this country until the last decade or so of the nineteenth century. Unsurprisingly, therefore, the *oldest* bogie passenger carriage in the National Collection is dated as late as 1897 – the East Coast third-class corridor carriage. By this time other things were changing as well.

Meanwhile, several British engineers tried to make eight-wheel coaches without bogies, and some extraordinary ideas emerged as attempts were made to cope with the curving problem without recourse to separately swivelling sets of wheels. By far the most celebrated approach – and pickled in aspic in the form of West Coast Joint Stock Travelling Post Office No 186 at the National Railway Museum – was F. W. Webb's patent radial-axle system. On this carriage, two sets of wheels (the inner pair) are fixed firmly to the underframe in the manner of a conventional four-wheeler, while the outer axles (one at each end) are each mounted on a separate frame which could move laterally relative to the coach body. It did this by means of restraining guides which caused the frame (viewed from above as it were) to describe a sort of part-circular movement whose origin (centre) was somewhere (theoretically at least) in the region of the coach centre-line. The theory was reasonable in that it kept the outer axles more or less at right angles to the line of rails, but the ride quality was not. The vehicles so fitted – and many of them carried

The six-wheeler was a highly characteristic British type and remained in use, particularly for parcels and luggage traffic, well into British Rail days. This Great Northern Railway example of 1887 is an early reflection of the increased use being made of railways by long distance passengers; apart from carrying the guard, its sole purpose was to convey passengers' luggage. It was a fortunate 'find' by Museum staff as recently as the early 1970s and was fully restored by British Rail Engineering Ltd at York in 1975.

East Coast Joint Stock corridor third class carriage No 12 of 1897. The gangway connection is prominent on the carriage end. Partially restored as early as 1952, the vehicle was given a comprehensive re-restoration in 1985–7.

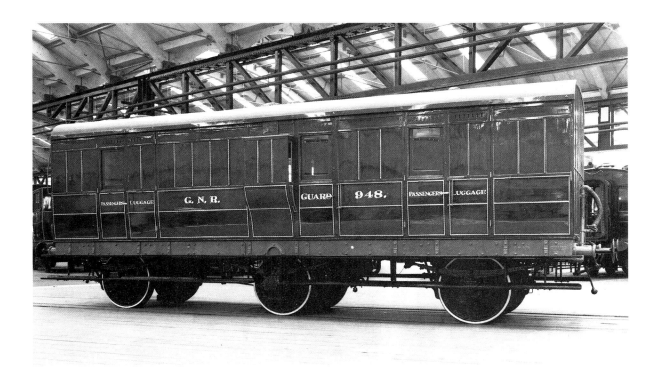

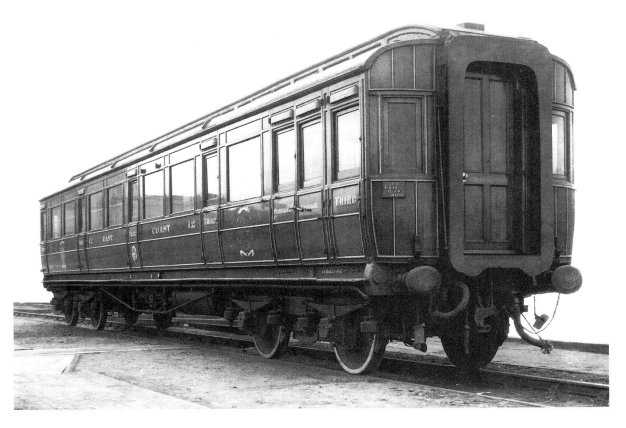

West Coast Joint Stock Travelling Post Office No 186, recently restored, showing in the main view the differences between the fixed axle (left-hand wheels) and the radial axle (right-hand wheels). The close-up view shows a detail of the spring attachment of each type of suspension.

people not post – were apparently prone to violent and alarming lurches of a quite unpredictable nature; but Webb took some time to be convinced that bogies were probably better.

The bogie was a liberator as far as carriage development was concerned, even though it took time to be established in Britain. In retrospect it is surprising that such a relatively simple device should have taken so long to become acceptable. In essence the carriage bogie is a separate vehicle to which the coach body is attached, most carriages usually having one bogie at each end. Its primary suspension (which keeps the wheel in contact with the rail) usually mirrored contemporary practice (wheel axles held in axleboxes supported by leaf springs working in horn-guides, for example). In this respect it was an orthodox four- or six-wheel vehicle similar to those discussed already; it is the bogie's attachment to the vehicle body that is so different. The bogie frame carries within it a moveable component which hangs, usually pendulum-like, from the bogie framework and which can move independently of the frame. This is called the 'bolster' and can carry its own springing and damping devices, quite independently of the primary suspension for the wheels themselves. The bolster also carries the pivoting mechanism and it is to the bolster that the carriage body is attached. This, in effect, puts a 'double' suspension between passenger and rail (the primary wheel suspension plus the bolster springing) and makes for enhanced ride quality.

The trouble is that a superficial examination does not reveal this cleverness. A typical bogie carriage seems to be sitting on top of its bogies whereas in reality it is hanging from them via the bolster. Nor is the bogie itself visually exciting but it is vital to the story. Fortunately, one of the best developments in the field – the 'double bolster' bogie designed by the celebrated Nigel Gresley of the Great Northern Railway and, later, the London and North Eastern Railway – is displayed in the museum without its body for

Close-up view of Gresley pattern carriage bogie. The primary wheel springs are at the lower right corner and prominent in the centre of the view is the 'knife edge' from which the moveable bolster hangs, free to move independently within the fixed frame of the bogie itself.

all to see. (It is particularly interesting in that it was also designed to carry the adjoining ends of *two* separate carriages on one bogie. This principle, called articulation, saves weight and money but at the cost of some flexibility in use.)

In the later nineteenth and twentieth centuries some bogies were given six wheels to spread over more axles the heavier weight of some specialized vehicles, such as sleeping and dining cars. Unlike the six-wheel carriage, the six-wheel bogie never deployed a wheelbase too long to be acceptable in terms of curvature. In consequence, railways could, by late Victorian days, contemplate 40 tons or more dead weight per carriage if carried on six-wheel bogies; some superlative vehicles resulted which are well represented in the National Collection.

Other technical advances were taking place simultaneously with the development of vehicle suspension. Although they were rather mundane, they were none the less important for the passenger. Lubrication and braking were just as vital as suspension in the quest for speed allied with safety.

The previously discussed fat axlebox had a limited ability to prevent overheating of the moving parts, should speeds become excessive. Tight-packed grease, melting under the action of friction, was not the most effective form of lubrication at speed and until a better system evolved, utilizing oil, this problem could not adequately be solved.

Higher speeds and more rigorous forms of signalling made it more and more essential that some form of reliable braking be devised. Many methods were tried but not all survive for the visitor to see. Perhaps the most curious involved the inveterate F. W. Webb who, with a business partner named Clarke, invented an extraordinary system whereby vehicles could be slowed down by means of a series of guards, distributed down the train, 'winding in' a mechanical chain system which brought the brake blocks into contact with the wheels. The story is well recorded in technical accounts, but regrettably the Museum cannot display

The interior of the broad gauge body was completely reconstructed by the Museum workshops and reveals (lower right) that the wheels projected inside the passenger compartment, concealed by a metal cover.

its absurdly naive characteristics.

Although passenger trains always had some form of braking, however simple, it took the Newark brake trials of 1875 to push the railways, reluctantly, to the view that some form of automatic (or at least semi-automatic) braking of a complete train *by the driver of the engine*, was the way forward. At the time, two systems were head and shoulders above the rest: the so-called 'air' and 'vacuum' alternatives. Although the air brake was probably the better, it was the vacuum brake which found favour amongst the majority of British systems, and it is this form of braking which is displayed on the surviving late nineteenth-century vehicles in the National Railway Museum Collection.

In simple terms the vacuum brake functions by virtue of air pressure, acting against a vacuum created in an enclosed cylinder in which a moving piston separates the air from the vacuum. When the vacuum exists, the brakes are held 'off' with the wheels free to move. Destruction of the vacuum causes the piston to move and apply the brakes through a series of mechanical linkages to the brake shoes. The vacuum itself (in fact, only a partial vacuum is required) is created

by a mechanism on the locomotive and distributed by continuous 'train pipe' from the locomotive to the rear vehicle via all the vacuum cylinders in the train. Connection between vehicles and between locomotive and leading carriage is by means of flexible hoses, conspicuously mounted on the ends of the vehicle. If the driver wishes to slow or stop the train, air is deliberately admitted to the train pipe, thus applying all brakes simultaneously. Should a coupling between vehicles fail, the connecting hoses will separate and air will naturally rush in, thus 'automatically' applying the brakes on both parts of the divided train and providing the necessary fail safe factor.

This relatively simple innovation made all the difference to the ability to operate safely at higher speeds and was only superseded on most trains in Britain during the 1970s, replaced by the more rapid acting and now almost universal compressed air brake. In simple terms these operate in a reverse mode to the vacuum system. Several railways adopted them in steam days, generally utilizing the Westinghouse principle, and vehicles which regularly operated over railways which had adopted air brakes had to be fitted with both vacuum and air systems. This was known as 'dual' braking of which the Museum possesses several examples. Although it was the vacuum system which became the 'norm' for locomotive haulage, air brakes were employed on electric multiple unit stock from a very early stage.

It was in the field of passenger amenity that the railway carriage displayed its most spectacular changes. None the less improved amenities came about slowly and were generally in response to perceived commercial advantages rather than altruistic motives; this was certainly true in the case of the great step forward precipitated by the Midland Railway in the 1870s and '80s, admirably represented by the preserved six-wheel carriage No 901. In the mid 1870s, more or less simultaneously, the Midland Railway abolished second class, upgraded third-class accommodation to equal or better than second-class quality, put third-class

carriages on *all* trains and brought first-class fares down to something like former second-class levels. To say that this unilateral action reverberated round the boardrooms of its rival systems is to put it mildly. Not only did the Midland adopt these aggressive commercial tactics to attract customers from its rivals, but it also embarked upon a programme of building new and better carriages, of which No 901 is entirely typical. Its six-wheel chassis, suspension and braking system are conventional enough and its body structure mirrored that of most railways; the revolution was inside the coach with the provision of soft upholstered third class, hardly differentiated from first class save for the lack of arm rests and somewhat smaller seat and compartment dimensions.

No doubt other railways tut-tutted about 'pandering to the lower orders', but such were the economic facts of life that once one major trunk line threw down a gauntlet, the others had to pick it up or lose business. (In this context it must be remembered that the Midland stretched from London to Carlisle and as far as Bristol in the South West, linking most major centres between. It therefore came in contact or competition with most of the really big English systems and, at Carlisle, made 'end-on' connection with three

The Midland Railway six-wheel composite (first and third class) carriage, with luggage compartment, is one of the most important vehicles in the collection.

The first and third class compartment interiors of Midland six-wheeler No 901.

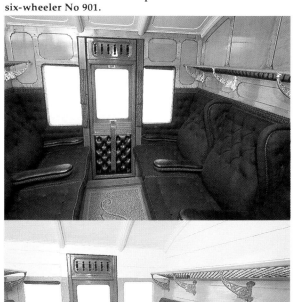

of the five principal Scottish railways. It was probably the most truly national of all the pre-1923 systems and its influence was profound.) In due course, most large railways followed the Midland's abolition of second class, but some of them took their time to remove three class facilities and second class survived on a few boat trains until the mid 1950s to make connections with existing 'three-class' services on the European mainland. Abolition of the second class explains why most trains in Britain during the first half of the twentieth century displayed first- and third-class markings for what was, in essence, our present two-class system.

As an ordinary carriage, Midland No 901 makes possibly the most important social statement in the collection, but about the same time, the first tentative moves were also being made towards more specialized and elaborate provisioning for the passenger. Again the Midland was in the vanguard, but by the 1880s and '90s most of the big companies were evolving new ideas as they fought to attract custom and provide that 'little bit extra' in the way of service. Those who argued the virtues of competition undoubtedly had much evidence in their favour during the last quarter of the nineteenth and early twentieth centuries in terms of improved carriage amenities. However, satisfaction of the demand for heating, lighting, lavatories and facilities for eating and sleeping nearly always entailed larger and heavier coaches.

Some of the first improvements were in the matter of heating. In the early days, even first-class passengers needed to wrap up well in cold weather. In due course the foot warmer began to appear – a metal water container which was filled with hot water at the start of a journey. Its efficacy rapidly wore off until replaced by a chemical mixture in the container which stored more heat in a given volume and, when shaken, reacted in such a way as still to generate heat when the chemicals were near exhaustion. Needless to say, F. W. Webb was involved in some of the developments! However, the most elegant solution to the problem was to use steam from the locomotive boiler and pipe it through the train via radiators inside the carriage. It added to the 'plumbing', increasingly visible at the carriage ends but did wonders for travel conditions. An alternative system, somewhat confined to more specialized vehicles, took the form of a self-contained, circulating hot-water system fed by a solid-fuel boiler carried in the carriage. This required the services of an attendant to keep the boiler alight and tended to be limited to such vehicles as sleeping cars and special saloons of the later nineteenth century. The Museum has but one nineteenth-century example of this system: the Duke of Sutherland's private saloon of 1899–1900. The idea continued to a limited extent into the twentieth century – for example the Wagons-Lits car of 1936 (see page 33).

The provision of lavatories, given the social mores of the time, was regarded as a somewhat delicate, nay sometimes unmentionable business. An early solution to the problem, apart from lengthy 'comfort-stops' at stations, was to separate two compartments with an intervening third section, containing a pair of lavatories, one for each adjoining compartment. Each compartment therefore had its own toilet, but it was manifestly obvious when a passenger made use of it, especially if the doorway was 'camouflaged' by a seat, as was sometimes the case. This system could go to quite ridiculous lengths and is exemplified by a bogie carriage in the collection from the London & South Western Railway and dating from 1904. This has six compartments, two for each of the three classes (the LSWR was one of the slower systems to abolish second class) and each compartment has its own lavatory! The carriage also has a section for guard and luggage, so was effectively a self-contained, one vehicle train and was a not uncommon solution to the problem of serving a separate destination not covered by the main train. Such a carriage would be attached to a long-distance train and detached at the appropriate junction from whence it would be taken, perhaps down a connecting line to its final destination.

Some railways compromised by fitting only a limited number of lavatories to which access was confined to the immediately adjoining compartments, leaving some sections unserved, not infrequently the third-class portions. It has to be said that the otherwise enterprising Midland Railway

This characteristic lavatory compartment, apart from the somewhat florid decoration of the ceramic ware, is by no means untypical of British carriage practice at the turn of the century. It is inside the former North Eastern Railway Dynamometer Car and dates from 1906.

London & South Western Railway tri-composite (three-class) carriage of 1903, fitted with no fewer than six lavatories. The vehicle was originally restored, superficially, as early as 1948 for the Waterloo station centenary and is shown here at that period still carrying its Southern Railway number 6474. In 1985–7, the NRM carried out a further complete restoration of the vehicle, including giving back its original and correct running number, 3598 and rebuilding the guard's lookout to the correct original pattern.

Queen Victoria's saloon as originally built in 1869 as twin six-wheelers with gangway connection between the two parts.

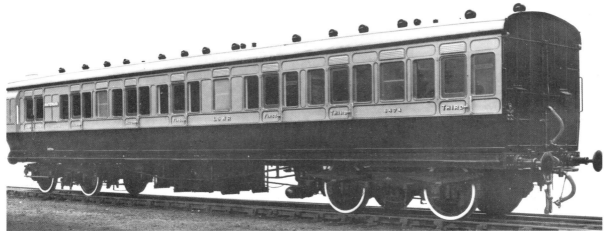

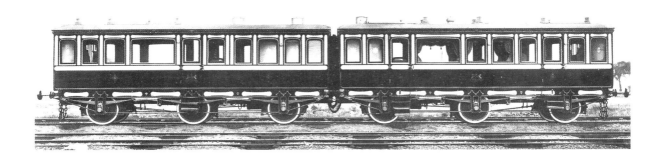

The two splendid twelve-wheel dining cars of the pre-First World War era. The Midland carriage of 1914 is virtually 'as built' but the so-called 'Royal' diner No 76 of 1900 has a newer (1938) chassis and is wearing the two-colour LMS Royal Train livery of the 1923–40 period. This was, in essence, the LNWR colour scheme (pre-1923) with LMS markings and was retained on the Royal Train at the specific request of HM King George V.

regularly adopted this 'limited provision' policy, although it did at least provide lavatories for both classes. The principal drawback was that in this situation, the traveller had to be something of a connoisseur of the subtleties of carriage design in order to be sure of meeting his bodily needs.

The logical solution, of course, was to provide a continuous passageway down the carriage, thus allowing maximum flexibility of passenger mobility within the vehicle and needing but one or two lavatories, normally one at each end. Most bigger railways began to introduce this type of vehicle, known as a corridor coach, during the 1890s; a particularly fine example, the already mentioned East Coast Joint Stock No 12, dating from 1897, survives in the Museum collection. Moreover, it is third class throughout its length. It also displays another late Victorian development – the connecting gangway between adjacent vehicles; it is the oldest passenger-carrying vehicle in the National Collection so equipped. The introduction of the gangway in Britain is generally attributed to another vehicle in the Museum, Queen Victoria's saloon of 1869; as built it was two six-wheelers connected by a gangway. The ensemble is now one unit, the two original bodies being united on a new chassis in 1895. Not for the first time, the conveyance of Royalty by rail turned out to be instrumental in producing features later adopted for all travellers, a point which will be explored later.

The interiors of the two twelve-wheel dining cars are equally magnificent. The view of the Royal dining car, shows, as well as the intricate wood veneers, a semi-formal layout of appropriate catering artefacts. The Midland view – and it is hard to believe it is *third* class – shows a more conventional dining car interior, again using 'in period' artefacts from the collection. The use of character costumed figures to enhance the exhibit was first tried out with the Midland dining car.

While the corridor itself was partly stimulated by the lavatory problem, the gangway between ordinary carriages was added principally to allow passengers to gain access to such vehicles as dining cars, of which normally only one per train was provided, if at all. The dining car is a self-contained restaurant on wheels with kitchen, pantry, food storage facilities and, of course, dining seats. Although the idea dated from 1879, when the Great Northern Railway ran the first one between Leeds and London, the real revolution in 'on-train' catering took place, like many improvements, during the 1890s when the 'continuous corridor' long-distance train first appeared. Previously, stops had been made to allow passengers to eat at station dining rooms or hampers of food, often provided by the railway company, were taken on the train.

Not surprisingly, the dining car was initially a perk for the first-class passenger, but by the end of the century, led by such major systems as the Midland, the Great Western, the East Coast route and the London & North Western, third-class passengers could also be catered for. The Museum has two prize specimens of the genre, an LNWR first class of 1900 and a Midland third class of 1914. In both cases the circumstances of their survival were fortunate.

The LNWR example was preserved principally because it served exclusively as the Royal dining car from 1904 to 1956. Apart from a new chassis in 1937–8 and a few minor internal modifications, No 76 is still very much as built. It is quite a tribute to the late Victorian carriage builders that a vehicle wholly typical of those provided for ordinary travellers was regarded as 'Fit for a King' without significant alteration. It is displayed in the Royal travel section of the Museum.

The Midland car survived until 1950 when it was spotted by the former Curator of BR Historical Relics, the late John Scholes, who had it partially restored during the 1950s. During 1985–6, the National Railway Museum took the process one step further, by giving it back its missing seats (18 out of an original 30) in replica form, along with some period costumed passengers, waiter and chef. As such it now features in the 'Travelling by Train' gallery.

Both these dining cars – and indeed the majority of their heavy, long-gone dining and sleeping car contemporaries – display six-wheel bogies. They also have a characteristic roof shape, known as clerestory, which was very popular at the time; its feature is a raised centre section running the full length of the vehicle above the main roof. This type of roof, also present on East Coast No 12, was designed to improve lighting and ventilation (the latter connected with improved heating).

Originally, artificial carriage lighting was primitive: an early device was a portable candle holder which dangerously 'hooked' on to the seat upholstery. By mid-Victorian times, oil lamps were the norm. These pot lamps, as they were often known, were generally inserted through a hole in the roof. By day, these holes were blanked out by a cover plate. Midland No 901 displays this type of fitting, though the lamps now carry electric light bulbs for Museum display purposes. It was quite an elaborate ritual to 'light-up' an oil-lit train as darkness fell. A porter would wheel along the platform a large trolley loaded with already filled and lit oil lamps while a second employee would walk along the roof of the train to remove the protective covers, catch the lamp as it was thrown up to

him by his colleague on the platform and finally place it into position. By all accounts, accidents were rare.

The advent of compressed oil gas allowed a central reservoir of fuel, usually carried in pressurized cylindrical tanks below the carriage, to be piped to lights. These usually had a 'pilot' flame, as in many present-day gas appliances. When the main gas supply was turned on, generally by means of a master control at the carriage end, all lights were fully illuminated simultaneously. These lamps were often quite tall and tended to get hot, so their common position high in the well-ventilated clerestory roof made sense on all counts. This can be seen clearly in East Coast No 12, although once again, the genuinely original gas lamp housings are now lit electrically for convenience and safety. As the name suggests, oil gas was manufactured from petroleum oil rather than coal. The carriage cylinders were filled from gas distribution points in sidings and stations.

Gas lighting had a long innings but it was primarily concern for safety which led, at the end of the Victorian period, to the introduction of electric lighting. Power storage was at first a problem, and it was only with the development of a dynamo driven by a belt from one of the carriage axles that the difficulty was finally resolved. However, compressed oil-gas cooking in dining cars was normal well into the post-Second World War period, and some gas lighting survived on older carriages.

All these improvements, most of which stood the test of time for the whole of the steam period, were made in a brief span of about three decades at the end of Queen Victoria's reign and were little changed afterwards. The carriage had 'grown up', as it were, in one generation and the National Collection fully reflects this. If, however, one had to choose one vehicle from this time which encapsulates all the developments, it would be the splendid private saloon built for the 4th Duke of Sutherland at the end of Victoria's reign. With the exception of continuous gangways, this vehicle shows some-

thing of every significant nineteenth-century carriage development, whether it be heating, lighting, ventilation, roof structure, braking or suspension on the technical side, or such things as kitchen, lavatory, dining and sleeping accommodation from the amenity aspect. To have all these features in one vehicle was certainly untypical; for it was perhaps the most opulent British example of that rare conveyance, the self-contained family saloon, available for hire by the well-to-do. It also proved highly significant in setting the interior style and amenities of all subsequent twentieth-century Royal saloons.

Exterior view of the 4th Duke of Sutherland's private saloon, built by the LNWR at Wolverton 1899–1900.

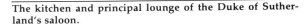

The kitchen and principal lounge of the Duke of Sutherland's saloon.

Freight Vehicles

Having taken the carriage story up to the beginning of the twentieth century, it is time to return to the freight wagon. The haulage of goods was the bread and butter of the railway business and generated more revenue for most of the bigger companies than the more spectacular passenger train. However, this importance had little or no significant influence on vehicle technology for more than a century. It is an astonishing fact that the BR standard four-wheel 16 ton mineral wagon, designed in 1950, was built along mechanical principles which were quite familiar by 1840! The fact that it was also the most numerous single design of railway vehicle ever built in Britain, to the tune of 206,444 examples between 1950 and 1959, almost says everything about the dinosaur-like rate at which the bulk of freight vehicles evolved in Britain. 'Trucks' they were often called and 'trucks' they mostly remained.

The basic British goods wagon continued to be carried on a four-wheel chassis of the type originally introduced in carriages by the Liverpool & Manchester Railway. In some respects, it was not even as good, in that dumb buffers were widely used (instead of the sprung equivalent) and couplings remained of the non-adjustable three-link type. In due course, oil axleboxes appeared on some vehicles, but they did not become standard until the twentieth century. Braking was rarely fully automatic until close to our present day; most wagons had to make do with relatively primitive hand brakes, sometimes on one side only. Its unsophisticated design was echoed by the operational methods. The sorting out of

A somewhat dramatic view, from the Museum archive collection, of that most common of all British goods vehicles – the standard 16-ton mineral wagon. There are thirty in this particular picture and it is doubtful if they ever looked as smart again!

vehicles to make up trains at their assembly points, called marshalling yards, and in goods yards was a time- and labour-consuming business. It was often performed in atrocious conditions involving danger to the shunters dashing between moving, unbraked vehicles with a pole in their hands (to couple or uncouple the trucks) and trying to grab the brake handle to slow down an over-enthusiastically propelled vehicle. Many men were killed and injured in the goods yards.

That these primitive arrangements should have survived for so long in the home of mechanized railways was a source of some bewilderment to many countries which had long adopted better solutions to the freight problem. The vulnerability of British Railways in the 1950s and '60s to growing road competition was, to a considerable degree, the legacy of the loose-coupled, unbraked four-wheel freight wagon. The problem was not fully tackled because of its sheer magnitude. Equally, there was no equivalent pressure group to the passenger, demanding improved design; it was of little concern to the customer how the railways chose to handle their traffic, providing it arrived safely and on time.

Part of the problem in modernizing methods was that both railways and private industry had invested heavily in providing suitable handling facilities such as goods sheds, warehouses, sidings and livestock pens. These were mostly designed for the four-wheel wagon. When it became apparent that larger and more sophisticated

'A picture can be worth a thousand words': these two Midland Railway Edwardian views demonstrate most graphically the total involvement of the railway with the business of moving the nation's commerce in the pre-1923 period. The general view shows Ancoats yard, Manchester with wagons from at least nine different railway companies represented, not to mention those of private owners; while the cattle pens at Derby in 1909 more than adequately portray the infra-structure of a now vanished activity – livestock conveyance by rail.

Private owner mineral wagons, at their peak, were numbered in hundreds of thousands, many bearing bold indication of their owners. Few remain in preservation but these archive views show typical examples.

quently many are better able to compete with the twentieth-century alternatives.

Viewed against this background it is not altogether surprising that the Museum's collection of freight stock lacks the comprehensiveness which characterises its locomotive and carriage holdings. Moreover, and this has to be admitted, earlier generations of 'preservers' seem largely to have ignored the freight story. In fact, it was not until the opening of the new National Railway Museum in 1975 that really systematic attention was given to this imbalance – and by then it was rather too late to fill many of the early gaps. Nevertheless, a perusal of Appendix II will reveal that the collection is now quite big and, in perhaps its most important aspect, that of cargo *variety*, is really quite good.

The basic freight vehicle is the open wagon, essentially a rectangular box on wheels in which could be loaded anything from loose coal to packing cases of machinery. The railways had hundreds of thousands of them and the private collieries (and other major users) had almost as many, if not more, frequently decorated in elaborate colour schemes bearing bold lettering advertizing the firm concerned. The open wagon was eventually categorized as either 'mineral' or 'merchandise'. The load-carrying capacity increased over the years, and construction gradually changed from all-wood structure (except for wheels and axles, etc) via wood body on steel chassis to the final all-steel versions of the 1940s and '50s, but there was little fundamental or revolutionary change.

When handling vulnerable cargo, the railways often put a protective tarpaulin sheet over the open wagons, and this gradually evolved into the permanently covered vehicle, known as a 'van'. Once again hundreds of thousands of these were built, generally following a similar line of evolution to the open wagon; but most were railway owned, rather than split roughly 50/50 between railway/private as were the mineral wagons.

These two vehicle types sprouted many

vehicles could be made, the investment in fixed assets was already so high as frequently to deter expensive modernization of these facilities to cope with bigger vehicles. Most customers actually preferred the old four-wheeler and the railways did not mind – four-wheelers were cheap to build. Moreover, there was no really effective competition, save between the railways themselves, and there was no point in one system building bigger and better wagons if its neighbours could not handle them. So the inertia built up.

Another aspect of the problem was the fact that Britain was first in the field. During those early days, there was no appreciation of how big a railway vehicle could be made and still retain stability. In consequence, British railways were built to a modest 'loading gauge', with restricted clearance dimensions between the rails and fixed structures. Other countries, developing their systems later, could learn from the British experience and make their systems capable of handling larger and more refined vehicles. Conse-

The common merchandise van was another highly typical freight vehicle type, somewhat neglected by the Museum's predecessors. Since 1975, considerable steps have been taken to improve matters but much restoration work remains to be done and this archive view must serve to represent one type which has managed to escape the slaughter. The continued simplicity in terms of brakes, suspension and couplings, was characteristic of most British freight stock until the 1950s.

Despite its traditional appearance, a 'fully fitted' goods van was an altogether more sophisticated vehicle and this fine large scale model of a North Eastern Railway fish van shows many of the significant differences, in particular the automatic brake hoses and the adjustable screw couplings. It still has a conventional handbrake lever but was perfectly capable of higher speed operation than the common loose coupled type.

The NRM's preserved and restored cattle wagon No B893343. Built by BR in 1951 to a basically GWR design, it still reveals traditional thinking in vehicle building. It does have automatic brakes and was one of the vehicles used in the very last traditional livestock working on British Railways. The 'XP' branding denotes suitability for higher speed.

Mineral traffic has always been a staple railway freight operation. This archive view shows an inter-war train on the LNER, prominent in which are four high capacity coke wagons of a type preserved by the NRM. A former North Eastern Railway mineral locomotive similar to the type shown here is also preserved by the Museum.

specialized variants for particular cargoes: livestock vans, vans for perishable cargo, refrigerated and insulated vans, milk vans, parcels vans, banana vans, etc. Many of these types are represented in the collection but most of them betray their common ancestry. Open wagons also spawned specialized types where a particular traffic could be defined without the need to consider the 'standard' goods yard. For mineral traffic, for example, the large four-wheeler was operated direct from coalfield to user. The Lancashire & Yorkshire and Great Western railways (both big coal carriers) developed some quite large four-wheelers for this purpose and the North Eastern Railway built trains of high-sided, high-capacity coke wagons for trans-Pennine use between the North East and the Furness district. An excellent example of one of these vehicles features in the collection.

The importance of iron and steel business to the railway is reflected in special long-wheelbase wagons developed for such things as metal tubes and rods. Bogies eventually appeared underneath especially long wagons designed for carrying loads like steel girders. In turn, these evolved into vehicles with a depressed centre section for the carriage of large items of machinery

varying from power station generators to complete tramcars! Examples of these specialized vehicles all feature in the collection.

Amongst the more unusual types of vehicle were elephant trucks, circus wagons, theatrical scenery vans, carriage trucks (for conveying horse-drawn vehicles) and, in a later generation, aeroplane vans. The railways had common carrier obligations and, provided the load itself would not foul the fixed lineside structures, the system proved capable of handling the most unusual cargo from time to time.

Another particularly important traffic, and one still very much handled by the railway, was that of bulk liquids, especially oil related products, and the Museum has a fine collection of tank wagons, stretching from an 1889 BP vehicle to a modern 100 ton petroleum tank. Most intervening stages are represented, including a 1937 built six-wheeler for bulk milk traffic, fitted with a 'glass-lined' tank.

Within all this variety, and much more has gone unmentioned, certain categories were considered sufficiently valuable to merit passenger train speeds. This required more sophisticated suspension, braking, coupling and, in some cases, heating and ventilation. Vehicles in this category became generally referred to as 'non-passenger coaching stock', and many of them did look more like carriages than freight wagons. The Museum has a good range of these vehicles too, oldest of which are the nineteenth-century Travelling Post Offices (TPOs), one being a replica

A pair of characteristic archive views of the sort of unusual loads quite regularly handled by the railways in their heyday. They are from the Midland and London & North Eastern Railways respectively.

A good, preserved example of the depressed centre or well trolley wagon, BR No 900402, code named 'Flatrol' and built in 1949. Capable of carrying a 40 ton load it is shown in semi-close-up with the front end of its load (former Tasmanian Railways narrow gauge Beyer-Garratt articulated locomotive, on loan from the Ffestiniog Railway). Of particular interest is the 'Instanter' three-link loose coupling with a 'variable length' centre link.

Three typical tank wagons as preserved by the NRM. From left to right they are: BP Oil Tank No 512 (1889), National Benzole Oil Tank No 2022 (1954) and ICI Liquid Chlorine Tank No 47484 (1951). All three were restored by sponsorship from their original owning companies.

of the pioneer 1838 vehicle and another the eight-wheel, radial chassis West Coast TPO. The speedy conveyance of mail was always important and the railways quickly demonstrated their ability to produce a quantum improvement over the road system. As a result, mail trains or part mail/part passenger formations soon achieved the importance they retain today.

The TPO was, as its name suggests, a complete mail service on rails. It was equipped for *en-route* sorting, along with an ingeniously clever mechanical system whereby mail could be dropped from or picked up by the moving train. This was effected by nets and hanging brackets which are displayed and explained on West Coast No 186. It even had a public posting box on the side, removed before the train started. Another interesting feature on this vehicle are the end gangways; not only are they the oldest such examples in the collection (revealing the very early importance of intervehicle mobility on mail trains) but they are also offset to one side in response to the interior layout of the vehicle. The only essential difference (other than form of construction) between this vehicle and its successors operated by British Rail a century later, is the lack of pick-up/delivery apparatus. This facility was withdrawn in 1971 because of the greater ease, economy and mobility of bringing all the mail by road to the stopping points of the mail trains.

Non-passenger coaching stock was not, however, confined to mail. Such perishable commodities as meat, fish and milk were often consigned by passenger train to ensure speedy transit, and many of the vehicles for such traffic were built to cope with the extra speed of such services.

Milk was an early candidate for preferential treatment and could be carried in either milk churns or bulk, which has already been mentioned. Churn traffic was a common feature until almost the end of the steam period, and the Museum possesses a fine example of such a vehicle – a Great Western Siphon van, the word 'Siphon' being a telegraphic code name. Often the size of passenger carriages, these vans were built in four-, six- or eight-wheel (bogie) configuration and were fully up to high-speed standards, sometimes including gangways.

Special too were vehicles designed for horses and prize cattle. The conveyance of expensive pedigree animals was, from an early stage, recognized as a form of revenue which might attract a higher price structure than the 'cheek by jowl' method adopted for flocks of sheep or herds of 'beef on the hoof' whose ultimate destination, reached by means of the humble cattle wagon, might well be a slaughterhouse!

Thus, there developed a special form of vehicle designed for the carriage of the more privileged four-footed species. It even had space for 'en route' fodder and a travelling groom. Curiously, the latter was never regarded by the railway as a 'passenger' per se(!) but, at least, he did have a seat, a light and, sometimes, warmth. These vehicles were built well into the BR period and the Museum's two examples, a horse-box and a special cattle van, both date from the 1950s. It would have been more interesting had one of them been of an earlier age; but even so it is fortunate that the basic *type* has survived.

Later, when the railways insisted on road coaches travelling 'empty', there developed the carriage truck, originally open topped but later, for more valuable cargo, becoming

This archive view of a sister vehicle to the preserved TPO No WCJS 186, LNWR No 35, shows the arrangement of pick up nets and delivery brackets, known as 'traductor arms' used for 'on the move' collection and delivery of mail. The coach is fitted with conventional bogies.

Interior view of the letter sorting racks on preserved WCJS No 186. Note the offset door (left, background) to allow room for the letter racks yet still permit staff movement between vehicles.

covered with a roof and looking exactly like a large goods van. However, the ends of the van had double doors so that the vehicle could be loaded over the buffers from a special loading bay. So important was this traffic that many railways insisted that at least one empty horse-box and carriage truck should always be located at principal stations, ready for immediate use. Eventually, the term 'carriage truck' began to encompass the carrying of motorized vehicles and sometimes became known as a motor car van; the principle remained the same and led to the modern Motorail car-

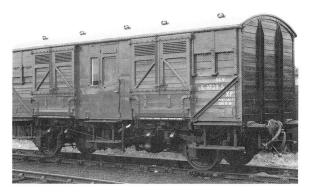

Special Cattle Van (SCV) No S3729S of identical type to the example preserved by the NRM. The freight vehicle ancestry is obvious but note the attendant's compartment in the middle. At the time of writing, the Museum's example awaits restoration to its original (1951) condition.

carrying service. Again, the Museum collection offers examples of these types of vehicle, both from the pre-nationalization era. The older of the two is an LNWR open carriage truck dating from 1908 and which remained in use for over forty years; the newer is a Great Western motor car van (code named 'MOGO') from the mid 1930s.

Of all the various specialized vehicles, whether for freight or other use, the most characteristic type was the brake-van. Regardless of the specific kind of traffic all trains had to carry a travelling guard – whose nomenclature is self-descriptive and goes back to road coach days when he did, genuinely, guard the coach, often with a firearm! One of his principal duties was to ensure the safety of the whole train, especially the brakes; it is the guard, not the driver, who is ultimately in charge of any train. The driver takes instructions from his guard, save in modern cases where driver only trains are permitted, and this is only allowed when, amongst other essential requirements, the braking system is entirely 'fail safe' should anything befall the driver.

The guard rode in a special vehicle at the back of the train which could be braked from within the vehicle – hence the term brake van, or sometimes 'guard's van'. These vehicles, primarily but not exclusively used on goods trains, made a few concessions to creature comforts and usually had a solid-fuel heating stove, a desk at which the guard could maintain his journal, a few bench-type seats and rudimentary lighting. During the cold night hours in winter, they were often the cosiest and warmest places in mar-

An early example from the archive collection of the carriage of motor cars by rail on a conventional 'flat' wagon. In due course, the NRM hopes to stimulate this scene with a genuine vintage car and a purpose-built carriage truck.

By the time of publication, the NRM's preserved ballast brake, LMS No 197266, should present a similar appearance to this 'as built' view of No 197263, photographed in 1932. The large, almost marine-like wheels for lowering the 'ballast ploughs' are visible at each end.

Preserved Matisa tamping machine No 74/007. The projecting spade-shaped extensions are forced down (mechanically) into the stone ballast at the side of the track and then vibrate the ballast into its correct position.

Preserved North Eastern Railway steam breakdown crane No CME 13, built in 1907. This exhibit is in working order and, since 1975, has been in use on the North Yorkshire Moors Railway. The wagon at the far end is known as the crane 'runner'.

shalling yards, and many are the half-frozen railwaymen who have sought refuge with the guard to gain some warmth and sustenance before a goods train departed and they had to get on with the task of making up the next one.

Naturally, the Museum has several of these distinctive vehicles, ranging from a typical, wood-built late nineteenth-century example of the London & South Western Railway to a very substantial mid 1930s bogie brake-van of the Southern Railway, fitted with rather more running refinements, including automatic vacuum brake. The last brake-vans for British Railways were built in 1962 and one of the Museum examples is the LNER design on which the final BR version was based.

Another interesting species of brake-van, again typified by a 1930s example, this time from the London Midland & Scottish Railway, was utilized with track maintenance trains. This van, variously referred to as a 'ballast' or 'plough' brake, has snowplough-like fixtures below the floor which could be lowered, by the guard, to just above rail-top level. They were used to spread the newly laid stone ballast across

the whole width of the track when track relaying took place, the ballast itself being carried in special open wagons, often of hopper shape, from which it is discharged on to the newly laid track.

Mention of this operation serves as a reminder that not all railway vehicles were for revenue traffic. Unlike the road haulage industry, where provision of the right-of-way falls on to the general taxpayer, the railways have to maintain their own infrastructure out of revenue. This has always been the case and, in consequence, a wide variety of specialized vehicles has been developed over the years. It would be physically impossible for the Museum to have saved examples of every variant, but its holding is reasonably catholic, ranging from a very early hand-operated crane of 1850 to some very modern, semi-automatic track-maintenance vehicles of a kind similar to those in use on the modern railway. Of this particular group of exhibits, perhaps the most spectacular are the steam breakdown cranes and the locomotive testing vehicles.

Accidents, even on such an ultra safety-conscious system as a railway, will always happen and railway vehicles, especially locomotives, are usually heavy. Since accidents of even a minor nature usually block the line for traffic, it is important that the railway possesses large mobile cranes capable of shifting almost any impediment. They were usually moved to the scene of the 'mishap' (as the railways euphemistically called such incidents, however serious) by a locomotive and were accompanied by vehicles carrying tools, equipment and, of course, personnel. The centre-piece of the breakdown train was always a steam-operated crane of which the Museum's NER example, dating from 1907, is not only reasonably typical but is still in working order. Interestingly, breakdown cranes were usually manufactured not by the railway but by specialist outside contractors such as Cravens or Cowans-Sheldon.

Longevity was a characteristic of much railway equipment and, in retrospect sometimes an Achilles' heel; but there is no prima facie reason why something should be scrapped because it is old. A particularly good example of durability is one of the Museum's locomotive testing vehicles, the NER dynamometer car of 1906 which was not only still capable of recording *Mallard*'s record-breaking exploits of 1938 but remained in service until replaced in 1951, a very different era with very different locomotives from those it was first designed to test. Its interior equipment, always a source of fascination to visitors, has all the solidity and permanence of most Edwardian railway equipment, but it is a tribute to the sophistication of the early twentieth-century railway that its equipment should prove so relevant and durable.

Durability was a principal reason why the

A 'through the window' view of LNER (ex-NER) Dynamometer Car No 902502, showing a wonderful array of vintage test equipment.

basic railway vehicle – especially on the freight side – changed little until more or less the end of the steam era. Increasing use was made of more 'modern' structural materials (usually metal replacing wood) and vehicles got bigger and heavier. Some freight vehicles, but not many, received automatic brakes and tentative attempts were made to run these as set trains at higher speeds to improve transit times. Any goods wagon carrying automatic brake was known as a 'fitted' vehicle and, if present in a train, had to go behind the engine, thus permitting the driver to augment his braking power; but examination of a fairly typical BR period example of the type, for instance the 1960 banana van, will reveal how little the basic concept had changed.

For this reason, and many others, some discussed in this survey, the railways encountered severe problems when faced with growing road and motorway competition, particularly in the 1950s and 1960s. 'Small consignment' traffic and 'part wagon-load' cargoes quickly succumbed to the greater flexibility of the lightweight motorized van which could, and did, literally 'go anywhere' and it was not long before other traditional sources of revenue 'dried up'. Away went the fish trains and the livestock services, along with the early morning milk train and many others until in 1969, for the first time in a century, freight revenue fell below that of the passenger services.

The radical modernization of freight vehicles is too recent to be able to predict what the future may hold; it is certainly too soon for the Museum to have many examples. However, it is possible to see that the railway will tend to concentrate on those traffics for which it is now best suited – long-haul, high-speed transit of broadly homogeneous cargoes. These seem likely to fall into far fewer and more tightly defined categories.

Part of the technical response to the problem of modernizing services has been a resolution of the vexed question of braking; modern freight stock can now move fast with full and automatic brakes. This has largely dispensed with the need for a brake van and, if the train still carries a guard, he now rides in the locomotive if the train is fully braked. The loss of many small goods yards has meant that the hindrance to larger vehicles has largely gone and the new generation of freight vehicles is generally much bigger and capable of carrying very heavy loads. The Museum's Phillips petroleum tanker, built as recently as 1970 and having an all-up weight of 100 tons, is characteristic of the modern freight vehicle, while important steps on the way are represented by the 1962 Speedfreight wagon (for container movement) and the Presflo wagon of 1961 for the bulk carriage of cement powder.

A 1960 built BR Banana Van No B882583 as preserved by the NRM. These vehicles emerged at the very tail end of what might be called 'traditional' wagon construction in Britain, but they were automatically braked and capable of 'express' speeds.

The 'new look' in freight vehicles, Phillips Petroleum 100-ton tank wagon No PP85209 was built as recently as 1970 and presented to the Museum in fully restored condition by the original owners in 1984.

Twentieth-century Passenger Stock

The story of the passenger vehicle was left at the end of the Victorian period. Since most of the ideas for future development were established before the twentieth century, the process since then has been more evolutionary than revolutionary. Largely because of the successful concepts of the later nineteenth-century carriage designers, the twentieth century has concentrated on refinement and improvement, which has produced some of the finest and most beautiful railway vehicles owned by the Museum.

Within this broad generalization, a few specific trends can be seen, all of which are well represented in the collection. Firstly, a specialized form of passenger operation began to develop, best summarized in the phrase 'self-propelled'. The success of the street tramway at the start of the twentieth century provided fierce competition to the railway in the short-distance field; to counter this, the railway began to investigate cheaper options than a set of carriages and locomotive. Early efforts were exemplified by the 'steam railmotor' – a very small steam locomotive built integrally with a single passenger coach. The Museum possesses but one example of this mode which was converted into a saloon carriage quite early in life. It's restoration will require substantial funding and is by no means certain.

The problem with the steam railmotor was bound up with its partial success in generating traffic. More passengers meant adding an extra carriage or two; but the small self-contained power unit, chosen for its economic virtues, could not cope with the additional load, so the railmotor tended to be confined to lightly used routes and vanished from the scene quite quickly.

To move larger numbers of people on suburban lines, electrification turned out to be the most effective if not universally adopted method, and the Museum has a good cross-section of important steps in this direction. The earliest is a 1914-built example for the LNWR (painted, however, in its later colour scheme because of structural changes made after 1923), followed by a comprehensive selection of vehicles built for the electrification-conscious Southern Railway of the 1920s and '30s and an LMS-built sliding door unit of the early 1940s. All examples are somewhat basic in their interior accommodation, the principal objective being to maximize seating capacity.

A third form of self-propulsion, the diesel multiple unit, makes use of the ubiquitous diesel engine and the Museum has every intention of preserving a BR example from the c. 1960 period when possible. However,

GWR diesel railcar No 4 as originally restored by BR in 1960. It was subsequently re-restored by the NRM as part of the Museum contribution to the 'Great Western 150' celebrations of 1985.

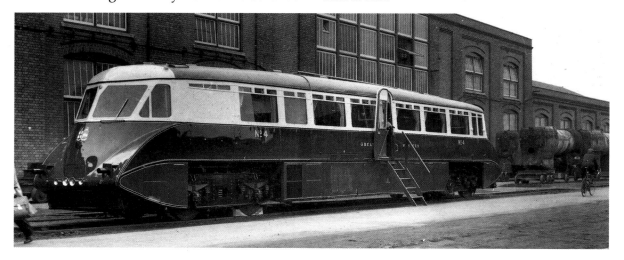

a significant pioneer in this direction was the GWR which introduced diesel railcars with *mechanical* propulsion in the 1930s. One of the first to be built (in 1934) was saved for posterity and is now in the National Collection. Its bodywork is quite distinctive and was built along motor bus principles by the well-known bus manufacturer AEC of Southall. Inside, the layout is a cross between contemporary rail and road practice, but is of interest in being an authentic reflection of current trends in interior decoration.

This mirroring of current fashion was a second noteworthy trend in railway carriage design generally. In their better carriages, the railways spared no expense to achieve some supremely beautiful effects. When combined with the equal attention given to painting, lining and decoration of the outside, the railways may be said to have reached the apogee of passenger comfort and opulence at a time when virtually all surface land transport was by train. It began late in Victorian and early Edwardian times and continued during the period up to the Second World War. Two superb examples of this 'grand epoch' may be singled out, both associated with the ever-increasing international nature of rail travel. These are the Pullman car *Topaz* and the Wagons-Lits sleeping car No 3792 (the latter acquired in 1978), both of which have undergone extensive restoration since then.

Topaz, built in 1913, is a supremely beautiful carriage and has been restored to as near original condition as possible. Its red velvet chairs, intricate wood veneers and inlays, polished brass table lamps with silk shades and elaborately decorated exterior are redolent of a vanished age of elegance. It is displayed in the colours of the South Eastern & Chatham Railway on which it ran (rather than the more familiar 'umber and cream' which most Pullmans sported), and is paired with the equally beautiful and elaborately decorated Wainwright 4-4-0 No 737. Together they make a breaktaking spectacle.

Equally memorable is the ruggedly built Wagons-Lits No 3792. Constructed in France in 1936 though built to the British structure gauge, it is of typical continental appearance reminiscent of the Orient Express. It was strongly built to withstand the rigours of cross-channel ferry boat operation between London and Paris on a celebrated train called the 'Night Ferry', It does not display the traditional wood veneers of many Wagons-Lits cars, being of 'all-metal' construction to meet shipboard fire regulations. At 55 tons it is also believed to be the heaviest type of vehicle to carry fare-paying passengers in Britain. The 'Night Ferry' ran from 1936 to 1980, using some of the original vehicles to the end, and a study of the interior of No 3792 will reveal just how much thoughtful provision went into its design. Like *Topaz*, it too is displayed with an appropriate locomotive and the two ensembles stand side by side in the 'Travelling by Train' gallery.

It was not only the first-class passenger who received care and consideration. Third-class passengers received their fair share too, nowhere better exemplified than by LMS convertible sleeping car No 14241, built in 1928 and normally placed on show in the main hall 'core' collection displaying significant stages in vehicle evolution. By night, the seats converted to beds with pillows and blankets (all for a modest 6s [30p] supplement) but most noteworthy is the lack of draughty compartment doors and the gradual enlargement of windows. Access

was by end vestibules only with no individual compartment doors, and although the vehicle still displays traditional wood construction with elaborate decoration, it was thoroughly modern in its amenities. The introduction of third-class sleeping cars was not confined to the LMS; all of the British systems made significant contributions to the general improvement of facilities for ordinary passengers, although the Southern, alone, did not offer third-class sleepers.

Very visible changes during the period include the gradual replacement of wood sheeting by metal panelling as an outside 'skin', thus giving a smoother and more modern appearance to much of the stock. There was also a considerable simplification in carriage livery. The original liveries had tended to reflect the traditional wood construction of vehicles, with lining liberally distributed where capping strips of wood were used to protect joins in the main panelling. With smoother sided metal-skinned vehicles, most railways adopted more austere decoration, partly for economy but

Exterior and (insert) a part interior view of Wagons-Lits 'Night Ferry' sleeping car No 3792 built in 1936 and restored by the Wagons-Lits company at Ostende in 1978 to as near as possible to its c. 1947–8 condition, the date when the 'Night Ferry' service was resumed after the Second World War.

also because it was perceived as more modern. With larger 'picture' windows and an increasing use of armrests and courtesy lights, even in the third class, the ordinary British railway carriage could stand comparison with anything in the world at the end of the company period in 1947.

By this time, integral steel construction of vehicles had begun to appear. For some twenty years after nationalization in 1948, the Mark I standard coach became com-

LMS third class sleeping car No 14241, built 1928, as restored to near original condition by British Rail Engineering Ltd, Wolverton, in 1978. Note the large windows and outside doors confined to the ends of the vehicle only. The couplings, steam and brake hoses and electric light connections are all prominent on the vehicle end, typical of the 'plumbing' and ancillary apparatus carried by latter-day steam age passenger rolling stock.

'Day' and 'night' arrangement of the compartments in LMS sleeping car No 14241.

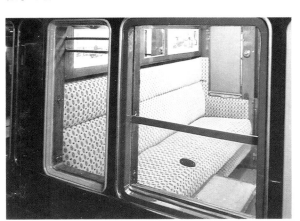

Exterior view of the preserved 1960 built Metro-Cammell first class Pullman car *Eagle*.

Some characteristic decorative paintwork on preserved coaches at the NRM. The vehicles represented are Queen Adelaide's saloon (1842), the Midland six-wheeler (1883) and the Royal dining car (1900).

monplace. In terms of structural strength it represented quite an advance but it perpetuated most of the pre-nationalization interior design concepts. Centre gangways rather than side corridors began to receive preference, particularly in third-class (now second-class) vehicles where they allowed either more or larger sized seats than side-corridor types; but it was not until the 1960s that the next step forward began. The Museum already holds some examples of the move towards modern-day coaches in the shape of the 1960-built Pullmans of the modern era, withdrawn only in 1978, and the first ever British Rail Mk II carriage of 1962 – the progenitor of the modern generation of main line stock.

Amongst all this variety, one group of carriages must stand supreme – the Museum's collection of Royal saloons and associated vehicles. They have already been the subject of their own separate Museum book,* which is why they receive relatively short measure here; but they represent a truly unique and internationally celebrated feature of the NRM display. They form the largest and most varied collection of such vehicles any-

Palaces on Wheels by D. Jenkinson and G. Townend (HMSO, 1981).

where in the world. Most have their own special place in the Museum's second major gallery; but even at a more fundamental level they would be important since, between them, they encapsulate virtually the whole story of railway passenger vehicle evolution from the 1840s to the 1950s, offering both a mirror to society and a story of technical evolution. Ever since Royalty took to the rails in the 1840s, the vehicles provided have always been at the forefront of current technology. Thus, Queen Adelaide's coach of 1842 is the finest contemporary first-generation four-wheeler owned by the Museum while Queen Victoria's saloon, was a pioneer in sound insulation and gangway connection when built in 1869. It was the 20th Century which saw things reach their most spectacular, starting with Edward VII's saloons of 1902, inspired by the Duke of Sutherland's saloon and built at the same place, the Wolverton Carriage Works of the old LNWR.

The East Coast companies replied during 1908–9 with an equally beautiful pair of saloons, this time in varnished teak rather than elaborately decorated paint, one built

Queen Adelaide's coach of 1842, possibly the finest preserved contemporary four-wheeler still in its original condition anywhere in the world.

East Coast Royal Train brake van, built in 1908 by the GNR and restored at Doncaster to its LNER (c. 1925) condition in the late 1970s. The varnished 'teak' finish was very much a characteristic of the East Coast trains until British Railways' days.

Interior of Queen Victoria's saloon of 1869. The Royal Blue trim was chosen by the Queen herself; the interior was not essentially changed when the carriage was rebuilt in 1895.

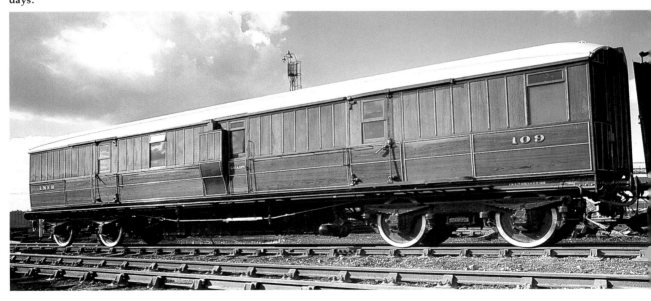

Contrasting Royal interiors, linked by two Queen Elizabeths. The older view shows the East Coast saloon No 395 of 1908 built for King Edward VII and later used by Queen Mary and Queen Elizabeth the Queen Mother; the modern interior is of LMS Saloon No 799 built in 1941 for HM Queen Elizabeth, when consort to HM King George VI and later used by HM Queen Elizabeth II until her Silver Jubilee year in 1977.

at York, the other at Doncaster. Both these vehicles, along with a fine luggage van also associated with the East Coast Royal Train, also survive.

The massive provisioning of mobile homes for King Edward VII and Queen Alexandra meant that the two principal north–south companies (LMS and LNER) had no reason to add to their Royal fleet during the 1920s and '30s, but the onset of the Second World War saw a second phase of Royal Train building. First off the mark was the LMS with a pair of armour-plated and air-conditioned saloons for the greater safety and comfort of the King and Queen during this difficult time. Built in 1941, they replaced for the most part the 1902 saloons. After the war, with armour plating removed, they continued to be the principal saloons and were used by HM The Queen and HRH The Duke of Edinburgh until 1977. In this year, they were withdrawn from service and in 1978 transferred to the NRM.

The second 1940s element is represented by two fine GWR saloons, conceived during the war but built in 1945 as part of an

Former GWR Royal saloon No 9006, used by HM Queen Elizabeth the Queen Mother until 1979 is a popular exhibit with visitors, not least because the table is laid with Her Majesty's own china which she donated to the Museum.

unfulfilled pre-war proposal for a new GWR Royal Train. Used for most of their life by HM Queen Elizabeth the Queen Mother, they were transferred to the NRM in 1983, having become obsolete in terms of braking and heating.

Finally, in the 1950s, BR added new saloons of more modern type to the Royal Train and these too became redundant during 1986–7, thus giving the Museum a selection of modern flush-sided Royal saloons of the 1940s and '50s from which to form a third generation mini-Royal Train, now displayed alongside its Edwardian and Victorian forebears with another appropriate locomotive.

Like everything else in the collection, one can never draw a concluding line to the rolling stock story in an industry which continues to develop – and this is as true of the Royal vehicles as anything else. But as they stand, they amply summarize the vehicle story so far.

Chapter 2

Locomotives

by John Van Riemsdijk

The oldest locomotive in the National Railway Museum is *Agenoria*, built in 1829. The earlier history, as far as original material is concerned, is mainly in the parent Science Museum in South Kensington.

It was Richard Trevithick who invented the steam locomotive, but none of his survives, unless, as is possible, the engine and boiler in the Science Museum were once the vital parts of his London locomotive *Catch me who Can*, which was demonstrated in 1808. It was also Trevithick who used the exhaust steam to draw up the fire, and so gave the world that authentic voice of railways, the exhaust beat, and that signature of steam, the plume of exhaust.

The Science Museum has *Puffing Billy* of 1813, which is probably the oldest complete railway engine in existence, and it has the original *Rocket* of 1829, together with its most serious rival, Timothy Hackworth's *Sans Pareil*. *Rocket* combined, for the first time, a boiler barrel with many firetubes inside, a water-jacketed firebox, and a simple arrangement of outside cylinders driving directly on to crankpins in the driving wheels. With this small machine, the railway engine came of age and all normal subsequent steam locomotives have been based on its design. *Agenoria* was a more complex contemporary of *Rocket*, and its main interest, apart from sheer antiquity, is that it is almost identical to the first locomotive to work in north America: *Stourbridge Lion*, an export from middle England.

Robert Stephenson built *Rocket* (of which the NRM has a working reproduction) but his father George was the main builder from

Agenoria **of 1829, the oldest locomotive in the National Railway Museum.**

1814 until 1825 when he built *Locomotion*, No 1 of the Stockton & Darlington Railway, the first public railway to use steam traction. *Locomotion* is part of the National Collection, and the date on which it hauled the inaugural train, 27 September, is also the date of the opening of the National Railway Museum, 150 years later, in 1975.

Three Styles of Locomotive Construction

Although the steam locomotive first appeared in Britain, by the end of the nineteenth century Britain had lost its pre-eminence in locomotive engineering to France and the United States of America. But the original models upon which the schools of locomotive design were founded all derived from the fertile brain of Robert Stephenson.

The frames of *Rocket* were an assembly of iron bars to which the boiler was firmly attached, as were the axlebox guides and springs. The cylinders were fixed on each side of the boiler, on plates which were not at first fixed to the frames. This construction allowed some flexibility which was advantageous when early tracks themselves were fairly flexible. *Rocket*'s success in the trials at Rainhill produced orders for more of the same design, and at the opening of the Liverpool & Manchester Railway in 1830 there were five of them.

Rocket itself was the nineteenth engine built by Robert Stephenson & Co. The twenty-sixth was the last development of the type by the firm; named *Northumbrian* it was the first to have the water-jacketed firebox incorporated within the boiler shell, and it also seems to have been the first to be

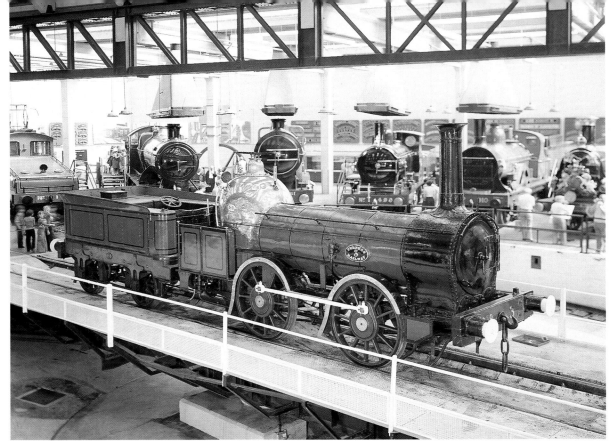

The Bury bar-framed style – 'Coppernob' No 3 of 1843 on the turntable in the NRM. In the background are many other engines discussed in this chapter.

provided with a proper smokebox. These features subsequently appeared on all normal steam locomotives, but the bar framing became the basis of the typical American locomotive.

The National Collection is sadly lacking in representatives of locomotive construction in this country between 1829 and 1866, nor is there much to be found elsewhere in Britain. Most of what remains from this period is unrepresentative of the progress being made, but the relics are supplemented by two important full-size reconstructions of Great Western Railway broad gauge engines: the non-working Stephenson 2-2-2 *North Star* and the working Gooch 4-2-2 *Iron Duke*. The Hackworth type 0-6-0 *Derwent* of the Stockton & Darlington Railway, though of a type which contributed nothing to the future, is something one is glad to have as amazing proof that obstinate conservatism was already present before railways as we understand them had reached their majority. But two of the survivors of the period

under discussion clearly show the seeds of future development and rank as objects of prime importance: the Bury-type 0-4-0, commonly nicknamed 'Coppernob No 3' and the LNWR 2-2-2 No 1868, formerly named *Columbine*.

Edward Bury and James Kennedy built an 0-4-0 named *Liverpool* for the Liverpool & Manchester Railway, which was tried out in 1830. This engine had bar frames, cylinders between them at the front and joined to the smokebox, and a cranked driving axle. It was the first locomotive to have inside cylinders as these are usually understood, the cylinders being more or less horizontal. It was not the first to have a crank axle: *Novelty* had one at the Rainhill Trials. A feature which gave Bury and Kennedy engines a distinctive visual character was the domed top to the firebox, clad in copper (hence 'Coppernob') which resulted from the box itself being basically a vertical drum attached to the horizontal drum forming the boiler barrel. This piece of history is enshrined in 'Coppernob', an engine built for the Furness Railway sixteen years after *Liverpool*, but similar to that first design.

The second of Robert Stephenson's three innovative styles of construction was the one which became most typical of British practice in the next forty years. The first representative of the style was the *Planet*, which appeared in September 1830. It was a 2-2-0, but otherwise had the same layout as the Bury engine, with inside cylinders driving on to a crank axle just ahead of the firebox; but the framing was quite different from anything seen before. The main frames were outside the wheels and made of long timbers with iron plates on both sides to take the axleboxes and springs. The weight of the engine was taken on to the axles by these frames. The boiler and smokebox were stoutly fixed to them, but this would not have been strong enough to withstand the thrust of the pistons, the cylinders being fixed in the smokebox, nor would the widely spaced bearings in the outside frames have given enough support to the crank axle against the piston thrusts, so four extra frames were fitted inside, joining the cylinders to extra bearings on the crank axle, which did not take engine weight. So different frames were provided for different functions – an excellent principle at a time when materials were of doubtful quality.

Planet and its kind weighed about 8 tons and the short wheelbase made such engines unstable at speeds of over 20 m.p.h., so in 1833 Stephenson added a third axle behind the firebox, to steady the engine and permit a larger grate to be provided. The first such engine, built for the Liverpool & Manchester Railway, was a 2-2-2, named *Patentee*. This was the true ancestor of the British locomotive. Within a couple of years of its appearance, improved 'Patentees' were being exported to inaugurate railways abroad, and the National Collection has one domestic example: the reconstruction of the Great Western's *North Star* in Swindon Museum. This represents a locomotive which was actually altered to the broad gauge of 7 ft having been originally built for a narrower one, 5 ft 6 in, and intended for the New Orleans Railway in the USA. But by 1837, the relatively rigid Stephenson multi-framed engine had already proved unsuitable for American tracks, so the engine was supplied to the GWR where it proved much superior to the other types available. The nearest thing to an original 'Patentee' type which survives in this country is *Lion*, a Liverpool & Manchester 0-4-2 of 1838 and owned by the Merseyside Museums.

The external framing and the multiplicity of inside frames of the original *Patentee*, were soon modified as better materials came into use, but the crank axle, which gave a great deal of trouble for the next twenty years, remained a feature of the great majority of British locomotives. But before describing some of those locomotives and the various styles of framing which marked the evolution from six frames to two, mention must be made of the third style of locomotive construction originated by Robert Stephenson.

In 1841 he produced the first 'long boiler' locomotive. It had no outside frames and all three axles were beneath the boiler barrel, the firebox overhanging at the rear. The reason for the design was primarily to extract more heat from the fuel: the short barrels of the previous boilers proving inadequate for this, with the result that the locomotives threw sparks and frequently ran with red hot smokebox doors. The boiler barrel could not be lengthened in the 'Patentee' type without lengthening the wheelbase, and this was unacceptable because turntables were too short and because the wheelbase of locomotives was still rigid so that only short ones could run safely round the sharper curves. The first long-boiler engine, and most of those used in Britain, had inside cylinders, but the use of such engines in Britain was short lived, except on the Caledonian and the Stockton & Darlington railways. A late example of the type used on the latter railway was built in 1874 by the North Eastern (which had absorbed the S&DR) and survived to take part in the railway centenary procession of 1925, by which time it had been well restored by the LNER (which had absorbed the North Eastern on its creation two years earlier). This engine, NER No 1275, is now part of the National

The sole surviving British long boiler engine: NER (S&D type) 0-6-0 No 1275, newly restored for the S&D Centenary in 1925.

Collection, a precious reminder of Stephenson's third concept which, though little used in Britain, can fairly be described as the origin of most locomotive design on the European continent. Quite apart from the historical importance of the type in the European context, this third Stephenson style established the use of outside cylinders, inside frames and straight axles which was to dominate the last years of the British steam locomotive.

Thus Robert Stephenson originated the three great schools of locomotive design that were adapted to the varying requirements of most of the countries of the world, and which, enormously developed, were eventually to coalesce in the mid twentieth century.

Development of the British Style

The British style is above all the 'Patentee' layout, but there were always some exceptions and also some notable experiments. One of the early exceptions, and what remains of one of the experiments, are both to be found in the National Railway Museum and both wear the colours of the London & North Western Railway. One of these is the outside cylinder 2-2-2 No 1868, formerly named *Columbine* of 1845, built at Crewe for the Grand Junction Railway. The

other is *Cornwall*, a much larger 2-2-2 built with the parts of an earlier experimental express locomotive.

Columbine, by which name the engine is still popularly known, was one of the earlier examples of a series of over four hundred 'Crewe' type locomotives owned by the LNWR. Often referred to in books as 'Allan's Crewe type', this design was not due to Allan, one time locomotive foreman at Crewe, nor was it the first to be built there. Its creator seems to have been William Buddicom, who took the design with him to France when he became engineer to the Paris–Rouen Railway.

Columbine, weighing but 16 tons and with 6 ft driving wheels, is the oldest preserved example of an express locomotive anywhere. Before her time there was differentiation between passenger and freight locomotives on some lines, but the express

Crewe type 2-2-2, LNWR No 1868, formerly No 49 *Columbine*.

engine had not emerged as a distinct type. There were well over a hundred engines more or less like *Columbine* and the last was built in 1858. There was also a greater number of 2-4-0s of the type, with smaller driving wheels, but these were not express engines.

The first generation of 'Patentees' gave much mechanical trouble, and by the end of the 1830s the detail design was being improved everywhere. But some railways decided, for the time being, against crank axles and elected to put the cylinders outside the frames. The question was: how could one best arrange the framing? The Crewe solution was to put the bearings of the driving axle (and coupled axle, when 2-4-0s of the type were built) into the inside frames only, but to retain the outside frames for the carrying wheels. The cylinders themselves were inserted into the sandwich in somewhat inelegant fashion, but the construction was very strong and this odd-looking front end was last built as late as 1901 for a 4-4-0 of the Highland Railway.

When John Ramsbottom succeeded Francis Trevithick as locomotive superintendent of the Northern Division of the LNWR, he enlarged the Crewe single driver design and took away the outside frames, thereby producing his 'Problem' or 'Lady of the Lake' class which was numerous, famous and long lived. But many of the older engines lasted as long as the century. And one of Ramsbottom's first acts was to rebuild *Cornwall* into its present form as a kind of final version of the old Crewe express engine. *Cornwall* had started life with its boiler slung beneath the driving axle and a most peculiar looking ensemble resulted. The usual LNWR maximum speed was 40 m.p.h.; *Cornwall* represented an attempt to raise that speed by having large driving wheels so placed that they could be more heavily loaded but she was altogether too awkward to build, maintain and operate. So the speed limit (it was not actually enforced but allowed for in the timetables) remained at 40 m.p.h. for about the next forty years. *Cornwall* was rebuilt, with a conventional boiler

in a conventional position, with Crewe-type framing, and her high horizontal cylinders and large wheels made her the most aesthetically satisfying of her breed.

It is worth noting that one begins to speak of aesthetics when one reaches the locomotives of the mid 1840s. First the eye is caught by express engines, large wheels being more graceful than small ones and more care being taken in the finish of machines in the public eye. But within ten years humbler machines were also being equipped with graceful chimneys and shapely steam domes, while carefully contrived curves appeared in frames and footplating. And we have the first evidence that paint was being applied by coach painters, trained in the tradition of gentlemen's carriages, to locomotives as well as coaches. The leaders in all this were not the railways so much as the private locomotive builders, who hoped to sell their products to directors with discerning eyes. It was still a period when much locomotive design was done by these

This fine contemporary model of Ramsbottom 2-2-2 *Lady of the Lake* is on loan to the Museum and is painted in the original Ramsbottom LNWR green livery, probably the only surviving authentic paint sample of this early style.

Cornwall, **newly restored by the NRM in 1985 with its unique, but historically correct, polished brass dome cover.**

The reproduction of GWR *Iron Duke* **of 1847 at Kensington Gardens in 1985. Note Brunel's broad gauge track.**

firms, and this practice never wholly died out, though it became very rare in the twentieth century.

The steam locomotive was always a machine which derived its shape from its necessary functional elements, if we except the few instances of streamlining which occurred in the twentieth century. In this it was quite different from diesel and electric locomotives or motor cars, and more to be classed with aeroplanes, sailing ships or bicycles. The possibilities of embellishing it were disciplined by its natural shape, and the particular skill of the embellisher lay in emphasis rather than concealment of that shape. As the nineteenth century advanced, the shape of British locomotives simplified because less elaborate constructions became possible with the improvement in available materials, but the paintwork became more flamboyant. In the middle years of the century much of the artistry went into the actual shaping of metal. *Columbine* is not in her original livery, which was a rather plain green, and many of her details have been altered over the years, but her safety valve on its low dome in the middle of the boiler barrel shows the careful original design of this detail, and the radial slots in the driving wheel splashers are well contrived to con-

tinue the form of the spoked wheels beneath. The splashers of paddle steamers had such slots, and their provision in locomotive splashers was perhaps an unconscious reference to the romantic idea of travel, whether by land or sea.

This romantic idea brings us naturally to I. K. Brunel, perhaps the greatest romantic of the early railway age, but fortunately also an engineering genius. Brunel conceived the broad gauge of 7 ft for the Great Western Railway, and when the National Railway Museum was being set up, it was apparent to the authorities that the most serious omission from the material available was a Great Western broad gauge locomotive. The *North Star* reproduction in Swindon Museum was not available, non-working and far from adequate to represent the motive power of more than half a century of broad gauge operation. Nothing could be done in time for the opening of the NRM in 1975, but the Science Museum was able to repair this omission by building a working reproduction of the first of the celebrated 4-2-2 express engines with 8 ft driving wheels, *Iron Duke*, designed by Daniel Gooch for Brunel. The original *Iron Duke* was built in 1847, and the same basic design continued to work express trains on the broad gauge until it disappeared in 1892. The reproduction *Iron Duke* was finished in 1985, in time to inaugurate the celebrations of the 150th anniversary of the founding of the GWR by running in Kensington Gardens with one reproduction covered carriage.

The working reproduction is not technically exact, but a very close approximation to the original machine. Because it has to comply with modern safety regulations, it has modern brakes, gauges, and trustworthy modern materials in its construction. It is not quite as powerful as the original, but far more powerful than it needs to be for what it has to do. In fact, it is the product of an extremely ingenious rebuild of an existing modern locomotive, one of two presented by the National Coal Board, which provided the boiler, cylinders and much of the motion work, as well as reuseable metal and fittings. Its tender and the reproduction carriages with which it now runs were made by British Rail for the Museum, at an ex-Great Western works in Cardiff.

The undoubted advantages of the broad gauge applied most strongly in a period when materials and machine tools were obviously far less developed than later on. Boilers were made of iron, and the techniques of shaping wrought-iron plate precluded the complex shapes which later enabled standard gauge locomotives to be equipped with powerful boilers. The fuel in the early days of public railways was always coke to prevent the emission of smoke. High rotative speeds of the driving mechanism had to be ruled out for fear of bending something, and the techniques of balancing reciprocating masses, then being worked out in continental Europe, were not applied in Britain for several more decades. Coupling rods could not be used at high speed and were found only on freight engines.

This is the context in which in the 1840s, broad gauge locomotives with 8 ft driving wheels were able to pull 100 ton trains at 60 m.p.h. from London to Swindon. *Columbine* could perhaps have managed 60 tons at 45 m.p.h., but on neither gauge were engines normally expected to work so hard.

There were twenty-nine of the original 'Iron Duke' class, with the authentic 'Pantentee' sandwich frames outside, and with three, not four, inside frames. They were replaced by new engines of closely similar design after about a quarter of a century; they carried the old names, and these lasted till the end of the broad gauge. *Iron Duke* dimensions were not reached in standard gauge locomotives until the end of the century, and much the same goes for the speeds of Great Western expresses.

The use of framing outside the wheels continued for something like a century after the appearance of the *Planet*, although the last engines built in this way, for the Great Western in the 1930s, were really rebuilds using existing material. The outside frames of later nineteenth-century engines lost their wood and timber composite construction as larger iron and, later, steel plates became available. These so-called double-framed engines not only showed considerable advantages of strength at a time when material weakness was a problem; they also allowed more freedom in firebox design and made a larger grate area possible without lengthening the trailing wheelbase, a point of especial importance when the trailing wheels were coupled, because long coupling rods were undesirable until they could be made of steel, in the 1870s.

One of the greatest exponents of the

Much improved but still essentially a 'Patentee': Kirtley's Midland Railway 2-4-0 express type No 158A of 1866.

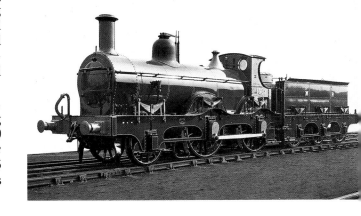

double-framed engine was Matthew Kirtley of the Midland Railway, yet his greatest contribution to British locomotive engineering had little to do with framing: it was the solution of the problem of burning coal rather than coke, without producing smoke. The experiments were done between 1856 and 1860 by Charles Markham under Kirtley's direction, and resulted in the now familiar brick arch spanning the fire, which directs the flames backwards towards the firedoor before they sweep upwards and round the whole firebox on the way to the firetubes in the boiler barrel. The firedoor itself had a deflector plate above it inside the box, and provision for allowing in air (secondary to that which entered below the grate via the ashpan) which was deflected by the plate to where it was most needed to ensure complete combustion and smoke consumption. This arrangement has been used worldwide ever since. Its design, and that of William Adams' bogie with spring-controlled side-play, which came five years later, were the last major British contributions to steam locomotive design all over the world.

Kirtley remained faithful to double frames until 1874. One of his mixed traffic 2-4-0s, No 158A, of this construction is a particu-

larly interesting item in the National Collection, and may regularly be seen at York. It is one of only two coupled engines with double frames in the collection, the other being the GWR *City of Truro*. But the Kirtley dates from 1866, while the 'City' is from 1903. Another Midland double-framed engine except for its leading bogie is the graceful 4-2-2 No 673, which was built to the designs of Samuel Johnson in 1899. This engine is from the period of the brief revival of the single-driver express engine, encouraged by the invention of steam sanding gear to increase the wheels' grip on the rails when starting and climbing steep gradients. Both these locomotives are in the rich Midland red livery, which was long familiar because it was adopted by the LMS after the grouping of 1923. But the 2-4-0 was originally in the bright green which preceded the red until 1883 onwards. By the time of its withdrawal it had gone through several boiler and other more cosmetic changes and, along with its few equally long-lived sisters, was one of the last survivors in Britain of a once very common construction.

One of the last standard gauge 4-2-2 types: S. W. Johnson's double framed design for the Midland Railway, built in 1899 and now restored to its 1909 condition as No 673.

The use of outside framing, to take the axleboxes and springs of carrying wheels only, lasted much longer than full double framing, but there are so few representative locomotives preserved from the 1850s and '60s that we have to come to Edward Fletcher's North Eastern 2-4-0 No 910 of 1875 to find a good example of the mixed frame arrangement. The National Collection has two other later 2-4-0s which also exhibit this characteristic: the later North Eastern 'Tennant' engine No 1463, and Great Eastern No 490, an engine which lasted till near the end of steam traction on British Railways.

Fletcher's No 910 represents the slightly earlier and more flamboyant style. It exemplifies the way in which the outside framing and the footsteps could become essays in the design of curves, and the base on which elaborate splashers with elegant fretwork could be erected. The whole is painted with many lines of many colours and surmounted by a boiler adorned with a dome positively arrogant in its splendour. Even the number plate of 910 is cast in figures which suggest the art nouveau movement of twenty-five years later. This engine is the best example of Victorian ornamentation in

Exuberant Victorian aesthetics and sound engineering design in Edward Fletcher's mixed-frame 2-4-0 express engine No 910 of 1875 for the North Eastern Railway.

Hardwicke, **brand new outside Crewe Works, in 1892.**

the Museum, the later examples being basically simpler and more austere in form, if not in decoration.

However, the future lay with inside frames only and it is interesting to compare No 910 with its design contemporary, LNWR 2-4-0 No 790 *Hardwicke*. *Hardwicke* was built in 1892, basically to a design by Francis W. Webb first introduced in 1874, and itself only slightly different from a previous design by John Ramsbottom. *Hardwicke* is some 8 tons lighter than No 910, an additional weight saving resulting from the use of driving wheels 6 ft 6 in in diameter, as against 7 ft; but nothing in the records suggests that the LNWR engines were slower or less powerful. *Hardwicke* owes her preservation to her performance in the 1895 races to Aberdeen, when she averaged 67 m.p.h. over the 141 miles from Crewe to Carlisle, including the thirty-mile climb to Shap (average gradient 1 in 188 with the final four miles at 1 in 75) with a load of 72 tons.

One of the greatest, most original and most influential protagonists of inside framing was William Stroudley who, after working in Scotland, became locomotive superintendent of the London, Brighton & South Coast Railway in 1870. The LBSCR was not much of a railway before he joined it, but the quality of his work soon gave it a new reputation. The National Railway Museum has two of his locomotives: the small 0-6-0 tank *Boxhill* and the 0-4-2 express locomotive *Gladstone*. *Boxhill* is one of the 'Terriers', the small, light engines built for suburban train working, initially on the South London line. Fifty of these engines were built between 1872 and 1880, and the last was taken out of service by British Railways in 1959. Several are preserved in working order and still doing duty on preserved railways. The 'Terriers' weighed only 25 tons, but their performances astonished the engineering world, as they could outpace and outpull many much larger tank engines. Their brilliance was due not only to the absence of unnecessary weight, but also to very good design of every detail, especially of the cylinders and valves, to make the best use of

Royal in colour only, GER No 87, the preserved example of James Holden's small but powerful shunting tank, was one of several such which found a superior role working the suburban services of the Great Eastern. It was built in 1904.

steam. James Holden of the Great Eastern was to learn from them, and produced a series of somewhat larger, 0-6-0 tanks between 1889 and 1904. Many of them operated the commuter trains out of Liverpool Street station with the same vigour that the 'Terriers' had shown with lighter trains out of Victoria. A late example, No 87 of 1904, adorns the York collection, a beautifully restored reminder of the hectic 'Jazz' services of the GER, the most intensive steam-worked suburban services anywhere in the world.

Stroudley's *Gladstone* was no less successful, but rather less orthodox. He had built 2-4-0s and the lightest and most elegant of 2-2-2s, but instead of progressing to a design with a leading bogie, he decided that his big express engine would be an 0-4-2. He had built tank engines of this wheel arrangement, which rode excellently at speed, and had tried an 0-4-2 tender design for mixed traffic. The first 0-4-2 express locomotive came in 1878 and *Gladstone* was part of a later batch in 1882. Other railways were critical

Gladstone **of 1882 shows Stroudley's simple elegance and his unusual choice of colour, but is here decorated as for a Royal journey, on the LBSCR.**

because, though the 0-4-2 had a long history as a freight or secondary service type, Stroudley fitted 6 ft 6 in driving wheels and clearly was making the equivalent of a 4-4-0 express engine. He was indeed, but he was making a much lighter engine for the same power, and gaining design freedom around the firebox. *Gladstone*, with some 20 sq ft of grate, weighed just under 39 tons, which was 7 tons less than contemporary 4-4-0s with similar dimensions. There were forty-two engines of this broad type, and they lasted between forty and fifty years, *Gladstone* herself having forty-five years of service before being preserved privately by the Stephenson Locomotive Society and placed in the old York Railway Museum, which was then owned by the LNER.

British Locomotives in the late Nineteenth Century

This is not a technical treatise – there are plenty of such accounts in railway literature for those who would know more – but it is well nigh impossible to describe any form of locomotive without reference to certain technical aspects so, before considering the final designs of the archetypal British style, a few technicalities must briefly be mentioned.

The second half of the nineteenth century saw the replacement of iron rails by steel ones, a process which reduced the rolling resistance of trains very substantially – a hundred ton train in 1900 was trifling, but a hundred ton train in 1850 was a hard pull. Enlarged rail sections and strengthened bridges made possible greater loads on the axles; oddly enough, this could actually reduce the weight of locomotives, because fewer axles were needed to carry a given weight, and axles with their wheels and the extra framing they require are heavy.

Within the locomotive itself, several developments need to be mentioned, mostly concerned with the essential process of steam raising and the more efficient use of such steam when raised. The injector, a device to force water into the boiler against the pressure of the steam within, was invented by Henri Gifford in France in 1859. It was fitted to most locomotives at once and replaced the feed pumps (driven off the motion) or the donkey pumps with their own cylinders and flywheel. The injector works by combining steam from the boiler with water from the storage tanks and forcing them down an ever more constricted passageway (generally of tapering cone shape) until they built up a combined pressure greater than that of the boiler steam, at which point the mixture can be 'injected' into the boiler. It is, in effect a 'non-return' valve since, once inside the boiler, the mixture immediately loses its pressure and so cannot return from whence it came. During the nineteenth century, full-pressure steam from the boiler was used to work the injector.

Some designers sought to save fuel by preheating the water, using exhaust steam. In Britain this practice was largely discontinued because it gave more trouble than it was worth, but in the twentieth century the invention of the exhaust steam injector achieved the same result with less trouble. On the continent and in North America, feed water heating devices using exhaust steam were highly developed.

Once generated in the boiler, steam is admitted to the cylinders by means of a separate moving component known as a valve, which alternately opens and closes the 'steam ports' at each end of the cylinder. To operate this valve, a form of mechanism is required known as a valve gear which is a crucial part of the locomotive; it controls the admission of steam to the cylinders and determines the quantity of steam used and the direction of travel. In almost all British nineteenth-century locomotives, the Stephenson link motion valve gear was preferred, though many alternatives were available, some to be found on locomotives in the National Collection.

The main changes in the design of the boiler were at the firebox end. The high firebox, which doubled as the steam dome, gave way to a more modestly raised firebox. The effect can be seen on the *Iron Duke* reproduction. This often provided the excuse for a bold brass beading. In the 1840s flush-topped boilers were already being built, the firebox outer casing being simply a continuation of the barrel, and this type eventually predominated until the square-topped Belpaire type arrived. First made about 1860 in Belgium, it was not adopted by a British main line railway until the Manchester, Sheffield & Lincolnshire (later Great Central) did so in 1891. Most of the locomotives incorporating these technical improvements were still essentially versions of *Patentee*, with inside cylinders, a crank axle somewhere near the middle of the wheelbase and a narrow firebox fitting between the frames just behind it.

There are so many examples of these locomotives that it is perhaps best to simply note what is to be found in the National Collection and what is sadly absent from that and indeed any collection. There are only two inside-cylinder single drivers, other than the broad gauge reproductions. One is the elegant Midland 4-2-2 already cited as an example of double framing, and the other is the 2-2-4 tank engine *Aerolite*, which is preserved in its final form as a two-cylinder compound, the sole surviving example of that once quite numerous system on the NER. The two cylinders are of different sizes – small high pressure and larger low pressure. The 2-4-0s have already been commented upon, but there is also an outside cylinder 2-4-0 tank in the collection: one of Beattie's London & South Western engines, dating from 1874 but much rebuilt, and now the only survivor of the work of an important and influential designer, but not a 'Patentee' type.

Two most popular types of late nineteenth-century passenger tank are represented in the collection by one example of each: the 2-4-2 and 0-4-4. Curiously, the 2-4-2 tank scarcely existed south of the Thames, or in Scotland, but the LNWR, GWR, MS&LR (later GCR), NER, GER and LYR all made extensive use of 2-4-2s, and it is one of the last named company's engines which is on view in York. No better choice could have been made, for the LYR engines eventually numbered 330 and the later superheated ones were actually more powerful than many contemporary express engines. The preserved engine is the first of the series, No 1008 of 1889, withdrawn late in 1954 and weighing 56 tons. She was designed by John Aspinall who eventually, and most unusually for Britain, became general manager of the railway – a position usually not accorded to an engineer in Britain.

There was no such obvious choice in the case of the 0-4-4 tank. The preserved engine is one of the last type built by the LSWR to the design of Dugald Drummond, an excellent 60 ton machine of 1899 and a type still greatly in evidence in the London area during the last years of steam.

A conspicuous omission from both the National Collection and the whole preservation scene, is the inside-cylinder 4-4-2 tank. The first of these appeared in 1888, eight years after the first of the well-known outside-cylinder engines of the London, Tilbury & Southend Railway which were designed by Adams. A later and larger Tilbury tank is in the collection, and an example of Adams' outside-cylinder 4-4-2 tanks for the LSWR also survives on a preserved railway, but the inside-cylinder type has completely gone. Yet these engines were very numerous and were built in a wide variety of sizes, from the small 1888 engines of the Taff Vale Railway to the express engines of the LBSCR class I3, one of which was the first British passenger engine to be superheated and proved convincingly superior to the saturated LNWR 4-4-0 in the working of the 'Sunny South Express' which connected Birmingham to Brighton. Had it lasted a few more years it would undoubtedly be preserved today, but we must be grateful for the preservation of the outside-cylinder variety, and especially for the Tilbury engine, No 80, *Thundersley*. The Tilbury line used 4-4-2 tanks for almost everything: it had seventy and the LMS built another thirty-five of Tilbury design, the last in 1930.

Discussion of the inside-cylinder 4-4-2 tank brings us to its tender equivalent, the typical British 4-4-0. The inside-cylinder 4-4-0 was actually introduced in tank engine form by William Adams on the North Lon-

don Railway in 1865, but the tender type originated in Scotland, on the North British Railway, with two 37 ton engines built in 1871. One of these went to the bottom of the Tay in the famous disaster, but was recovered and lasted until 1919.

One of the greatest of the early exponents of the inside-cylinder 4-4-0 tender engine was Dugald Drummond. He had worked under William Stroudley in Scotland and had followed him to Brighton. At first he followed Stroudley's ideas in everything, except that Drummond adopted the Adams bogie. His first 4-4-0s were built for the North British in 1876 and later ones for the Caledonian. They were brilliant locomotives but none has survived. However, Drummond eventually succeeded Adams on the LSWR and in 1899 produced his T9 class, of which No 120, withdrawn in 1963, happily belongs to the National Collection. Part of their success can be credited to their long, deep fireboxes, giving 24 sq ft of grate. To accommodate this box behind a cranked axle, the coupled wheelbase was extended to 10 ft, a record for 1899 and a figure never exceeded in this country, though frequently equalled in later years. Not many years before, 8 ft was considered the maximum safe length for the coupling rods of an express engine, but the progress of metallurgy in the late nineteenth century justified Drummond's confidence.

Including No 120 and the untypical *City of Truro*, the National Collection has five inside-cylinder 4-4-0s, and the Scottish Transport Museum in Glasgow has two more. At York, the oldest is Wilson Worsdell's NER Class M1 No 1621 of 1893, a very pretty locomotive but by no means in its original state. When built, engines of this class had no superheaters, and their slide valves were outside the frames. The chimney was set further back than now, and the profile of the front end was particularly proud and pleasing. The large, brass windowed cab and the single beaded splasher remain as they always were; the whole effect of the engine shows that elegance can be achieved with simpler outlines than those of

Fletcher's resplendent 910. No 1621 was superheated by the LNER, and lost her outside steam chests long before, but it was those outside steam chests that gave the engine its ability to run really fast, for this was one of the racers of 1895. Nos 1620 and 1621 were running at speeds into the eighties with hundred ton trains over the hilly and twisting route between Newcastle and Edinburgh, in the races to Aberdeen. No 1621 was a big engine in those days, the first to exceed a weight of 90 tons with her tender. Interestingly it was the much-maligned Thompson (CME of the LNER in succession to Gresley) who saved No 1621 in 1945,

The preserved Drummond LSWR 0-4-4T No 245, seen as running in Southern Railway days as No E245.

Rail crusher and racer of the North Eastern: W. Worsdell's 4-4-0 No 1638 as built, with outside steam chests. The preserved No 1621 began life in this form.

Functional form lovingly enhanced by paint: Harry Wainwright's class D 4-4-0 No 737 of 1901 seen at Ashford after restoration as a Museum exhibit in SECR colours.

Gresley having earlier turned his thumbs down to a proposal to save No 1620!

The other inside-cylinder 4-4-0s in the National Collection were preserved less for technical excellence than to represent the pregrouping railways to which they once belonged. Both were good, standard engines in their day and both show resplendent liveries. One is a saturated steam engine of 1901 and the other a superheated engine of 1920, so they are very different in power and weight. The older engine is No 737 of the South Eastern & Chatham Railway – a joint management concern running the old South Eastern and London, Chatham and Dover systems. Designed, in the technical sense, by Robert Surtees, but under the supervision and with the artistic direction of the locomotive superintendent, Harry S. Wainwright, No 737 is one of Class D, inexpensive to build but of a rare beauty and adorned in many coats of paint of many colours. But the shape is entirely natural,

even functional, and the adornment is all calculated to emphasize that shape. The Wainwright 4-4-0 is for many the perfect ideal of locomotive beauty.

The engine with which No 737 may be contrasted is the much heavier Great Central 'Director' class locomotive *Butler-Henderson*, designed by J. G. Robinson, who was also a great locomotive artist and left numerous classes of beautiful-looking machines behind him. The superheated 'Director' was perhaps his best, though not his largest, passenger engine, but it was his 2-8-0 freight engine which was his masterpiece, and of that more will be said when we finally leave the story of inside cylinders. We are indeed nearing the end of the inside-cylinder story as far as the National Collection is concerned, and all the rest share

The hardest and most profitable of duties: a Great Western 'Dean Goods' on a fifty wagon freight train near Didcot in British Railways days. The total life of the class was seventy-four years!

Saddle tank No 1247 of 1899 shows the GNR livery in which it started life. It worked freight round London for sixty years.

one common feature – six driving wheels, coupled together and mostly without supplementary carrying wheels, the 0-6-0 type.

Most inside-cylinder six-coupled engines were for mixed traffic and freight haulage. The 0-6-0 tender engine probably earned more revenue for the railways of Britain than did any other type, and almost all had the 'Patentee' layout. The long wheelbase inside-cylinder 0-6-0 was built from 1834 until 1941, and tank engines of the type were built even later, the last for main line work probably being the Great Western taper-boiler pannier tanks of 1947. One of these is happily in the National Collection.

There are four 0-6-0 tender locomotives in the Museum's care, and their dates run from 1897 to 1942, while their weights range from just under 37 tons to just over 51. Their driving wheel diameters are substantially similar (4 ft 11 in to 5 ft 3 in) and all four are fitted with the vacuum brake, because all were regularly used on passenger trains (continuous brakes for ordinary freight and min-

eral trains did not come to Britain until after their withdrawal). The oldest of the designs, the Great Western 'Dean Goods' is arguably the best, despite the lack of a superheater, because these engines were amazingly powerful for their size, and fast and economical as well. The most powerful, and the ugliest locomotive in the whole collection, is O. V. S. Bulleid's Southern Q1, but its looks belie its nature, and under the wartime lack of finish is a machine of very high quality indeed, which went about its tasks of heavy haulage with less noise and fuss than many a 2-8-0. Of the other two, the Great Eastern J17 represents a most successful and long-lived design first built in 1900, and LMS No 4027 of 1924 represents one of the most numerous of British 0-6-0s – over 700 were built – but unfortunately not one of the best. Versatile they were and considerable revenue earners, but their axleboxes regularly overheated and they often sheared the crankpins in their wheels, their mechanical design being largely inherited from less powerful Midland Railway predecessors without superheaters. The regular York-based representative of this quartet is the Great Eastern example.

Derived from the 0-6-0 tender engine, the 0-6-0 tank was to be found in the stock of almost all British railways of any size. Three types have already been mentioned, two being mostly used for passenger trains, but the majority of these engines were used for shunting and short-haul goods trains. The fourth National Railway Museum example is a most attractive saddle tank design used by the Great Northern Railway, No 1247 of 1899. There were over two hundred GNR saddle tanks, built between 1874 and 1909 by Patrick Stirling and H. A. Ivatt. No 1247 was withdrawn after exactly sixty years of service, bought by Capt W. G. Smith and, after many more years of work on preserved railways and some specials on British Rail metals, was presented by him to the NRM.

The 0-6-2 tank was another numerous type, used for all types of duty, even some fast passenger work on the North Staffordshire Railway. One of the NSR engines, dating from 1922, is in the National Collection and so is one of the engines of the Taff Vale Railway, No 28 of 1897. The Taff Vale was a large and profitable undertaking, operating within a quite small area of South Wales, which contributed 274 locomotives to the GWR when it amalgamated in 1922. It was

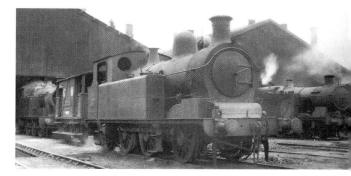

The now preserved Taff Vale 0-6-2T is seen here as GWR No 450 at Cardiff (Cathays) in company with some of its GWR built taper boiler derivatives.

A Great Eastern 4-6-0 in original condition, posing with new coaching stock built by the LNER for the Hook of Holland continental boat train.

Preserved LNWR 'Super D' 0-8-0 seen here as LMS No 9395. The engine is preserved in this modified LMS form with the addition of a tender cab.

then using 0-6-2 tanks for all its heavier passenger, coal and general freight workings, but this was the pattern all over South Wales, where there were a large number of busy independent railways using 0-6-2 tanks. When they were all part of the enlarged GWR the new management produced a further series of such engines at Swindon, a new but typically Swindon design which recognized the supreme usefulness of the type.

Perhaps the most significant omission from the collection in the inside-cylinder, six-coupled category is the 4-6-0 type. Many were built for a number of British systems but none was officially preserved. Most of them were no better than the bigger 4-4-0s and 4-4-2s, but fortunately for posterity, one of the best of the breed, a Gresley rebuild of a Great Eastern example (Class B12) is privately preserved.

The natural extension of the 0-6-0 tender engine, for heavy haulage, is the 0-8-0. Inside-cylinder versions of this wheel arrangement were numerous on only three British railways: the GNR, LYR and LNWR. The GN engines were typically neat products of H. A. Ivatt, but lasted only about thirty years because the LNER was able to buy a large number of 2-8-0s of Great Central design from the War Office after 1918. It was not until the 1930s that the LMS built enough of W. A. Stanier's 2-8-0s to be able to

scrap the numerous LYR and LNWR 0-8-0s, and fortunately one of the latter lasted long enough to escape the cutter's torch and enter the National Collection. No 485 was built in 1921 and is preserved in its final condition as LMS No 9395. Though these engines never ran fast, they could pull hard and had sufficient merits to tempt the LMS under Stanier to embark on a massive modernizing and rebuilding programme lasting well into BR days. Its success undoubtedly saved money by delaying the need to build too many Stanier 2-8-0s before the war. The LMS also built a modernized series of 0-8-0s, based on the LNWR type and the result was an engine very good in parts, but with most of the faults of the Midland-inspired superheater 0-6-0s built in. This most modern of inside-cylinder 0-8-0 classes had a very short life and none is preserved, but it is much more appropriate that as its sole two-cylinder 0-8-0, the National Collection should display the far more common LNWR design, including its later modifications.

The Modern British Locomotive

The reader may wonder how the narrative can have gone thus far without mentioning

The outside cylinders and 8 ft driving wheels of Patrick Stirling's No 1, built for the GNR in 1870, give it a unique look of grace and movement.

one of the most famous locomotives preserved anywhere, and a particular gem of the National Collection – Patrick Stirling's first 4-2-2, with 8 ft driving wheels, built in 1870 – the 'Stirling Eight Footer'. Also left out of the story so far is the Adams 4-4-0, No 563 of 1893, a machine of comparable elegance and even longer active life. The reason is that these engines do not have inside cylinders. They are brought in here to introduce the modern British locomotive.

To deal with the LSWR engine first, Adams developed the leading bogie with sideways movement controlled by springs for his inside-cylinder 4-4-0 tanks for the North London Railway. He then, in 1868, adopted outside cylinders for these, and originated the best-known type of North London locomotive. One of these was preserved for some years by the LMS, but then broken up on the orders of W. A. Stanier, a deplorable emulation of the deeds of his great former chief on the Great Western, G. H. Churchward, who had ordered the breaking up of preserved broad gauge 4-2-2 and 2-2-2 locomotives at Swindon Works. The Adams outside-cylinder 4-4-0 culminated years later in his LSWR express engines. By using outside cylinders for his big engines, Adams was able to lengthen the fire grate within a given coupled wheelbase, and make the valve gear easily accessible to fitters and footplatemen. He could enlarge all the vital bearings, and he could provide large steam chests with large valves and free steam passages. Another speciality he used in most of his engines was an annular blast-pipe, which produced a more even draught effect on the whole bank of firetubes. As a result of all this, the 4-4-0s were the most efficient express locomotives in the country when they were new.

The use of outside cylinders must be associated with balancing of the reciprocating masses of the motion work; this came late to Britain because it was less important with inside cylinders. But Adams understood these matters, and in other ways also paid particular attention to the way his engines rode. Evidence of this can be seen in

Severely functional but immensely stylish, William Adams' LSWR 4-4-0 of 1893 pointed to the future trend of design more surely than its contemporaries.

the beams for equalizing the weight on the coupled axles, visible between the wheels. In many ways these engines were ahead of their British contemporaries, and while Adams learned from continental practice he was also perhaps the last British designer to have a major influence abroad.

Patrick Stirling believed that big wheels gave a better grip on the rail, but wanted to keep his boiler as low as possible; the boiler could be closer to the driving axle if the latter had no cranks so the cylinders went outside, but were kept warm by the handsomely curved smokebox wrapper. The leading bogie was simply pivoted, without sideplay, and the low trailing axle allowed plenty of freedom for the design of firebox and ashpan. No 1 was the first of these engines, of which there were fifty-three, the last and largest dating from 1895. All had gone, except for No 1, by the end of 1915. The engine weight increased in successive batches from 38 to 49 tons and the grate area from under 16 to 20 sq ft. These were great locomotives which performed well with remarkable consistency. In the 1895 races to Aberdeen, they were the only single drivers, and they brought their trains to York every night with handsome gains on the normal timings, averaging around 60 m.p.h. with trains of up to 175 tons, but never running faster than about 75 m.p.h. In the eye of the general public they were the epitome of beautiful machinery. If they seemed old

Basically an Adams design, T. Whitelegg's largest LTSR 4-4-2 tanks were still being built by the LMS in 1930. *Thundersley* of 1909, now preserved, is here decorated for the Coronation of King George V and Queen Mary in 1911.

fashioned to some railway engineers of the 1890s, they none the less pointed the way to more modern designs more surely than the inside-cylinder 4-4-0 so much in favour.

But while one may cite the example of Stirling, and even more that of Adams, the fact is that the modern British locomotive owed most to what was happening abroad. The ten-wheeler was already well established in America in the 1860s for freight service and by the 1880s was commonly built as a mixed traffic 4-6-0, a type which also appeared in Europe at this time. The 4-6-0 appeared in Britain, nominally as a goods engine, on the Highland Railway in 1894. The designer, David Jones, had hitherto remained faithful to outside cylinders with the Crewe type of framing, but now he put the frames entirely inside, while retaining external cylinders. These engines were so useful that they often worked passenger trains, and were followed later by a version with larger (5 ft 9 in) driving wheels. A 'Jones Goods' is preserved in Glasgow, a fitting pointer to the Scottish lead in modern locomotive design.

The Atlantic type (4-4-2) came to Britain in 1898 in the form of Ivatt's No 990, later named *Henry Oakley*, the first of a very successful class and one of the prized items in the National Collection, now displayed correctly (being superheated in LNER days) as LNER No 3990. This graceful and to our eyes quite small engine may be a technical landmark, but it is no less an illustration of skilful labour relations. Enginemen were notoriously conservative, and the superb reputation of the Stirling singles meant that no successor would be readily accepted. But Ivatt produced an engine which was entirely familiar, with a similarly arranged, but longer, firebox, similar outside cylinders and just four coupled wheels, of a diameter reasonably reduced in view of their greater adhesion and the need to fit a larger boiler barrel. The men took to these engines at once, and performed some fine feats with them, but their reputation has been overshadowed by what followed. After four years, and having the confidence of the running and maintenance staff, Ivatt did what he no doubt planned all along and put a much larger boiler with a wide firebox, the first in Europe to be applied to a whole class, on to the same design of chassis. The first of the large Atlantics, No 251 of 1902, is clearly the first of the 'big engines' in the National Railway Museum. When equipped by Gresley with the large superheater, they could on occasion perform like Pacifics, as when No 4404 took over a 585 ton train unprepared, and averaged over 60 m.p.h. with it, producing 1200 drawbar horsepower for $1\frac{1}{4}$ hours.

Ivatt's big engine weighed 70 tons and in terms of weight, the other ten-wheeled express engines which followed in the next twenty years were much the same, but the grate area was generally less, as was the power exceptionally sustainable. Both the 4-4-2 and the 4-6-0 types were built extensively, and except for the locomotives of the Great Western and the Glasgow & South Western, the 4-6-0s were generally less satisfactory than the Atlantics. On the North Eastern and the Great Central, early express 4-6-0s proved less satisfactory than comparable Atlantics. On the Caledonian, the largest McIntosh 'Dunalastair' 4-4-0s could do everything his 4-6-0s could do. On the LNWR the small inside-cylinder 4-6-0s were scarcely the equal of their contemporary 4-4-0s, while Dugald Drummond on the LSWR produced four types of 4-6-0, only the last of which could equal the performance of the best of his 4-4-0s, but certainly not exceed it. In view of this sorry story, it is not surprising that the only pre-grouping 4-6-0 in the National Collection is one of Churchward's Great Western engines, which were magnificent.

If the work of Churchward is underrepresented in the National Collection, the same is not true of private preservation on preserved railways, where his designs are abundant. But the publicly owned *City of Truro*, *Lode Star* and the 2-8-0 No 2818 in the NRM do at least represent the three significant phases of Churchward design. Its distinguishing marks were a willingness to learn from overseas practice and great attention, paid personally and not just left to draughtsmen, to some details which were seen as vital. His design features were all tried out thoroughly before he produced his definitive designs. Most of the experiments were done while Churchward was still nominally under the able but ageing William Dean. *City of Truro* represents this phase, for

The first British 4-6-0, David Jones's Highland Railway locomotive of 1894, built for freight but equally useful for passenger service, now in the Glasgow Transport Museum.

The first British 'Atlantic', H. A. Ivatt's No 990, later named *Henry Oakley*, as built in 1898. A logical successor to the Stirling 'Eight Footer'.

Ivatt's secret weapon: the large 'Atlantic' boiler of 1902 which brought the wide firebox to Europe.

Churchward's GWR 2-8-0 No 2818 outside the NRM.

this is basically a Dean engine, but it has the benefit of Churchward's conclusions about valve timing and the type of taper boiler, with sloping and subtly curved Belpaire firebox, which Churchward copied from the 4-4-0s of the Pennsylvania Railroad. When he came to build an entirely original design, the 4-6-0 No 100 *William Dean*, in 1902, he copied the American arrangement of outside cylinders, with the two castings bolted together on the central line of the locomotive, fitted bar framing at the front end and adopted the American position for the valves set far inwards and driven by the internal Stephenson gear by levers on cross shafts. The design of the taper boiler progressed rapidly to the well-known 'Swindon No 1' type. This was the genesis of the highly successful 'Saint' class.

No 'Saint' is preserved, although the Museum has a good model (page 138), but the nearest thing is the equivalent 2-8-0, of which the Museum's example was built in 1905. In the comparative trials held in 1948, following nationalization, of the steam locomotives of the four group railways, this

pure Churchward design proved to be the most economical of the heavy freight engines. The Author's experience is that it was exceptionally sure footed on starting and also capable of quite high speed, if one was foolish enough to attempt it. Using smaller boilers, a large family of Great Western standard types followed the 4-6-0 and 2-8-0 types, including several varieties of 2-6-2 tank, the 'County' 4-4-0 and its equivalent 4-4-2T. Later, the first British mixed-traffic 2-6-0 was evolved from the standard parts. Churchward's four-cylinder engines with Walschaerts valve gear, which include *Lode Star*, will be dealt with later.

The eight-coupled outside-cylinder main line freight engine, in the form of a 0-8-0, first appeared in Britain on the Barry Railway in South Wales in 1886. Several other railways assayed the type, and in 1901 came the first of a long line of outside-cylinder 0-8-0s on the North Eastern. These were elegant, small-boilered machines and ninety were built before a similar engine with a greatly enlarged boiler appeared in 1913, of which there were 120. The National Collection has an example of the final type, with three cylinders: No 901 of 1919.

Excellent though some of the 0-8-0s were, it was Churchward's 2-8-0 that pointed the way to the future, when the addition of superheating generally increased the front-end weight and made leading carrying wheels desirable. This was well exemplified on the Great Central on which J. G. Robinson had introduced in 1902 a saturated (non-superheated) outside-cylinder 0-8-0 for mineral trains; he enlarged the design in 1911 to a superheated 2-8-0 version of which 126 had been built by 1914. No less than 521 were subsequently built for the Ministry of Munitions. The engines, popularly known as 'RODs' after the Railway Operating Division of the Royal Engineers which had operated them in wartime, were robust, reliable, powerful and easily maintained, with a boiler virtually the same as that of Robinson's Atlantics, having a Belpaire firebox with some 26 sq ft of grate. They weighed around 74 tons, the same as Churchward's engines after superheating. The National Collection has one of the first of the Robinson 2-8-0s, a worthy companion to the GWR engine. Of some 1700 later British 2-8-0s, the

The North Eastern Railway started building locomotives with two outside cylinders in 1899 but the National Collection has the last three cylinder type as exemplified by this ex-works view of No 901 when newly built.

LBSCR class I3 4-4-2 tank, on an express including a Pullman car. These brilliant engines first proved the value of superheating in Britain. Alas, none was preserved.

The Collection also has one of Robinson's Great Central 2-8-0s, of which 521 were built for the War Department. This one is on the LNWR, on loan after return from overseas.

The preserved *Sir Lamiel* **(SR No 777) in action on an enthusiast excursion, crossing the Scarborough bridge, York, on 29 July 1982.**

National Collection possesses none, a matter of some regret but mitigated by the fact that three types are represented by private preservation.

This narrative must now return to the introduction of superheating – a means of giving extra heat to steam after it has lost contact with the water in the boiler in order to provide it with more power to do work. In the nineteenth century various designs of steam dryer, or low temperature superheater, had been tried in Britain and abroad, but the main features of the modern, high temperature, superheater were devised by Dr Wilhelm Schmidt of Cassel in Germany. The event which proved decisive, as far as British railway history is concerned, was the decision of Douglas Earle Marsh, of the LBSCR, to fit superheaters to five of his large express 4-4-2 tanks, the well-known I3 class already referred to, built in 1908. At the request of the LNWR, one was tested against a LNWR 4-4-0 with no superheater over a 90 mile run between Rugby and East Croydon, with the 250 ton 'Sunny South Express', running at a little over 50 m.p.h. What astonished the railway world was not the performance in terms of power; both engines handled the train with no difficulty. But the tank engine, with only just over 2000

gallons on board, covered the 90 miles without running short of water and did the round trip on about 3 tons of coal. The 4-4-0 needed 3000 gallons and 4 tons of coal.

This was particularly significant in view of the considerably increased train weights, starting in the 1890s with the general introduction of bogie coaches offering a higher standard of comfort. While axle loadings were restricted, fairly light ten-wheeled engines were necessary for the heaviest passenger duties. But generally, higher axleloads became acceptable at about the time that superheating came in, and this produced a revival of the 4-4-0. This fact led the LNWR's chief mechanical engineer, C. J. Bowen Cooke, to produce one of the finest of the older British express classes, the 'George the Fifth' type, a 4-4-0 with a superheater, long-travel piston valves above inside cylinders, and a 10 ft coupled wheelbase enclosing a deep firebox. These engines were as good as most contemporary ten wheelers, and they were worked extremely hard with spectacular results. It is a matter of deep regret that one of these wonderful machines did not survive to be preserved. It is one of the few genuine 'lost causes' in an otherwise very comprehensive national collection.

It is also necessary, in this analysis of the move towards the modern steam locomotive, to refer again to locomotive valve gears.

The best of all valve gears was devised by Egide Walschaerts in Belgium in 1844, and reinvented independently by Heusinger von Waldegg in Germany in 1848. It requires less power to drive than Stephenson gear, is less subject to wear, is more precise in its action and is far easier to design. In fact, most of the Stephenson gears in the locomotives so far discussed were incorrectly designed, a fact which showed itself in the inability of the gear to be linked up to short cut offs – the admission of steam to the cylinder for only a short portion of the piston stroke, thus making maximum use of the expansive potential of steam at no extra fuel cost.

The only engines so far mentioned which had Walschaerts gear were some of the later and privately preserved 2-8-0s. The arrangement of two outside cylinders with valves on top and Walschaerts gear outside, so familiar in the later years of British steam, had its first modern application in some 2-6-0 mixed-traffic engines designed by H. N. Gresley for the GNR in 1912. Perhaps more significant were R. W. Urie's ten mixed-traffic 4-6-0s which appeared at the beginning of 1914, the H15 class. Although they lasted on average for forty-five years, none was preserved, but the National Collection has two important derivatives. One is the 'King Arthur' class 4-6-0 *Sir Lamiel* of 1925, the result of a revision, by R. E. L. Maunsell of the Southern, of Urie's big-wheeled later version of his 4-6-0. The other derivative was quite different: another mixed traffic 4-6-0, LMS No 5000, one of the famous Stanier 'Black Fives' introduced in 1935. Its number would suggest it was the first example built, but No 5020 of the same class was the first into service.

The public images of these two types could hardly have been more different. The seventy-four 'King Arthurs' (the total includes the twenty Urie engines as improved by Maunsell) all bore romantic names, were painted green, and spent much of their lives taking holiday-makers across the south of England. They worked boat trains, they raced westward with the 'Atlan-tic Coast Express', they even worked the 'Southern Belle' Pullman express between London and Brighton for a time. The 842 mostly unnamed 'Black Fives', on the other hand, worked everything from pick-up goods to express passenger trains, and their range of action extended from London to the north of Scotland. The 'Black Five' is commonly described as a Stanier derivative of the GWR 'Hall' class, devised by C. B. Collett by the simple expedient of fitting 6 ft driving wheels to a 'Saint', and so it is; but the 6 ft 4-6-0 in Britain had its origins in that Scottish school of locomotive design which Urie brought south with him to the LSWR when he followed Drummond.

The 2-6-0 or 'Mogul' wheel arrangement had already been long used in America when it was introduced to Britain by William Adams in 1878. These engines had outside cylinders with valves on top. Several inside-cylinder types followed on the GWR and in Scotland, while Churchward produced a first class outside-cylinder 2-6-0 in 1911. However, the first of the true imitations was the Gresley engine already mentioned as initiating the modern use of Walschaerts gear. In 1917 Maunsell, then of the SECR, produced the first of what was to be a numerous and excellent family of Moguls with taper boilers and Belpaire fireboxes, very like those of the GWR, but employing outside Walschaerts gear and quite high superheat. They were used mainly for freight on the Southern but could run fast with passenger trains, especially at peak holiday periods.

Among the best of British 2-6-0s in this Walschaerts valve gear 'family' were the engines which came from the Horwich Works of the LMS from 1926, the first of which is the only 2-6-0 in the National Collection. This was the first new LMS design, though it owed much to George Hughes of the LYR whose works Horwich had been. The big cylinders of these engines had big piston valves to suit. They were most capable engines, powerful on freight work and brisk on passenger trains. Some Scottish drivers preferred them to the later 'Black

Fives', and there was indeed little difference in the vital boiler dimensions (though the design was very different) nor in tractive effort. The 2-6-0, at 66 tons, was 4½ tons lighter than the 4-6-0, a fact accounted for by the extra wheels of the later engine.

Sir Henry Fowler designed a highly successful 2-6-4 tank on the basis of the Horwich 'Mogul'. There was some reduction in designed power, but the free running and general versatility remained, and this type was built in large numbers, developed by Fowler's successors Stanier, Fairburn and the younger Ivatt, and appeared but little changed as a British Railways Standard class after nationalization. Stanier's first version was a variant with three cylinders, of which a batch was built specially for the Tilbury line from 1934. The first of these engines belongs to the National Railway Museum, an interesting companion to LTSR 4-4-2T No 80, coming as it did so soon after the last batch of 4-4-2 tanks built for the Tilbury line in 1930. The preserved Stanier 2-6-4T is clearly a somewhat less characteristic example than a two-cylinder machine would have been, but it is the only big modern style passenger tank in the collection.

More Than Two Cylinders

There are two reasons for having more than two cylinders. One is to increase the power, when the limits imposed on the maximum width of the locomotive prevent further enlargement of outside cylinders. It then becomes necessary to add one or two inside cylinders. The other reason is to improve the balancing of the locomotive, and this perhaps requires a word of explanation.

With two cylinders, the cranks are set at right angles so that one cylinder can overcome the dead centres of the other. This means that the pistons, crossheads, part of the weight of the connecting rods and some other parts move back and forth in a sequential, not an opposed manner. Unless something is done about this, the whole engine tends to move jerkily, and the drawbar pull is a series of tugs. The effect gets much worse with increasing speed and can be very uncomfortable for passengers. It is possible to balance these various parts by the addition of weights in the wheels and elsewhere, but this destroys the rotating balance with the result that the wheels thump up and down as they turn at speed, and hammer the

One of the best LMS locomotive designs was the first to appear after the grouping, the Horwich 'Mogul' (a colloquial name for the 2-6-0 wheel form), a powerful and a lively express engine, an example of which is seen here at speed in cold weather near Derby.

The preserved Stanier three-cylinder LMS 2-6-4 tank No 2500, designed for the Tilbury line, is seen here in steam at Bressingham, Norfolk. Its livery is not completely accurate (a minor point) and will be rectified when, as expected, it actually returns to York (T. J. Edgington).

rails. This is known as hammer blow. The permanent way engineer does not like it and limits the axle loading he will allow, to compensate for it. The bridge engineer doesn't like it either.

The proportion of reciprocating weight which the designer chooses to balance is a compromise between hammer blow on the track and a jerky drawbar pull. There is no way out of this with only two cylinders, except by fitting reciprocating counterweights, never done in Britain. However, if there are plenty of coupled wheels, the hammer blow can be divided among them and its effect on the rails reduced, but the total hammer blow, which worries the bridge engineer, cannot. To make matters worse, the proportion of reciprocating mass to be balanced has usually to be greater if the cylinders are outside, because the disturbing forces are further apart and tend to make the engine 'hunt' or waggle along the track. With inside cylinders this effect is reduced to about one third.

In a four-cylinder engine, the inside and outside cranks can be opposed at 180 degrees on each side of the engine and the reciprocating masses balanced, avoiding either hammer blow or irregular drawbar pull. There will still be faint sideways disturbances, but the problem is really solved. The same is true in a three-cylinder engine,

though less obviously so, and again no hammer blow need arise, but the lateral disturbances are rather greater. So only an engine with two outside cylinders is prone to ride roughly, 'pump' the drawbar and inflict some damage on track and substructures and at times itself. In spite of this its simplicity and ease of maintenance has ensured its popularity, and great refinement has been brought to its design. But all the finest of larger British locomotives have wisely been fitted with three or four cylinders.

The first four-cylinder locomotive of normal type in Britain was a 4-4-0 of 1897, by James Manson of the Glasgow & South Western Railway, in order to pave the way for higher axle loadings. The civil engineer, like many of his kind in those days, understood nothing of this. His 'gut feeling' told him that if there were more cylinders there would be more hammer blow, so there were no more four-cylinder engines on the GSW. By this time there were many four-cylinder locomotives working on the Continent. They were compounds, and among them a

The 2-6-4 tank ultimately took the place of all the many 4-6-2 and 4-6-4 tanks, of which latter type the most famous were the LBSCR ones, later turned into 4-6-0s. This picture with a tiny Stroudley 'Terrier' (of the type exemplified in the collection by *Boxhill*) is one of many such photo contrasts in the Museum archives.

1400 horsepower in a slim package: *La France*, the Great Western's Nord-type four-cylinder compound 4-4-2, on an express at Westbourne Park, London, in 1905. A similar engine, but superheated, is preserved in France.

type appeared in 1900 which surpassed in power, speed and economy any other, in Britain or Europe. This was the Atlantic of the French Nord Railway, and in 1903 Churchward bought one for the Great Western, two larger ones following two years later. From these he evolved his own four-cylinder design, with simple expansion and only two sets of valve gear, believing (wrongly as it happens) that his excellent valve arrangements would compensate for the lack of double expansion. Eventually Churchward produced a superb machine, which he fitted with the same boiler as the 'Saint'. *Lode Star*, in the National Collection, epitomizes the smooth elegance of the British steam locomotive, but her boiler derives from an American model and her chassis from a French one, while the intelligent harmonization of these disparate elements was a product of Churchward's own genius. The 'Stars' were developed in the 1920s into the famous 'Castles' and 'Kings'.

The whole engine hammer blow of a 'Saint' was nearly 18 tons at 85 m.p.h. That of a 'Star' was brought down to 3.7, while a 'Castle' gave 3.5 and the much larger 'King'

only 2.2. A 'Star' weighed 75½ tons (after fitting of a superheater), the 'Castle' was a little bigger all round, while the 'King' was said to weigh 89 tons, but probably weighed 3 tons more, and was considerably more powerful in proportion. Though these two types were designed under C. B. Collett, they followed Churchward's lead in all important matters and set a standard for British express locomotives by which all others came to be judged. It is therefore fitting that all three classes should be represented in the National Collection: *Lode Star* at Swindon, *Caerphilly Castle* in the Science Museum, and *King George V* in Hereford, in the care of Bulmers, but frequently out on the road in steam.

When W. A. Stanier, later Sir William, left the GWR to take charge of locomotive matters for the LMS, he very soon produced a Pacific version of the 'King' by putting a large boiler with a wide Belpaire firebox on to a slightly altered 'King' chassis. Stanier's

The Great Western *Caerphilly Castle*, in the Science Museum. This 1923 design was then the best in Britain, an enlargement by C. B. Collett of Churchward's four cylinder 'Star' class.

'Princess' Pacifics were twelve in number, and after some initial difficulties proved extremely useful to the LMS, with its long distances, fast schedules and heavy trains. The cylinder and wheel dimensions were exactly as in the 'Kings', and so was the high boiler pressure of 250 lb/sq in, but they had four sets of valve gear, Stanier believing it to be superior. When the challenge of LNER rivalry led him to design a streamlined Pacific, however, these enlarged engines had only two sets of gear at the suggestion of Stanier's chief draughtsman. Known as the 'Princess Coronation' class, these engines are now always thought of as 'Duchesses'. *Coronation* herself reached 114 m.p.h. on a celebrated trial in 1937, thereby just beating the current LNER record of 113 m.p.h. After the war, when the streamlining was removed from those engines that had it, the class did its finest work, regularly developing the highest horsepowers recorded in Britain, especially when taking heavy trains

over the climbs to Shap and Beattock summits on the West Coast main line to Scotland. On test, *Duchess of Abercorn* briefly recorded 3,300 indicated cylinder horsepower, the British record. This is rather less than the peak power of French compound Pacifics of similar weight, which could reach 3,700, but Stanier maintained that the British loading gauge made large compounds impossible, while the cheapess of British coal made the fuel saving of the compound unimportant. Those that knew the 'Duchesses' in their prime will not complain: the music of a four-cylinder exhaust is unforgettable.

After the transfer of *City of Birmingham* to the Birmingham Science Museum, there was, strictly speaking, no LMS Pacific in the National Collection. Less strictly speaking, there still is, thanks to the indefinite loan of *Duchess of Hamilton* by Butlins Ltd, which has enabled this engine to be restored, operated and exhibited by the National Railway Museum.

Other than the GWR *Lode Star*, none of the large number of four-cylinder 4-6-0s inherited by the 'big four' at the 1923 grouping

Sir William Stanier's *Duchess of Hamilton*, newly returned to working order at York station in May 1980. This was the last and largest British four-cylinder design, introduced in 1937. The first carriage is the Museum's preserved ex-Royal Train escort vehicle, LMS No 5155.

survives. Of all those long-vanished types, one must especially regret the LNWR 'Claughton' class, occasionally brilliant but also one of the most elegant looking locomotives ever designed. Though many were built from 1913, the First World War prevented any major modifications, and the death of their designer, C. J. Bowen-Cooke, soon after resulted in nothing being done when the LMS received them. Had the less wealthy LNER inherited them, it might have been a different story; this company had an excellent record of improving older types.

Apart from *Lode Star* and the enlarged 'Castle' and 'King' derivatives, the National Railway Museum also has a fourth four-cylinder 4-6-0 in its collection, the Southern Railway *Lord Nelson* of 1927, preserved in fully working order from 1980 to 1986. This engine appeared only a matter of weeks before *King George V*, but was briefly the most powerful British 4-6-0. It was the first of a quite small class intended for very specific duties, including some of the Southern's heaviest boat trains which were frequently double headed at the time. The 'Nelsons', although four-cylinder machines, were conceived with no regard to the balancing advantage of placing cranks opposite, or nearly opposite, the spacing of cranks taken in sequence being 90, 45, 90 and 135 degrees. This gave eight exhaust beats to a turn of the wheels, but the whole

engine hammer blow, at just over 5 tons at 85 m.p.h., was over twice that of the 'King'. It was still moderate compared to a 'King Arthur' which produced over 20 tons at that speed, a speed the 'Arthurs' frequently attained in the West Country. The 'Nelsons' had four sets of valve gear and were good engines but did not distinguish themselves until Maunsell's successor, O. V. S. Bulleid, fitted them with his simplified version of the French Lemaitre exhaust arrangement, which required a very large diameter chimney and spoilt their good looks. The preservation of a 'Nelson' was a little surprising, but from 1980 to 1986 there was the opportunity to hear those eight exhaust beats and one can still admire the curiously aristocratic appearance of this locomotive, even though its running days are probably over.

Other than in Britain, the vast majority of the world's four-cylinder engines were compounds, while the vast majority of the globally somewhat less numerous three-cylinder engines were not. It is therefore somewhat ironic that the National Collection's oldest three-cylinder machine should be a compound: Midland 4-4-0 No 1000 of 1902, displayed in its superheated and

In 1913, C. J. Bowen Cooke produced the 'Claughton' class four-cylinder 4-6-0 for the LNWR. No example of this supremely elegant class has been preserved but the Museum has a fine 1/16 scale model.

rebuilt form of 1914. This was the first of a grand total of 240 engines built by the Midland and the LMS, by far the biggest class of three-cylinder compound built anywhere in the world and also Britain's numerically largest 4-4-0 design of any type. The Midland compounds were the only long-lasting compounds in British railway history, and very good, economical, smooth-running engines they were, especially on the hilly routes of southern Scotland after the grouping. They could also be very fast. They went a long way towards reinstating the compound locomotive in British esteem, but not far enough to have successors, though several were designed but not built, including two types of 4-6-0 and one Pacific.

The three-cylinder simple expansion locomotive is particularly well represented in the National Collection. The North Eastern 0-8-0 and the LMS 2-6-4 tank have already been mentioned, but there is also the Southern 4-4-0 *Cheltenham* of the 'Schools' class, the LNER 2-6-2 *Green Arrow*, one of the Southern Railway light Pacifics *Winston Churchill*, a heavy Southern Pacific *Ellerman Lines* (cut away to show the interior, and able to be rotated slowly by electricity), and, above all, the most popular exhibit in

the whole National Railway Museum, the record breaker *Mallard*. If that list leaves some notable gaps, these are largely covered by the private preservation of *Flying Scotsman*, two 'Royal Scots' and three or four LMS 4-6-0s of Stanier's class 5XP. Sadly unrepresented anywhere are the three-cylinder Atlantics of the North Eastern which once wheeled their heavy trains so serenely between York and Edinburgh.

The three-cylinder simple really started as a tank engine, if we exclude some early experiments. During this development phase, the old NER influence was probably the most significant, particularly in the work of Vincent Raven. It is thus fitting that the NRM's sole survivor from this period should be the above mentioned 0-8-0. Sir Vincent Raven, as he eventually became, produced

More lost elegance: Sir Vincent Raven's three cylinder 'Atlantic' locomotives on the NER were smooth running and economical. They lasted long but none was saved. Again the Museum has a model. No 2165 is posed with a First World War ambulance train.

many three-cylinder types, including the Atlantics already mentioned, the last 0-8-0s and finally a Pacific.

H. N. Gresley succeeded Ivatt as locomotive engineer of the Great Northern just after Vincent Raven succeeded Worsdell on the NER, but Gresley was a younger man, and in 1923, when Raven was ready for retirement, Gresley became the chief mechanical engineer of the whole LNER system. Gresley had taken note of Raven's activities, and had already produced two three-cylinder designs: a 2-8-0, based on his own two-cylinder 2-8-0 of 1913, and the most powerful of all British Moguls, the astonishing K3 class. His first Pacific, *Great Northern*, appeared in 1922, and the third of them, *Flying Scotsman*, in 1923, and thus an LNER engine.

Gresley, like Raven, preferred to concentrate the drive of all three cylinders on one axle, though he was not able to do this in all designs. This concentration is to be preferred from the balancing point of view (as it is in the case of four-cylinder engines). Raven had put six eccentrics on his crank axles, but Gresley put none, because he used external Walschaerts gear and derived the motion of the inside valve from those of the outside valves. Gresley's 2:1 conjugated valve gear has often been criticized, and certainly gave some trouble in the beginning – it was first used on the large 2-6-0 – but eventually gave less trouble than the inside valve gears fitted to the last LNER Pacifics built by his successors. It looked extremely simple and logical, was easy to reach and left the space between the frames wonderfully empty for those who needed to reach the inside crosshead and the middle big end.

Gresley had thirty years as a locomotive designer, on the GNR and the LNER. He was aware of locomotive developments in America, France and Austria, and applied some of them in his locomotives. After half-a-dozen two-cylinder designs, he concentrated on those with three cylinders (except for an experimental four-cylinder compound with a water-tube boiler). His hundredth Pacific coincided with his knighthood, is named *Sir Nigel Gresley* and is happily preserved in working order, as is *Flying Scotsman*. The National Railway Museum has his *Mallard*, which reached the world record for steam of 126 m.p.h. in 1938, and the V2 *Green Arrow*, the first of a long series of 2-6-2s virtually as powerful as the 4-6-2s, a class which regularly hauled twenty-four coach expresses and eighty wagon freights during the war.

Mallard differs from the first Gresley Pacifics in two important ways (and one unimportant one – streamlining). The valve gear was greatly improved in the early Pacifics after comparative tests with a Great Western 'Castle'. After the Churchward valve setting was adopted, the engines were much more economical and ran more freely. The first streamliner, built for the 'Silver Jubilee' express, could reach 113 m.p.h., but *Mallard* reached her higher speed because of the second change in the design: the double Kylchap exhaust system. Gresley was a friend of André Chapelon, the great French designer, who drew out *Mallard*'s exhaust for him. Gresley planned that all his Pacifics should have this exhaust system, but this was only achieved many years later.

The remaining three-cylinder locomotives in the National Collection came from the Southern Railway whose early engines of this genre were a continuation of the SECR 2-6-0 family and very much the result of that fine engineer R. E. L. Maunsell. His undoubted masterpiece was the three-cylinder 'Schools' class 4-4-0. The requirement was for an express engine lighter than the 'King Arthur' or 'Lord Nelson' types, and able to pass through the restricted tunnels of the Hastings line. His three-cylinder U1 2-6-0 type was not powerful enough, and was restricted to 70 m.p.h., so Maunsell designed an engine with larger driving wheels and a slightly shortened 'King Arthur' boiler, which weighed just over 67 tons and had more than 28 sq ft of grate. The forty engines of the 'Schools' class were probably the most powerful 4-4-0s in the world and certainly the last and most modern. They eventually replaced 'King Arthur'

4-6-0s on many duties, notably on the Southampton and Bournemouth line. Having three cylinders of the 'Lord Nelson' type and concentrated drive, they rode beautifully and were favourites with operating and permanent way staff alike. Not surprisingly, several have been preserved. The National Railway Museum has *Cheltenham*, which owes its preservation to the Railway Travel and Correspondence Society, founded in that town.

O. V. S. Bulleid succeeded Maunsell in 1937. He had worked closely with Gresley from GNR days (he was in fact H. A. Ivatt's son-in-law). Electrification of the Southern's suburban network had helped to spread London south of the Thames, but the steam locomotive stock had dwindled and aged. With a war in prospect, further electrification could not be counted upon, but greater demands on the system could be expected. Perhaps Bulleid's best claim to greatness is that he foresaw this and was able, even in wartime conditions, to build no less than 140 new Pacifics. The first type was the heavy 'Merchant Navy' class: thirty engines, of which the NRM has one example, *Ellerman Lines* in its rebuilt form, sectioned and motorized as an instructive exhibit. These engines weighed about 96

tons and had $48\frac{1}{2}$ sq ft of grate. The rest of the Pacifics, the 'West Country' and 'Battle of Britain' classes, were 10 tons lighter and had 10 sq ft less grate area. Of these, the NRM possesses *Winston Churchill*, more or less in original condition.

The basic design of the Bulleid Pacifics was like that of Gresley's. The trouble was that Bulleid put all the experiments into one design. To be fair, many of the innovations only ranked as such in this country. The welded steel fireboxes, with thermic siphons, had long been common in America and had been a success in France. The box-like wheel castings were also common in America, 280 lb/sq in boiler pressure had often been exceeded in Europe and America, and things like air-operated firedoors and other conveniences were long established in some countries. Unfortunately, the coal consumption of Bulleid's original Pacifics was fantastic, largely because of the valve gear, which was a miniature version of Walschaerts, driven by chains, encased in an oil bath and anything but precise.

Mallard, **Sir Nigel Gresley's record breaker of 1938. Streamlined and with double Kylchap exhaust, this was the final form of his three cylinder LNER 'Pacifics'.**

Green Arrow **was the first of 184 2-6-2 mixed traffic versions of Gresley's 'Pacific', built from 1936. To some, these were 'the engines that won the war'. The locomotive is seen at Carlisle (Upperby) on the occasion of the return to steam on the Settle–Carlisle line, Easter 1978 (D. Jenkinson).**

R. E. L. Maunsell's three cylinder 'Schools' class 4-4-0s were the last and most powerful of the type. From 1930 they replaced 4-6-0s on some Southern routes. The preserved No 925 *Cheltenham* **is shown here in the 1946–7 Southern Railway colours with so-called 'sunshine' lettering.**

All the 'Merchant Navies' and many of the others were rebuilt with conventional valve gear, and then became as economical as any other modern locomotives. But even in their original form they were exceptionally fast and powerful engines, which rode smoothly and could compete with any equivalents in the land as regards performance. During those comparative trials held just after nationalization, Southern Pacifics produced the highest horsepowers recorded, and on some routes nothing so powerful had been seen before. But their consumption of fuel and water was by far the highest, and they used vast quantities of oil, because it escaped from the valve gear casing, and sometimes ended up on the wheels, causing slipping. Moreover, their annual revenue mileage compared with Gresley and Stanier Pacifics was poor. The rebuilt engines retained all the virtues of the original design, and eliminated most of the faults. Without the smooth casing, they revealed the proportions of their boilers and showed their large Lemaitre chimneys. One must be glad that some of these engines have survived in

The sectioned *Ellerman Lines*, the rebuilt form of Bulleid's larger 4-6-2 type.

both original and rebuilt forms, for they were the last really exciting design in the history of British steam, if not the best.

Nationalization and Modern Motive Power

The extensive comparative trials undertaken in 1948 were nominally intended to establish which features of the locomotives of the four group companies best merited inclusion in new Standard designs to be prepared by British Railways. In the event they had little influence save in the context of establishing some of the component parts to be used in new engines. The practice of no one railway showed overall superiority and it was natural enough that R. A. Riddles, a Crewe trained ex-LMS man, should, for the most part, continue to develop the steam locomotive along LMS (Stanier inspired) principles. New Standard designs were introduced (to avoid giving offence by perpetuating too many LMS types) but it was a little odd that there should be so many. There were 2-6-0s of three different sizes, two 2-6-2 tank designs, a 2-6-4 tank and two 4-6-0s – all essentially LMS derived engines, though the smaller 4-6-0 and the intermediate 2-6-0 were novel variations and some made use of

GWR-type boilers. The larger types were two sizes of Pacific (later augmented by a single more powerful engine) and a 2-10-0 freight locomotive, which was numerically the largest of all the Standard classes, with 251 out of the grand total of 999 British Railways designed steam locomotives.

The National Collection has examples of the most numerous Pacific type, the 'Britannias', and the large freight engine. There were fifty-five 'Britannias', weighing 94 tons with 42 sq ft of grate, dimensions very close to those of the older Gresley Pacifics, but the new engines had only two cylinders. They were therefore harder on the track than Gresley's three-cylinder engines, but were given a greater route availability rating, which enabled them to be used on the old Great Eastern main lines of the former LNER. The London Midland Region had inherited few wide firebox engines from the LMS, only 50 as against 386 built to LNER design and so was able to make excellent use of 'Britannias'. But the few on the Western Region, where there was no tradition of wide fireboxes, were greeted with suspicion, not to mention prejudice; though they regularly worked some expresses with perfect competence, they were not really needed or much liked. Like many engines with only two outside cylinders, they inflicted some damage on themselves, and were unreliable at first in consequence, but in the long run (and, as the first of the Standards, introduced in 1951, they had a longer run than any others) they won universal good opinions as powerful and reliable locomotives, and their decidedly un-British but handsome appearance was an effective symbol of the new order in the railways of Britain. Of all the Standards, this was the one most obviously needed in the passenger field.

The last steam locomotive type represented in the National Collection is the Class 9 heavy freight 2-10-0, the NRM engine *Evening Star* being the best known and officially the last of the class. Swindon Works gave it a passenger green livery and the magical adornment of a copper-capped

British Railways' official last steam locomotive *Evening Star*, **in steam at Swindon when new, on 11 March 1960. It was finished in passenger livery; pictures of this engine on a freight train are rare!**

Great Westernized chimney in anticipation of its ultimate status. *Evening Star* is a star among preserved locomotives, often seen in action at speed on passenger trains, and her whole class is sometimes seen as the best of all the Standard classes. The lives of these engines were so short (some ran for only six years) that their long-term value remains unknown.

It seems a little quixotic for Britain to build a 2-10-0 fifty years after the type first appeared in Europe and at a time when mineral traffic was in decline. Another curiosity of the 2-10-0s was the driving wheel diameter. The freight trains they might be expected to work seldom ran at more than 40 m.p.h., so the fitting of wheels which were appropriate to 60 m.p.h. suggests that the exact role of the Class 9s was uncertain. The 5 ft wheels entailed a long wheelbase and made the design of the firebox and ashpan more difficult. If a mixed-traffic machine was intended, a 2-8-2 with a 'Britannia' boiler might have been expected and was originally the type envisaged; but Riddles was concerned about the possibility of wheel slip with a trailing truck and insisted on a 2-10-0 with the largest wheels which could be associated with a wide firebox.

In due course, the Class 9s achieved their best work in just the sort of role that would

have been entrusted to 2-8-2s in most other countries. There were occasions when they were logged at speeds of 90 m.p.h., and there is no reason to doubt the ability of these engines regularly to reach this speed. However easily the steam might pass through the cylinders, at 90 m.p.h. the whole engine hammer blow and the oscillations of the drawbar pull would both be approaching 20 tons, which does no good to locomotive, track, bridges or the train, and the 90 m.p.h. exploits were soon suppressed by 'authority'.

But the occasional abuse of these locomotives at least showed the excellence of the mechanical design and one must regret that these splendid machines came too late to find a real role on the railways of Britain. Perhaps the nearest they came to one was on the Somerset & Dorset line, now long closed, where very heavy holiday trains had to be worked over formidable gradients at good speeds. The sight of them at work there was as stirring as anything ever seen on British metals, and is an enduring memory of the last British steam locomotive design.

We now turn finally to the non-steam items of motive power in the National Collection, diesel and electric. For the most part these date from the British Rail period – hence their inclusion at this point in the story; but a few interesting pioneers date well back into the company period and some background information is relevant, starting with the diesel story.

The internal combustion engined locomotive had the same sort of primitive beginnings in industrial locations as the steam locomotive, at the beginning of the twentieth century. It had achieved something like a definite form in a double-bogie diesel-electric heavy shunting engine in the USA in 1925. It remained mainly a shunter until after the war, though streamlined trains with diesel engines incorporated began to make their mark in the United States in the 1930s, and railcars were considerably used in France and Germany. The very limited pre-war use of the diesel in Britain included a few railcars, but was mainly in the form of six-wheeled shunters, and this type proliferated after the war.

It is not surprising, therefore, that numbered amongst the NRM's diesel collection is a more than adequate representation of the characteristic, if humble, diesel shunter. Compared with their steam counterparts it might be argued that there are too many (four standard gauge and one narrow gauge), but there are sound reasons. Firstly, there are three forms of diesel transmission to consider (electrical, hydraulic and mechanical) and a small 0-4-0 or 0-6-0 is a convenient way of covering all three types without absorbing too much storage space. Secondly, the Museum has regular need to move its rail-borne exhibits around the site and a simple way to do this is to use a fully working diesel shunter. The Museum has three such engines which cater for both these needs, the 1953 built Class 08 Diesel Electric, No 08 064, the 1960 Class 03 Diesel Mechanical No 03 090, both in final BR colours, and the 1960 Diesel Hydraulic, restored to its original colours as D2860. Of these, No 08 064 is particularly interesting since its ancestry can be traced back to the adoption of diesel-electric propulsion for shunting purposes by the LMS in the 1930s.

The BR Class 08 was a direct development of the standard LMS type.

This company was the British pioneer in diesel traction – along with the GWR in the railcar field – and it was the LMS which produced Britain's first main line diesel electric, No 10000, at the end of 1947. This engine was not saved for posterity and its absence from the National Collection may be regarded as just as regrettable as some of the lost steam causes already mentioned. However, much of the experience gained with No 10000 was subsequently built in to later BR diesels such as the preserved Brush Type 2 (see below), so all was not lost.

When the modernization plan, foreshadowing the elimination of steam on British Railways, was announced in 1955, the decision to offer the initial £1,200,000,000 was a political, not an engineering one. This was made obvious by the stipulation that the money should not be spent in the railway workshops, but with private industry. As a result a large variety of diesel locomotive types was produced by firms in competition, and many of them were unsatisfactory,

Preserved British Railways diesel-mechanical shunting locomotive No 03 090. This engine, fitted with an exhaust 'cleaner' was used inside the Museum during 1975 for the 'setting up' operations and is kept in full working order.

while the ones which were less so still required a period of development to iron out the teething troubles. This proliferation of types not only caused much trouble to British Rail at the time but has subsequently presented the NRM with more than one 'Judgement of Solomon' problem in terms of its preservation policy. It is not possible to save everything – in spite of the many blandishments from outside – if for no other reason than that it would unbalance the whole collection. Secondly, it is often not possible to bring a true historical perspective to bear until well after the time in question. Indeed, some observers maintain that future railway historians may regard the wholesale dieselization of the 1950s and '60s as a ghastly aberration and that full electrification would have been better from the outset. The NRM, in attempting to portray an ongoing story, has to come to terms with this problem and nowhere is it more difficult than in the case of locomotives. What, for instance is typical, what is significant and what is outstanding? These are difficult issues to resolve and, in a sense, the NRM collection already reflects the confusion and uncertainty. Take for example, the celebrated 'Deltic' diesels.

The Eastern Region remained unimpressed with the first generation of BR diesels which generally, at best, only equated to a V2 2-6-2 in power. Following the Gresley 'big engine' tradition, it acquired twenty-two 'Deltics', which could produce over 50 per cent more power but had only three-quarters of the weight of the first 136 ton 2000 hp engines. The prototype, built as a speculation by English Electric in 1955, resides in the Science Museum. The production 'Deltics' were only slightly different. With their opposed-piston, two-stroke engines, a total of 36 cylinders and 72 pistons, they were very expensive – about five times the cost of the largest steam locomotives – but they were the only diesel locomotives in the world able to run continuously at over 100 m.p.h. and gave magnificent service for some twenty years, until the High Speed Trains displaced them from the East

The only diesel-electric locomotive type which could be described as brilliant, even by world standards, was the English Electric 'Deltic'. Its two-stroke engines always left a trail of visible exhaust like this. The engine featured is the preserved No 55002 during its last years of British Rail operation.

Coast route in 1978. One of them, appropriately No 55 002 *King's Own Yorkshire Light Infantry* has a place in the NRM, but they were neither characteristic nor typical of contemporary BR diesel practice in general.

What, however, was characteristic or typical at this time? In the early days of dieselization the secondary services out of King's Cross experienced much dismal performance and amazing unreliability from three types of locomotive in the then Type 2 power classification. But a fourth type eventually displaced all the others. Introduced in 1958 and originally known as the Brush

The most successful diesel-electric 'maid of all work' has been the Brush, later Hawker-Siddeley, type 2 (Class 31). The Museum's example, the first of them, shows the pleasant appearance devised by the British Railways design panel.

Type 2, this was at first a 1,250 hp engine (some uprating has since taken place, with new diesel engines). Weighing just over 100 tons, they were 50 per cent heavier than the ageing 0-6-2 tanks which worked many of the trains they took over; they were also certainly 50 per cent more powerful and more versatile in consequence. This Class 31 type, to use its later nomenclature, was also reliable – at that time the rarest of virtues in a diesel. Many were built, and almost all are still in service on a variety of mixed traffic, including some fast passenger trains and some heavy freight. The first of them is deservedly preserved at York. Interestingly, H. G. Ivatt (the former LMS CME when No 10000 was built) was much involved in their design.

Another proven type from this first diesel phase, was the so-called Class 20 design, of which the prototype No D8000 (later No 20 050) was selected for preservation. Compared with D5500 it looks markedly different, not having an all-enclosed body style but it functions in much the same way. Its utilitarian bodywork (known as the 'hood' style) merely serves to protect the machinery, and the Museum takes advantage of this by opening up several of the hinged doors to enable visitors to see within. Indeed, one of the problems of non-steam traction is that outward form rarely reflects internal function, so it is hard at times to see 'how things work'. How many realize, for example, that a diesel electric is actually a mobile power station wherein the diesel engine generates electricity in order to drive the electric motors which actually turn the wheels?

For this reason, the NRM has found it necessary to display rather more 'bits and pieces' of non-steam traction in the form of generators and bogies, for example, in order to explain more fully what is going on. Amongst these may be mentioned a diesel-hydraulic power bogie from a 'Western' class locomotive; for as well as its fully functional diesel-hydraulic shunter, the Museum also has an example of the final fling of Great Western individuality, dating from 1963, proof that fifteen years of nationalization had not produced uniformity. The Western Region determinedly experimented with direct hydraulic transmission, with which the Germans had achieved some success, because the equipment was lighter, not needing a generator or traction motors amongst other items. In the long run, the electric transmission proved more reliable and easier to control, but No D1023 *Western Fusilier* and the others of the largest diesel-hydraulic type did some good work in their rather short lives.

Western Fusilier is not always at York, being still in full working order, but, along with the other locomotives mentioned, serves to contribute to a representative cross-section of the 'first generation' diesel-

Preserved and restored Class 20 diesel-electric No D8000, outside the Museum.

The power bogie, showing the traction motor between the wheels from a withdrawn British Rail Class 24 diesel-electric.

ization of British Railways. Pedants may argue the case for further examples but on the whole it is unlikely that more will be selected from this period, save for one or two examples of those longer lasting, more numerous and generally more effective units which are still (in 1987) going about their daily routines, having stood the test of time. Already, the prototype High Speed Train power unit No 41001 has been added to the collection, along with a mock-up of the production series cab.

Paradoxically, pure electric traction has a longer history than the diesel, and in Britain the first electric locomotives started work on London's Underground in 1890. One is preserved in the Science Museum, and a later underground locomotive, used on the LSWR's Waterloo & City line from 1898, is on view in York. There is also a somewhat maverick battery locomotive of 1917; but these are little more than tractors, and the oldest recognizable electric locomotive is NER No 1 of 1904. When the NRM opened in 1975, this was the only electric locomotive on view, and its preservation can only be described as a piece of luck. Two such locomotives were built for working coal trains on a line which was partly in a sharply curved and steeply graded tunnel on Tyneside. Steam locomotives produced asphyxiating conditions in that tunnel, and while things were far better on the Metropolitan and District railways' tunnel sections in London, those railways adopted the same policy as the NER and produced very similar locomotives. None of the London locomotives survives in anything like its original condition, so the one at York stands to represent the first style of main line electric locomotive in Britain.

The NER later built more and larger double-bogie electric locomotives for normal freight service on the Newport–Shildon line, which was also equipped with overhead wires, but none of these has survived. Perhaps the saddest loss, particularly in view of the electrification of the East Coast main line, is that of the NER's electric express engine, No 13. This was built in

North Eastern electric freight locomotive No 2, twin of the preserved No 1 of 1904, which represents the first generation of main line electrics.

An impressive view of the preserved 1500V DC locomotive No 26020 outside the NRM.

The now preserved electric locomotive No E5001 seen on 'Golden Arrow' Pullman service at Dover.

1922, when it was planned to electrify the main line between York and Newcastle. Designed by Sir Vincent Raven, it was an admirable design for its period, and under test it developed the designed 1800 hp with a 450 ton train. For forty years this machine was annually run on the Newport–Shildon line, electrified at 1500 volts. It was then scrapped, but the NRM has a fine model.

The first real main line electrification in Britain, in which freight as well as passenger trains were so worked and entailing the building of a large class of electric locomotive, was that between Manchester and Sheffield, undertaken by the LNER but completed in BR days. It was planned under Sir Nigel Gresley, and one of his last locomotive designs was the prototype double-bogie locomotive for the line. This machine was tested in 1941, and then laid aside until it was lent to Holland to help in the post-war revival of that country's railways, which included lines electrified at 1500V DC. Experience was gained there of the qualities of the design, while the Dutch named the engine *Tommy*. Eventually it returned to England and many more of the type were built. *Tommy* was scrapped some time before any of the others, as it was non-standard in some respects. It had technical and historical claims to preservation because, like LMS No 10000 in the diesel field, it was the first British main line electric locomotive to see extended service, and its post-war travels added to its interest. However, the NRM has one of the basically similar production series, BR No 26020 which went on show at the Festival of Britain in 1951 and headed the first official train through the Woodhead Tunnel in 1954.

The Museum also has a later double-bogie electric locomotive from the Southern Region, where eventually such machines were brought in to replace steam in the haulage of trains, such as many boat trains, and inter-regional service trains, which were not worked by multiple units. No E5001 is one of a class which spent most of its time running on lines electrified at low voltage and equipped with a third rail from which the current is collected – lines shared with the suburban and main line multiple unit trains. Of the 25kV AC electric locomotives which operate the former LMS route to Scotland, none has yet been acquired by the National Collection, although a Class 84 from the 'first-generation' 25kV 'build' is on loan until a more characteristic type is withdrawn. Main line electrification came late to Britain, but it has a long future, and the locomotive acquisitions of the NRM are likely to be predominantly of electric locomotives.

Like most other parts of the National Collection, the locomotive element can never be complete and much has, perforce, remained unsaid. The various steam, diesel and electric self-propelled units have scarce been mentioned, save in the rolling stock chapter; and exploration of many interesting sidelines which the collection might suggest has had to be suppressed, including the influence of British engineers overseas. This is an inevitable consequence, in spite of the declared gaps in coverage, of the Museum being in possession of such an immensely rich assemblage, and for this there must be cause for thanks.

Presented to the National Collection by the Chinese Minister of Railways, this 4-8-4 is one of twenty-four which were the largest single-unit steam locomotives ever built in Britain for service overseas. KF 7 (607) of 1935 worked until 1977 and symbolizes, in very impressive fashion, the British contribution to overseas railway activities.

Chapter 3

Right of Way

The railway is a highly disciplined form of transport and has been so since its origins, the mere fact of matching wheels and rails having imposed a basic discipline from the outset. However, with the development of the mechanized railway in the early nineteenth century, additional safety constraints were gradually imposed in the form of signalling; while the railway itself, as a fixed feature of the physical landscape, developed more and more characteristic forms as its growing sophistication made increasing demands upon the skills of that still relatively new specialist, the civil engineer, often in association with the architectural profession. The railway line, or 'right of way', can be simply divided into three principal elements: the fixed structures themselves; the track which was put down on or around these structures and the signalling methods.

These vital aspects of the railway story are not simple either to present or interpret in a museum; in the case of civil engineering and architectural structures, the problem is well nigh impossible for two main reasons. Even if the objects themselves were not generally far too large to move into a museum environment, many of the most significant are still in use on the modern railway. (The ability of engineering structures to carry loads and withstand stresses far greater than those first envisaged when the railways were built is a remarkable tribute to Victorian engineers.) The Museum can do little more than build up a comprehensive archive of drawings, plans and photographs to give a cohesive picture of this astonishing achievement. Space can be found for selective models of important structures and, in one small but important case, the Museum has managed to re-erect outside the famous Gaunless Bridge from the Stockton & Darlington Railway. However, to appreciate fully Britain's railway heritage of civil engineering and architecture, one must continue to examine the real thing *in situ*. Happily, current British Rail management is not unaware of its inheritance in these areas and has made major steps in both conservation and restoration of its more significant structures.

Fortunately for the Museum, the other two aspects of the story, permanent way and signalling, are easier to portray. In both areas the collections are considerable and the rest of this chapter is devoted to a consideration of their more important aspects.

Permanent Way
by David Mosley

The track, or 'permanent way', is the physical basis of the railway, and has several intrinsic advantages: vehicles can be guided along on a prepared track and do not have to be individually steered, while a smooth running surface reduces friction, helping to use motive power efficiently. The origins of guidance for wheeled vehicles goes back at least as far as the Romans, but it is generally agreed that the concept of railways came about in the mines of central Europe in the late fifteenth century. By the early seventeenth century, railways connected with the coal-mining industry were in use in Britain, a prominent example being that developed by Huntingdon Beaumont in 1603 at Wollaton near Nottingham.

The Midland Grand Hotel at St Pancras c. 1907 – typical of mid-Victorian railway architecture in its most ebullient and very permanent form. The hotel was opened in 1875 and is now a listed building. Part of Barlow's great train shed roof to the adjoining station can just be seen on the right.

The famous and celebrated Ouse viaduct on the London to Brighton main line. Built in 1841 and highly typical of the railway 'look' in terms of the bigger fixed structures, this fine example of early Victorian civil engineering is still in use today.

George Stephenson's River Gaunless Bridge, re-erected outside the NRM. The world's first iron bridge on a railway line, it was completed in 1823, but replaced in 1900 by a bridge suitable for greater axle-loads. It is fortunate that this pioneering structure has been preserved.

These earliest railways were of wooden construction and the Museum has an example of wooden rails dating from 1750. These were used at the Groverake mine near Blanchland in Co. Durham and are laid to the very narrow gauge of 18 in, thus giving some idea of the small scale of these earliest operations. As railways expanded through the coalfields, so methods were introduced to increase the longevity of the wooden rails; replaceable strips were fitted to the top of the rails, to be renewed as they were worn away by the wagons' wheels. By 1767 these strips were sometimes made of cast iron.

The formative years of the cast-iron rail are represented by two principal types. The 'plateway' was championed by such engineers as Benjamin Outram and John Curr and had an 'L-shaped' cross section, enabling road carts to run directly on the rail, thus avoiding interchange between the two modes. The Museum display features plate rails from the Penydarren Tramway, where in 1804 they proved somewhat fragile under the weight of Trevithick's pioneer steam locomotive, and from the Peak Forest Tramway. In the latter case the complexities of a turnout in plateway are vividly illustrated; the display is complemented by the stone blocks which acted as sleepers.

The plate rail was superseded by the edge rail. The forerunner of today's rails, edge rails were advocated by William Jessop as early as 1792 for use with flanged wheels. Made of both cast and wrought iron, early edge rails were 'fish-bellied' with a thicker centre section where not supported by stone blocks. Edge rails and flanged wheels are shown in a display featuring a wagon of 1815 from the Vale of Belvoir Railway whilst other fish-bellied, cast-iron rails come from the Liverpool & Manchester Railway and a less famous line between Mansfield and Pinxton in Nottinghamshire. Some idea of the extreme discomfort of early passenger travel can be gained from a 15 ft long section of malleable iron rail from the Stockton & Darlington Railway. An unsprung coach and rails set in chairs carried on stone blocks must have made for an unenviable ride!

The Museum's model of part of a 'lost' Brunel bridge – the Landore Viaduct, Swansea, over the River Tawe, which opened in 1850. The original, mostly of wooden construction, had thirty-seven spans varying from 40 to 100 ft and was a third of a mile long.

Some early engineers considered that the combination of smooth iron rails and the smooth treads of steam locomotive wheels would prevent the locomotive from hauling heavy loads. In an effort to overcome this problem, John Blenkinsop, working on the Middleton Railway in Leeds, patented in 1811 a special type of fish-bellied rail with projections on the outer face. These projections formed a 'rack' along which locomotives with an appropriate driving cog wheel could haul themselves when moving heavy trains. This system, used at Middleton until the 1830s, formed the prototype for today's 'rack and pinion' mountain lines. When Isambard Kingdom Brunel designed the Great Western Railway, it was to a broad gauge of 7 ft 0¼ in and with a radically different approach to the permanent way. Bridge rails with an 'omega-like' section were placed on longitudinal wooden baulks and held to gauge by metal tie rods, the whole being known as 'baulk road'.

In the early years of railway development, the differing approaches to the details of the permanent way were as numerous as the

Plateway: a plain wheel running along a flat rail with a guiding upright plate attached to the inside of the running surface. Plateway was widely used on early horse powered lines but the coming of the steam locomotive frequently tested the thin plates beyond the limits of their construction. The wheel is part of the Peak Forest truck, a full view of which is given in Chapter 1.

The classic railway configuration, flanged wheels running on edge rails: this example is from the Vale of Belvoir line which opened in 1815. The rails display the 'fish-bellied' appearance common at this period, the inherent weakness of the cast iron being compensated for by an increase in depth in the unsupported area. The stone supporting blocks are also evident.

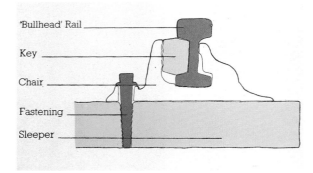

'Bullhead' Rail

Key

Chair

Fastening

Sleeper

A self explanatory diagram of track components of the steam age along with characteristic track components of the present showing flat bottomed rail on concrete sleepers with the rail held in place by 'Pandrol' clips.

many private companies. The variations in rail section, fishplates and chairs are represented by a large reserve collection of permanent way exhibits.

The permanent way of the steam age soon assumed a settled form with gradual improvements. Early ballast materials like ash and slag were replaced by high quality Beckfoot granite on the London Midland & Scottish Railway. The sleepers which supported the rails came to be of hard wood protected by a soaking in creosote, and on to these were fixed cast-iron chairs which carried the rails. These chairs, in many styles, all featured a wide base to spread the weight of a passing train. The rails were secured in the chairs by a wooden or metal key. The rails, traditionally in 60 ft lengths, were joined end to end with an all important gap of about $\frac{1}{2}$ in to allow for expansion in hot weather. The rails were connected by fishplates. As railway vehicles became heavier so the rail sections became more massive until the rails in use today may weigh as much as 113 lb per yard.

The first steel rails in this country were produced by Robert Mushet for the Midland

Railway and were laid at Derby station in 1857. They gave five times as long a life as contemporary wrought-iron rails and so ushered in the material which is now standard for all rails. Steel rails were usually of three types of cross section. In Victorian times some use was made of 'double-headed' rail which, it was intended, could be turned over and the second face used. In operation this idea proved impractical as the face held in the chair sustained so many gouges and irregularities that it adversely affected the quality of the ride once inverted. The most common rail type in the days of steam was the 'bull-head' with a heavy running surface but smaller bottom area supported in the chair. The numerous chairs and keys of the bull-head rail made it relatively costly to maintain, and after the nationalization of the railways in 1948 widespread replacement was undertaken with 'flat bottom' rail which is easier and less costly to maintain.

In the heyday of steam railways, maintenance of the permanent way was a vital but labour intensive activity. Armies of navvies undertook the initial building of the railway; indeed, the term 'permanent way' is the name for the finished railway as opposed to the 'impermanent way' used by the navvies and contractors during construction. The last major line to be constructed in the old style by navvies without large-scale mechanical aid was the Settle & Carlisle in the 1870s, but the replacement of large sections of track was also a labour intensive operation, as can be seen in the accompanying photograph from the Museum archives. Day-to-day maintenance was undertaken by gangs of plate-layers (their name is a throwback to the earliest days) under the control of a ganger. Each gang had its own section of line to maintain, and competitions were held annually to determine which section was the 'prize length'.

The Museum's display shows some of the major components of the permanent way in the heyday of steam, and the panels of track, complete with points, are presented as part of an operational signal display. The intro-

In the days of the private railway companies the replacement and maintenance of the permanent way was a most labour-intensive occupation. This Lancashire & Yorkshire Railway official picture shows replacement of sleepers at Bolton station on 16 August 1914.

A 'plough brake' in action: ballast is lowered into the space between the rails from doors in the floors of the wagons. It is then pushed into approximate position by the plough on the brake van and can be seen spilling out over the rails near the rear of the train.

duction of High Speed trains has brought about radical changes in the permanent way, and this modern type is also represented in the Museum. Gone are the wooden sleepers, now replaced by cast pre-stressed concrete with the position for the rails already in place.

Insulation is a feature of modern tracks as the rails carry a weak electric current to facili-

Track inspection in the old style. The Museum's 'Velocipide' in action.

A more modern track inspection/recording vehicle. On the occasion of the centenary of the Permanent Way Institution, a 'Neptune' stands outside the Museum. Behind is an early 'Matisa' tamping machine.

The two working sets of points on display in the Museum. Nearest the camera are the semaphore signals with their associated mechanical lever frame; the electrically operated points with their colour light signals are at the far end.

tate 'track circuiting'. As a train's wheels pass over the track, the circuit provided by the current is broken and the signalman is provided with a visual indication of the train's whereabouts. The flat-bottomed rail is therefore insulated from the sleeper by a plastic pad and the rail fastenings, the Pandrol clips, are also insulated. The Pandrol clip is one simple but ingenious way of securing the flat-bottomed rail to the sleeper. It is a steel spring clip which can be easily driven into place or removed as necessary. Its tensile strength makes it very much less susceptible to vibration and it does not work loose. It is also unmoved by 'rail creep', a tendency of rails to move slightly in the direction of travel of a braking train. Pandrol clips are cheap and easily replaced so compare favourably with the complexities of chairs and keys. Pandrol clips were first used on British Railways in 1959, and with well over 50 million now in use are the most common rail fastening.

These new components have combined to produce a more efficient but less rhythmical permanent way, often with continuous welded rail laid in lengths of over a mile. The need for expansion joints is overcome by the

massive section of the new rail and the laying of the prestressed track at a time of the mean temperature to be expected during the life of the rail.

The Museum's collection also includes a number of maintenance, inspection and track-laying vehicles, which were supplemented in June 1984 by a large collection of contemporary machines in a temporary exhibition to celebrate the centenary of the Permanent Way Institution. Of the Museum's own permanent way vehicles, by far the most romantic is the 'Velocipede'. This is effectively a tandem-tricycle which was moved along by a rowing action; originating in the United States in the 1870s, they were used for inspection and light maintenance duties. A more familiar vehicle to fulfil the same function is the Wickham trolley. Powered by a JAP motorcycle engine, the Museum's example was built by Wickham of Ware in Hertfordshire in 1933 for the LNER. Rather basic in appearance with canvas weathersheets, the trolley is light enough to be easily sidelined when not in use.

The LMS 'plough brake' of 1932 represents the beginnings of mechanization in the laying or large-scale replacement of the permanent way; a brake van fitted with small snowplough-like attachments underneath, the plough brake was placed in a ballast train and designed to push the ballast roughly into position as it was discharged from the hopper wagons. The permanent way gangs then pushed the ballast into the final position in, under and around the sleepers – a process known as 'tamping'. By the 1950s tamping was becoming mechanized, reflected in the Museum's Matisa machine from the period and a much larger and sophisticated Plasser lining control (to align the rails) and tamping machine from 1968. The latest vehicle in the collection, the Neptune Track Recorder, marks the beginning of the trend away from a labour intensive facet of railway operation to one which is now in the forefront of the high technology era.

Signalling
by J. T. Howard-Turner

A railway comprises, in effect, two main but complementary systems – a carefully designed, constructed, and maintained track, and the trains themselves which run on that track and which carry the traffic that earns the bulk of the revenue. However, it would not be practicable for trains to run other than at very low speeds unless stringent precautions were taken to ensure that their drivers were given adequate warning of any need to slow down or stop. The distance required to stop the train is obviously critical to the subject of signalling.

The great advantage of railway transport is the very low rolling resistance of steel wheels on steel rails, enabling very heavy trains to be operated at high speeds. But this carries with it the disadvantage that such heavy and fast trains require relatively long distances to be brought to a stand. For example, a passenger train weighing several hundred tons and scheduled to run for long distances at 100 m.p.h. or over, may require a distance of a mile or more in which to come to a stand. A loaded freight train, weighing perhaps over 1000 tons and travelling at over 60 m.p.h., may require a broadly similar distance in which to stop. These distances are enormously greater than those needed by motor cars, coaches or heavy lorries running at comparable speeds. The braking distance is greatly lengthened as speed increases.

It is virtually impossible for a train driver to stop his train from a high speed in time to avoid an accident, if the first warning he has is when he actually sees, for himself, that conditions ahead are unsafe for him to continue at his normal speed. The driver must have adequate warning, perhaps a mile or more away, of any necessity for him to slow down or stop where he is not expecting to have to do so. Therefore, the art of railway signalling is to provide such equipment and apparatus that trains can be driven at speeds far higher than would be the case if the driver had to see directly that everything was safe for him to proceed at high speed,

At Borough Market Junction was a relatively small 35-lever signal box with power frame which controlled one of the world's busiest railway junctions near London Bridge station. Opened on 17 June 1928, it was superseded as part of a major re-signalling operation in the mid 1970s, but before removal, it was carefully photographed and recorded so as to facilitate complete re-erection at the NRM. It is shown here in both its original location and as re-erected on one of the Museum's outdoor sites.

and to slow down or stop if it were not. Without any form of signalling a driver would probably have to proceed at walking pace through a tunnel (particularly a curved one), or even perhaps at night.

In early days the running of trains was somewhat akin to the running of horse-drawn vehicles on roads, in that drivers were expected to keep an exceptionally careful lookout and be prepared to stop if they saw that the way ahead was not clear or, if they were warned to stop, even if they could not themselves see any reason for such out-of-course delay. However, soon after the Liverpool & Manchester Railway was opened in 1830, it was realized that signals must be provided which drivers could see from afar, and which would therefore give them sufficient warning of any necessity to reduce speed or to stop. From the mid 1830s, all main line railways had some form of signalling, even if only at specific places. The earliest 'fixed' signals – so called to distingu-

ish them from flags or lamps held by staff beside the line – were provided at stations and (a little later) at junctions remote from stations, often separated by miles of track.

The first means of telling a driver that his train was close behind another train, was the 'Time Interval' system: when a train passed a fixed signal in the clear position, that signal was put to danger to protect the train, and was then kept at danger for a prescribed first interval of time, usually 5 minutes. When that had elapsed, the signal was made to indicate caution; and after a second interval, often another 5 minutes, had also elapsed the signal was placed in the clear position again. If a second train approached the signal while it was still at danger, it had to stop until the first time interval had fully elapsed, when it was allowed to proceed under caution. The signal was again put to danger and the Time Interval cycle was restarted. If the second train approached while the signal was at caution, it could continue at reduced speed while the driver and fireman kept a sharp lookout. The signal was of course put to danger again and the whole cycle restarted. If the second train did not approach until both intervals had elapsed and the signal showed clear, it could of course proceed at its normal speed.

The 'Time Interval' system was reasona-

This mechanism demonstrates a very early method of controlling various signals from one position. When the relevant stirrup was depressed by the signalman's foot, and then moved slightly away by a subsequent action, the stirrup remained depressed holding the signal to show a 'proceed' indication. When the signalman pulled the stirrup towards him and removed his foot, the signal returned to 'stop'. The iron structure supporting and guiding the stirrups formed a framework, from which the term 'frame' was taken to denote an apparatus containing a number of levers working signals, points, etc. The example shown came from the Manchester Sheffield & Lincolnshire Railway, probably about the late 1840s, and is the earliest mechanical signal frame in the S&T Study Collection.

A set of highly characteristic, former Great Northern Railway 'somersault' semaphore signals mounted on their original lattice bracket post symbolically control the rail access to the Museum's main display hall.

bly satisfactory provided that no untoward incidents occurred, but clearly did not cater for the possibility that train No 1 had passed the signal in the clear position, but had then come to a stand at a place from which it could not be seen from that signal. If train No 1 had stood long enough for the full time-cycle to have elapsed at the signal (which would then have been made to show 'clear'), there was grave risk of train No 2, running under a 'clear' signal, colliding with the rear end of train No 1.

It was eventually realized that space rather than time was a safer method of control. This new principle laid down that the man working one signal (A), and of course placing it to danger when train No 1 passed, was not allowed to place it again at caution (let alone to give the clear indication) for train No 2 until he had received advice from the man at the next signal (B) that train No 1 had reached and passed signal B. This advice was given by the electric telegraph, which was being developed simultaneously with railway communication. Where this

method was considered too restrictive on train working, it was laid down that if train No 2 reached signal A before train No 1 had reached and passed signal B, signal A could be placed in the caution position to allow train No 2 to continue on its journey, but in the full knowledge that train No 1 was not far ahead.

The second method, subsequently known as 'Permissive Working', was later abolished for normal passenger-train working, except in the vicinity of certain large stations or in other somewhat abnormal conditions. It was retained for lines used by freight trains. With these changes, signals on passenger lines were made to show either danger or proceed only.

The method of space interval working became known as the 'Block System', and has been the basis of railway signalling for well over a hundred years. The means of

A fair-sized mechanical frame by Stevens, the design dating from the 1890s, is shown here still in use at Allbrook Junction, north of Eastleigh (Hampshire) on the Southern Region. This photograph shows certain matters worthy of mention including various types of signalling instruments, indicators, and signal and point repeaters, mounted on the 'blockshelf' above the levers, and in the centre, the diagram of the layout controlled by the signal box.

A tappet locking principle was applied to certain 'miniature-lever' frames by which points and signals were operated by electricity, by compressed air or by compressed air under electrical control. Such frames are known collectively as 'power frames', the first ones in the UK having been installed in 1899. A very large installation of this type is seen here at Glasgow Central Station. Installed before the First World War, it had no less than 374 levers.

achieving the space interval between trains have changed with the times, the types of signals and their methods of working have changed, the equipment has changed and the basic concept has been greatly widened. For example, in modern signalling a driver will only be given a clear signal provided that safety of the track itself is proved, quite apart from an absence of conflicting movements.

The introduction of railways was a major factor in the rapid development of the electric telegraph and subsequently of special instruments and equipment for railway signalling purposes. Normal telegraph instruments for the transmission of messages gave transient indications only, but for railway signalling purposes continuous indications were normally needed.

Since the fundamental object of railway signalling is to enable drivers to run their trains at the highest permissible speeds in full confidence, it is imperative that misleading or wrong signals or incorrectly set points are impossible. This was achieved by fitting interlocking to signal box lever frames. Various forms of interlocking were developed from about the 1850s, and in some cases were protected by patents. As the railways grew, safety requirements became more stringent and traffic levels increased, necessitating more complex track work and consequently interlocking. Patent rights sometimes stood in the way of the development of some already well-established designs, so entirely new types of apparatus began to appear from the 1870s onwards. Moreover, not only were a number of the then privately owned railway companies designing and manufacturing their own types of apparatus to meet their own requirements and to avoid having to pay royalties to various signalling contractors, but several such contractors were in competition with each other.

It is against this background that the NRM has, over the years, assembled one of the finest and most comprehensive railway signalling collections anywhere in the world. As yet it is only partially exploited, but already in the Main Hall of the Museum are two working exhibits of about the middle period of signalling and interlocking, and various show cases. The first of the working exhibits shows a pair of points with relevant semaphore signals, all operated mechanically. There is still a considerable amount of equipment of this type in use on British Rail in the late 1980s, but the quantity is steadily diminishing as modernization takes place.

The second working exhibit also shows a pair of points and relevant signals; the points are operated by an electric motor and gearing and the signals are colour lights. The equipment formed part of the set up installed in 1926 at Holborn Viaduct station in London, and was saved for the NRM in the early 1970s when the area was resignalled. To the end of its life, that particular installation retained the original display arrangements for the use of two yellow lights (giving four separate aspects of red, yellow, double-yellow and green). It is important to note that the term 'amber' is *not* used in railway signalling in the UK.

In the adjacent display cases are examples of various types of signal equipment, and some thought is being given to the practicability of placing another signal box near the car park at the north end of the Main Hall.

The whole subject of railway signalling and telecommunication is so broad, much of it being an enigma to those not fully in touch with it on a daily basis, that the exhibits referred to above can only show a fraction of what has been involved in creating British Rail's enviable safety record. There is insufficient space in the Main Hall to enable safety considerations to be explained, or to show the many important and ingenious types of equipment that have been designed and developed over the last hundred and thirty years. A Signalling & Telecommunications Study Collection is therefore being put together. This study collection may be seen by those students who have a genuine need to visit it, but unrestricted and unescorted public access is not at present contemplated. The means whereby special visiting permission may be granted are given in Appendix III.

Chapter 4

Off the Rails

It is important to realize that the growing sophistication of transport during the nineteenth and twentieth centuries encouraged the railways to develop a whole infrastructure down the years until it was in a position to offer a totally integrated 'package' to a potential consumer: 'door-to-door' as it were, whether it be people or merchandise or even the livestock and implements of a complete farm. As a result the railways entered the business of carriage by road, water and even air as the years went by, but almost always in support of their principal business of trunk haulage by rail. The railways had a considerable stake in canals, the present National Bus Company had some of its origins in railway omnibus services of the 1920s and '30s and a small but very early part of the internal domestic network of what is now British Airways can trace its roots back to the Railway Air Services operations of the mid 1930s.

The NRM could not possibly hope to cover the whole story in terms of preserved hardware, although the balance is somewhat redressed by archive sources. Two elements are, however, well represented by exhibits: road vehicles and shipping, the latter mostly in picture or model form. It is these two areas which feature in the next few pages.

An Albion motor bus of 1929 owned by the LMS which built the bodywork. Destined for operation in Scotland, this vehicle, and others like it in the LMS Glasgow fleet, was ultimately transferred to Western SMT in 1931 which eventually became part of the Scottish Omnibus group.

In the mid-1930s, the GW, LMS and Southern Railways collectively took to the air under the umbrella of 'Railway Air Services' – an idea pioneered by the GWR a year earlier. Cross-country routes were chosen and this picture of a DH Dragon Mk II at Speke airport, Liverpool shows the inauguration of the Liverpool–Plymouth service on 7 May 1934.

Road Vehicles
by Lilian Hogg

It surprises many visitors to see road vehicles on display in a railway museum. It is a popular misconception that there has always been a feud between road and rail companies. This probably stems from the earliest days of railways when road hauliers, fearing for their livelihood, banded together as the Anti-Railroad Society. In due course the majority of these protestors threw in their lot with the railways and happily amassed fortunes as their cartage agents. Later still, the railways developed their own road services, but the memory of that original, brief antipathy lingers on.

From their beginning, railways provided a passenger and goods transport service that was cheaper and quicker than anything hitherto. Yet those pioneering railways had to rely heavily on existing road transport to fulfil their obligations. Many companies, for example, opened sections of their line before the whole route was complete and had to shuttle passengers from one section of line to another by stage-coach. It was also common for stations to be a little way out from the centre of a town, so omnibuses were hired by the companies to provide a passenger service between the station and the town centre. In those early days the vehicles used to ferry passengers were horse drawn. Some were stage-coaches still proud of their fanciful names, such as 'Highflyer' and 'Defiance' which were advertised in the Manchester & Leeds Railway timetable as available to meet the Manchester train at Littleborough.

More common for town services were omnibuses, similar to the original 1829 vari-

A London & South Western Railway horse ambulance. The false floor was rolled out to collect the injured horse. The animal was then held upright in the ambulance by a canvas belly band secured with winches.

The Museum's only passenger carrying road vehicle: a horse bus from the Kent & East Sussex Railway, built around the turn of the century.

ety pioneered by George Shillibeer in London. They had a body longer than a normal stage-coach with three windows in each side and a door at the back. These vehicles seated about twenty people and were pulled by three horses.

The only passenger road vehicle in the collection is a light single-horse bus which was acquired by the Kent & East Sussex Railway in 1913. It was used for transporting passengers between Rolvenden station and Tenterden town. Its style and date make it something of an anachronism, since by 1913 the larger railway companies had experimented successfully with motorbuses and charabancs. Unfortunately, none of these motor passenger buses was saved to come into the Museum collection, but many were photographed by the railway companies and the results may be examined in the Museum's photographic collection.

The Museum has a small but diverse collection of road goods vehicles, which provide examples of most of the major developments that occurred in the railway's haulage of goods by road. In the 1830s and

'40s the emerging railway companies dealt with goods in a similar way to passengers, in that they were only interested in getting customers to send their goods by rail; how it arrived at the station and how much that journey cost were matters best left to cartage agents. Goods haulage, however, soon became a major field of competition between rival railways and each company tried to maximize their share by offering a door-to-door service.

By 1860 the majority of railways had absorbed cartage into their overall operations. They provided stables, ostlers and vets, and a few even had farms to grow fodder and graze out retired horses. In pre-motor days, the horse enjoyed something of a monopoly as the prime mover of railway goods by road, but enjoyed is surely the wrong word to use, for the life of a railway horse was one of hard, unremitting toil, up to fourteen hours a day, seventy hours a week. The average working life of a railway horse was not surprisingly a mere five years. Yet the railway carters looked after their horses, exhibiting them at shows and very often walking off with a majority of the prizes. They also provided care for them when sick. In the road vehicle collection is a very sturdy, smartly turned out, horse ambulance owned by the London & South Western Railway, used to collect 'fallen' horses from the street.

Goods cartage undertaken by the railways was of two types: a fast or express parcels service and a heavy haulage service for bulk goods. The parcels services normally covered fairly short routes in towns, with many stops. The vans and horses were much lighter than for bulk haulage. Parcels vans were light covered wagons, weighing a minimum of 30 cwt, drawn by either one, two or three horses. These horses, nicknamed 'trotters', were mainly Cleveland Bays, Dales Ponies or Welsh Cobs. The Lancashire & Yorkshire parcels van in the collection is typical of those built at the turn of the century for single horse operation. In the 1930s horse-drawn parcels vans were still

The Museum's second major complex in 1908 when it was a bustling goods yard. Note the weighbridge, which was a vital piece of equipment in any goods yard.

being produced but with added refinements like pneumatic tyres, electric headlamps and disc brakes. This final design prevailed until the 1950s when horse-drawn vehicles were completely withdrawn.

Most heavy goods were loaded on to flat drays, lurries or rulleys (the name depended on the local vernacular, but design differences were slight). These drays came in a variety of sizes, and their weight determined the number of horses needed to pull them. The Museum has three drays, two from railway companies and one from an early cartage agent in Aberdeen. All are basic four-wheeled flats with wooden shafts. The latest of them has solid rubber tyres but the earlier two have the more usual wooden iron-rimmed wheels. As with parcel vans, the later drays were built with pneumatic tyres which, of course, reduced vibration.

Railways were called on to carry an extremely varied selection of goods, and many special vehicles were built to accommodate their customers. An 8 ton heavy duty dray at the Museum has a specially low floor for tall loads, and screw clamps for holding sheet wood, metal or glass. Such a dray was normally pulled by at least two horses, often more.

At the beginning of the twentieth century, railways began experimenting with mechanical means of propulsion for their road services. The GWR pioneered a motor bus passenger service between Helston and The Lizard in August 1903. Such was the success of this experiment that, ten years later, 242 passenger motor buses were in use by railway companies and 192 mechanical cartage vehicles were in operation.

Motorized cartage vehicles all aimed at improving the efficiency of goods handling by the railways, but there were quite a few problems to overcome before a completely satisfactory system was established. For express parcels deliveries the motor vehicles used were light four-wheeled, canvas-topped vans, a natural progression from their horse-drawn predecessors. Their main advantage over horses was speed and the ability to cover a wider delivery area. The Commer van in the Museum collection, built in 1938, was used by the LNER for their fast parcels service in London. The design was typical for such vans in the 1930s and '40s, when speed and reliability were crucial to keep up with the road competition that was

A horse drawn 8-ton dray owned by the Midland Railway. Photographed at Lawley Street, Birmingham in June 1909 by the railway's own photographer.

then developing. We are lucky to have this van, for most of the remainder of the fleet was destroyed during the Blitz in London.

For heavy haulage, which tended to be medium distance with infrequent stops, steam lorries had a brief heyday at the beginning of this century. The major manufacturers were Foden, Clarkson and Sentinel. The Museum has on loan a 6 ton four-wheeled steam wagon built by Sentinel in 1918. Although it is not strictly a railway vehicle, the design is identical to those supplied by the company to the Lancashire & Yorkshire Railway and it is painted in the colours of that system.

By 1930 steam for heavy haulage had virtually disappeared and the motor lorry reigned supreme, with petrol engines being

Horse drawn and mechanical equivalents of the express parcels van. The sides of the vans were often used to advertise other services offered by the company, in particular transport to holiday resorts.

Three mechanical horses in the collection. The blue is a Scammel, the maroon is the unique Karrier Cob 1G and in cream and maroon is the British Railways 'electric horse' built by Electricars of Birmingham.

replaced in due course by the diesel variety. The one major drawback with most goods lorries was that they had to remain idle while being loaded or unloaded. The horse, in comparison, could be uncoupled from an empty dray, coupled to a waiting loaded one, and continue working again with a very short turn-round period. To solve this problem the LNWR came up with the idea of 'demountable' flats for their motor vehicles. These could be moved around on top of an ordinary horse-drawn dray, fitted with longitudinal guide rails along which the 'demountable' could slide. The latter was then transferred to the motor lorry using similar guide rails fitted to its load platform. Lining these rails up and physically transferring the load was a dangerous, exhausting and time-consuming business. The GWR tried to solve the same problem by using motor tractors and trailers, but the trailers proved very unstable on public roads.

So despite all the mechanical achievements of the motor age, the old horse continued to be king in the goods yard. His regal, if plodding, progress in the streets, however, was leading to increased complaints of congestion from other road users, as indeed, was all horse-drawn traffic, whatever its origins. In due course the LMS issued a brief to the motor trade for a mechanical alternative to the horse for local deliveries. It had to be cheap, light, manoeuvrable and easily uncoupled from a dray. The result was the Karrier Cob. The original vehicle, LMS No 1G, survives in the Museum's collection. The 7 hp engine provided speeds up to 18 m.p.h. The narrow three-wheeled tractor and 3 ton carriage capacity provided both strength and manoeuvrability. The main drawback was the coupling system which had been devised to haul existing horse drays. It was a hand-operated hydraulic mechanism which lifted the dray so it could be coupled to the back of the tractor. The operation was slow and required considerable driving skills. Later Karrier Cob models improved on the coupling design, but by this time the Scammell company had brought out a tractor and trailer with an automatic coupling that both saved time and reduced the risk of accidents. Scammel and Karrier mechanical horses were widely used by all four of the grouping companies. Although their introduction started the process of ending the use of horses and carts, it was not until the late 1960s that the last railway horse was retired.

For longer distance road haulage to meet increasing competition, the railways introduced considerable fleets of motor vehicles during the 1920s and '30s, and also offered manufacturers complete distribution systems, including railway depot warehouses. With small consignments, increasing costs also saw the use of motor vehicles extending over greater distances from a limited number of rail-head distribution centres.

After nationalization in 1948, British Railways inherited a vast goods delivery empire of staff, vehicles and equipment, and set about a rationalization plan which involved cutting out duplicated services, mechanizing the goods warehouses and yards in the larger centres, and using road distribution to an even greater extent. In the early fifties an electric version of the mechanical horse was developed. This battery-electric vehicle, built by Crompton Parkinson Electric (owned by the Austin Motor Co), proved very successful, and an initial fleet of a hundred provided services at sixteen different centres throughout Britain. An almost identical type produced by Electricars of Birmingham was used on the Southern Region of British Railways. One of these vehicles is preserved in the collection. It can haul $2\frac{1}{2}$ tons and its battery will last 25 miles between charges. The maximum speed is 18 m.p.h.

The Science Museum, of course, collects historic vehicles, and the understanding of road haulage generally is therefore obviously enhanced by the collection at York.

Railway Shipping
by Michael Blakemore

In the 1970s the British Railways Board, through its Shipping and International Services Division, was the world's largest dock owner with seventy-six harbours, wharves and docks and 95 miles of quays. It should come as no real surprise that the railways became so closely involved with the shipment of passengers and freight by sea. Britain is, after all, a traditional trading nation, and even before the railways developed, was producing goods which were in demand in all corners of the globe. Some of the earliest railway ventures sought to connect the manufacturing centres with the great trading ports. The railway companies were nothing if not brimming with enterprise, and were soon asking why they should be content merely with depositing the customers and their products on the quayside when, for a little extra investment, they could take them on to the high seas as well? There was money to be made and the railways, the directors reasoned, might as well make that money as anyone else.

The first experiments in steamship operation were modest. In 1841 the Glasgow, Paisley & Greenock Railway put on two boats to carry passengers to the Firth of Clyde resorts, while the following year the directors of the London & Blackwall Railway speculatively introduced a ferry service between Blackwall and Gravesend. But the distinction of establishing the first railway-operated sea-going line belongs to the South Eastern Railway which, dissatisfied with its arrangement with the New Commercial Steamship Company to provide a Folkestone–Boulogne service, formed a subsidiary company of its own in 1844.

The strategy of founding independent subsidiaries to deal with shipping business had to be adopted, as at this time the railway companies were specifically barred by Act of Parliament from directly owning ships. Indeed the London, Brighton & South Coast Railway was taken to court by the SER which alleged that company capital had

been put into the Brighton's shipping subsidiary. The case was found proved and the LBSCR heavily fined, no doubt to the satisfaction of the SER which had itself been refused permission to invest in its own maritime offshoot.

The law was eventually changed in 1863, and in the ensuing years many of the companies whose lines reached the seaports tested the water and acquired fleets of their own. By 1913, 216 railway-owned ships were registered, and the maritime activities of the companies earned them an income of over £5 million a year.

Nor did the railways concern themselves just with the operation of their fleets; a great deal of energy was devoted to the development of harbour facilities. Fleetwood, for example, was entirely a product of the railway age and was developed by the Lancashire & Yorkshire Railway which grew to be the largest railway steamship company. Newhaven was expanded by the LBSCR after it had found Brighton unsuitable and Shoreham extortionate. Development of this sort continued in the twentieth century with the Midland Railway creating the port of Heysham (completed in 1904), while the ever-ambitious Great Central was instrumental in the founding of Immingham which was declared open by King George V

in 1912. But, of course, not all railway shipping interests were quite so extensive; at the other end of the scale were such as the Furness Railway with their homely pleasure craft on Lakes Windermere and Coniston.

The preservation of a locomotive or item of rolling stock brings problems enough; the preservation of a ship is another proposition altogether. This the Museum discovered in 1978 when the possibility was aired – and found impractical – of claiming the paddle steamer *Lincoln Castle*, the last Humber ferry. The Museum's record of the railway shipping fleets therefore consists of some forty scale models, supported by small exhibits and photographs. Often the models were commissioned by the owning companies and were displayed in glass cases at important stations on their systems. Complementing the models is a fine collection of maritime photographs, covering the activities of the railway docks as well as a sizeable number of actual ships.

Six of the models represent paddle steam-

The paddle steamer *Paris*, seen here at Newhaven, was built for the LBSCR in 1888 by the Fairfield Engineering & Shipbuilding Co at its Govan yard on the Clyde. She remained with the LBSCR until 1912 when she was sold to the Shipping Federation and was scrapped in 1924.

The Great Central Railway's new deep water dock at Immingham under construction in 1909. Its creation of the port of Immingham on a 1000-acre site in the Lincolnshire marshes south of the Humber estuary was the last major dock development undertaken by a railway company. Building work took six years, during which 2500 men were employed and the equipment used included 10 steam navvies and 39 cranes.

ers. Somehow the idea of the paddle steamer seems to belong firmly to the nineteenth century but they continued to be built for the railway companies well into the twentieth century – in fact the last, the previously mentioned *Lincoln Castle*, was not commissioned until 1940. An earlier example with a tale to tell is the *Paris*, built in 1888 for use by the LBSCR between Newhaven and Dieppe. In 1890 the company awarded her crew an extra month's pay for their efforts in bringing her safely home after she had been stricken in mid-Channel with a damaged paddle wheel at the height of a ferocious north westerly gale.

One of the more modern designs was the PS *Whippingham*, introduced on the Southern Railway's Portsmouth–Ryde service in 1930. She was one of that great armada of

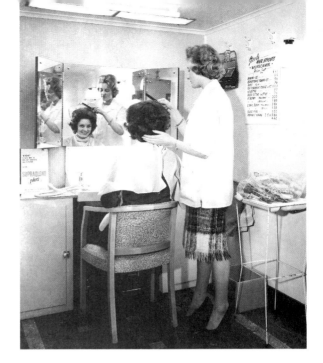

The Southern Railway's paddle steamer *Whippingham* was another product of the Fairfield Engineering & Shipbuilding Co. Launched in 1930 and shown leaving Ryde, she was withdrawn from service in 1963.

Changing fashions – the 'sixties look' is applied in the hairdressing salon of the *Duke of Lancaster* during a crossing between Heysham and Belfast in 1963. Built as a twin-screw steamer by Harland and Wolff of Belfast in 1955, *Duke of Lancaster* was later converted to a car ferry and employed on the Fishguard–Rosslare service before being withdrawn in 1979.

ships which, in May 1940, took part in the evacuation of troops from Dunkirk, and of the almost eight hundred boats engaged in this mission it was to this modest steamer that the distinction fell of rescuing the greatest number of men on a single voyage – no fewer than 2,700, more than double her intended passenger load.

This was just one of a whole series of wartime adventures of many ships represented in the model collection. Given Britain's dependence on its seaways, it was inevitable that the railway ships – especially the larger screw-propeller-driven vessels of the twentieth century – should be required to play their part in the national defence.

One such was the *Engadine*, constructed in 1911 for the SECR's sailings from Dover and Folkestone, and one of the first two British ships to incorporate a purpose-built car deck. Requisitioned for war service in 1914, *Engadine* became a seaplane carrier and on 31 May 1916, at an early stage in the Battle of Jutland, staged the first-ever launch of an aircraft during a naval engagement. Despite poor visibility, the pilot and his observer managed to sight and report three enemy cruisers before ditching in the sea, the only means at this time of 'landing' a seaplane.

Wartime escapades came the way of the *Côte d'Azur*, one of the French-built vessels of the Société Anonyme de Gérance et d'Armement which had taken over the ships of the Northern Railway of France (Chemin de fer du Nord) in 1923. Dating from 1930, *Côte d'Azur* is not, therefore, strictly a railway ship but is certainly worth a mention as a reminder that the French railways also played a role in the operation of Channel steamer services and continue to do so in the form of the nationalized SNCF. Called up for war duty in May 1940, she assisted in the evacuation of French troops from Flushing, Belgian civilians and troops from Ostend and British troops from Dunkirk. Whilst undertaking the latter assignment, she was hit during a bombing raid and went down, which should have been the end of the story. She surfaced again the following year under the German flag and was employed as a minesweeper in the Baltic, finally disappearing in the inhospitable waters around Stettin in 1944.

It is the coincidence of the development of

the railway fleets during the twentieth century and the international upheavals of 1914 and 1939 which has resulted in so many of the Museum's models representing ships with such colourful histories. Whilst only a few examples have been reviewed, it would nevertheless be wrong to assume that they all had such illustrious careers.

The SS *Ouse*, for instance, was one of the LYR's fleet of cargo ships plying between Goole and northern Europe. The *Ouse* spent nearly thirty years in the mundane general trading which was the cornerstone of the nation's economy until, in August 1940, while attempting to avoid a torpedo from an E-boat off Newhaven, she became just one of the 4,786 merchant vessels to be lost through enemy action.

The humble 'service' vessel is represented by a fine model of the grab and sand-pump dredger *Rhyl* which was built in 1911 for the LNWR to the design of its Marine Superintendant, Commander G. E. Holland. Based at Garston near Liverpool, *Rhyl* was employed on dredging duties along the Mersey and within the port itself, and at the time of launching was the only combined sand suction and grab dredger afloat. In January 1950 she passed into the ownership of the Docks and Inland Waterways Executive (which, following nationalization of the railways, took over the railway-owned 'trade' ports) and after years of faithful dredging was scrapped in 1958.

The collection is rounded off by three more modern ships from the British Railways era. These are two of the three 'Dukes' (*Argyll* and *Lancaster*) introduced in 1956 on the Heysham–Belfast service and the unimaginatively named *Holyhead Ferry I* which, when launched in 1965, was the first vessel with drive-on/drive-off facilities to operate between Britain and the Irish Republic.

Of course, 'modern' is a relative term. The 'Dukes' have all been withdrawn and the last to remain in British Rail ownership, *Duke of Lancaster*, now functions incongruously as, of all things, a country club moored on the North Wales coast. The *Holyhead Ferry I*, after a working life of a mere sixteen

Model of the twin-screw steamer *Côte d'Azur*, constructed by Forges et Chantier de la Méditerranée at Le Havre in 1930. *Côte d'Azur* fell into enemy hands in 1940 and was finally lost in 1944.

Model of the LNWR's grab and sand-pump dredger *Rhyl*, built in 1911 by Ferguson Bros Ltd, of Port Glasgow. *Rhyl* spent her entire career at Garston Docks from where she was withdrawn from service in 1958.

The *Holyhead Ferry I* was constructed for British Railways by Hawthorn Leslie (Shipbuilding) Ltd in 1965. The other side of this model features a cut-away panel (revealing contemporary 'Matchbox' cars) and illustrates the changing requirements of the car age. There never was a *Holyhead Ferry II*; by the time the original was succeeded on the Dun Laoghaire route, 'proper' names were back in favour!

years during which it did at least acquire the more inspiring name *Earl Leofric* whilst sailing out of Dover, was accounted for by a firm of Spanish breakers in 1981. And finally, in 1984, under the government's policy of selling-off profitable state-owned industries, British Rail's maritime subsidiary, Sealink UK, was purchased by the Sea Containers group, so bringing to an end a hundred and forty years of railway ships.

PRESENTED TO
ROBERT STEPHENSON ESQUIRE
CIVIL ENGINEER
BY A NUMEROUS BODY OF FRIENDS
IN TESTIMONY OF THEIR ADMIRATION OF HIS TALENTS
AND ESTEEM FOR THE INTEGRITY AND INDEPENDENCE OF
HIS PROFESSIONAL CHARACTER.
NOVEMBER XVIth MDCCCXXXIX.

Chapter 5

Not Just Technology

Although 'modern' transport systems are based on technology, the railways have played a large part in the social as well as technological history of this nation, and as a result this Museum holds certain collections which would grace the galleries of many a fine art museum.

The early railway companies soon realized that their new mode of travel could not pay its way merely by transporting people from A to B. It was no use moving hundreds of people many miles from home and abandoning them on station platforms with no facilities, so they built hotels. These were usually next door to or an integral part of the main line stations and were equipped with the most fashionable and exquisitely crafted artefacts, often designed to persuade the public that this was definitely the way to travel. For passengers wishing to go further afield, the railway companies built ships and fitted them out like floating hotels. Then came 'on train' catering and other developments until, beneath the smoke-covered exterior of the rail transport system, there was often a hidden world of polished mahogany, silver and crystal (at least for its wealthier patrons) never before associated with land transport.

At the same time craftsmen of all types were using their skills in other areas of the new transport system. Just as locomotives and carriages were being turned out in the most elaborate and colourful paint schemes with ornate lettering and company coats of arms, so too, carriage furniture was carved

This magnificent silver plated epergne and candelabrum stands 3 ft high. The engraved legend on the base states that it was presented to Robert Stephenson by his friends in testimony of their esteem in 1839. It would be hard to find a more appropriate item to symbolize the non-technological aspects of the Museum's collections.

and inlaid, intricate ironwork and stained glass appeared at stations, uniforms had brass buttons and gold braid, medals were struck to honour company servants, elaborate presentation pieces were made for retiring board members, souvenirs of all types appeared to commemorate the opening of a new line or station (or even a disaster!) – and almost *everything* carried the emblem of the company which made or commissioned it. Artists, too, realized there was scope for them even in this new world of technology and began painting railway scenes, taking commissions for boardroom portraits and perhaps most importantly, painting the now famous railway advertising posters.

This attention to ancillary detail was not just a whim on the part of the railway companies; it also made practical and economic sense. Being private organizations they had to be competitive and, human nature being what it is, Mr X was quite likely to travel with company Y rather than company Z because he preferred the colour of the engines or the comfort of the carriage seats, so naturally the individual owners did their utmost to attract fare-paying passengers to their particular railway. Britain's railway heritage is therefore not simply the machines and rails and not only of interest to engineers and steam enthusiasts! This chapter tries to show prospective visitors something of the extent to which the National Railway Collection is most definitely 'not just technology'.

Silver, China and Glass
by Gwen Townend

One would not expect these three commodities to figure prominently in a transport collection but the railway companies used

... and everything carried the name or emblem of the originating company.

them extensively, albeit mainly in the fields of catering, commemorative and presentation artefacts. There are other instances of these materials being used, but in these cases they usually feature as an integral part of a carriage or building and are therefore not so readily preserved and displayed except in the form of a whole carriage or, by taking sections of now demolished buildings and fitting them into appropriate displays, perhaps with a photograph of the original building. Although not intended as a review of catering, this section will inevitably be concerned with catering artefacts because of the nature of the materials under discussion.

The basic collection in this field was inherited from the museum's two predecessors at York and Clapham, which, being railway administered, could readily acquire all significant items as they became redundant. Although we have the 1968 Transport Act facility, acquisition of certain items is not quite as easy as it was and we augment the collection by purchase and accepting donations or bequests. This means we do not always acquire everything we would like but no museum can collect everything just because it is old or attractive and on the whole we have a comprehensive collection.

Items from buildings and carriages are normally acquired through British Rail as these do not readily come into private hands, nor are they always easy to salvage. In recent years, however, the structural alterations being carried out by British Rail have enabled us to claim several interesting architectural specimens in the form of stained glass, ornamental iron and stonework. This type of acquisition needs careful consideration because such items are difficult to display in isolation and are generally accepted only if they can be sensibly fitted into an appropriate theme or if they are unique.

The collection of souvenirs and commemorative items in the silver, china and glass category have, by and large, not come from British Rail since they were made by the railway companies either for purchase by the public or for presentation to company servants. Acquisition of such pieces has therefore to be by purchase or through individuals donating family relics to the Museum; this has resulted in some unique and interesting personal items finding a place in the collection.

Looking at the accompanying illustrations, it is obvious that much artistry and craftsmanship went into the manufacture of these decorative items and one might be tempted to think it was just all for 'show'. This was not the case at all. In fact everything, with perhaps the exception of souvenirs, had a specific use, and the form they took merely reflected the fashion and lifestyle of the period of origin. The railway has always been fashion conscious: when trying to attract custom, the needs and tastes of the prospective clients must be followed if customers are not to disappear. If the artefacts produced by the private railway companies often appear to be more lavish than their British Rail counterparts, it is largely because current fashions are less ostentatious. British Rail can still provide, as with their new Pullman services introduced in 1985, an elegance and style of service which would equally be appreciated by our Victorian and Edwardian ancestors. At the time of writing the Museum is proposing to obtain a set of these new Pullman artefacts and they will be just as significant in the context of the collection as are their predecessors.

The 'silver' in the collection is all plated holloware and the 'china' is often earthenware. It is known that some of the more prestigious railway hotels had solid silver items at one time, but unfortunately none has reached the National Collection. Whether the visitor be a student or someone wishing to reflect nostalgically on past eras, this collection tells something of the lifestyle of this nation as well as how we travelled, almost every piece being typical of its period. Phrases in common usage today such as 'Victorian opulence', 'Edwardian elegance' and even 'Sixties Nasty' can be understood at a glance from some of our displays. Heavily chased silver, brightly coloured over-gilded china and 'fussy' souvenirs of the Victorian era cannot be confused with the more delicate elegance of the Edwardian period or the overtly 'plastic' nature of the 1960s.

At the same time it does not make economic sense to destroy everything and start again when fashion changes so there is always an 'overlap' with only the new items being in the current style. For example, the Edwardian 'Art Nouveau' style was reflected in *new* buildings and rolling stock at the time but much of the railway network was still ostensibly Victorian. As styles became plainer articles could be used longer without appearing 'dated' and, in the case of silver in particular, the railway companies often erased the old lettering and had the pieces re-engraved. This was particularly noticeable from 1923 onwards when the many small companies were grouped together into the 'Big Four'. It would have been very wasteful and expensive to destroy

No expense was spared when serving the Royal Family. The point engraved crystal and delicately coloured Limoges porcelain was made specifically for Queen Victoria's use in the royal waiting room at Perth station. The crockery is blue and gold banded Royal Worcester (backstamped only), used on the Royal Dining Car into the reign of the present Queen and gold banded china face-stamped with the crest of the LNWR.

all the pieces from the pre-grouping era so many were re-engraved and put back into service with the new companies. Some very old pieces were never re-engraved and were withdrawn from use still bearing their old company name and many such pieces are in the National Collection.

In the 1930s, the drastic fashion change to 'Art Deco' coupled with the now considerable age of many artefacts encouraged the railway companies to adopt a replacement rather than re-use strategy. The 'Grand' Victorian hotels could not be replaced but any new ones – the Queens, Leeds is a good example – were built in the 'Odeon' style. Even the company emblems were changed to the new art form with monograms looking like coffee pots (LMS), the High Speed design of the LNER, and the circular 'shirt button' design of the GWR, all equally epitomizing British design in the 1930s.

During the Second World War, catering and similar services were much reduced. Not surprisingly, the silver plate, now often looking somewhat old and tired, had to 'soldier on' and any necessary replacement crockery or glass was utilitarian in design. Any items in the collection which are plain white with black lettering were probably made during this period.

Immediately after the war equipment could not be immediately improved and markings remained a hotchpotch because the newly nationalized British Railways could not re-mark everything *en masse*. Eventually, a new corporate image evolved and the artefacts in the silver, china and glass category began to look more or less as we know them today. Any remaining silver was again re-engraved with the emblem of the new nationalized company whose emblem itself has changed several times during the last forty years. Crockery became rather plain and usually only back-stamped to indicate ownership, the exception being some hotelware which remained patterned to denote a particular prestige hotel, the Charing Cross Hotel and the Royal Station Hotel, York being typical. For the first time, stainless steel and plastic were being used in mass catering so the 'silver' became stainless steel, the china became earthenware and the offerings from the buffet cars were served on plastic and paper.

New buldings also echoed the 1960s trend for glass and concrete while souvenirs were more likely to be made of plastic than china. Even the Pullman Car Company started to use that particularly nasty variety of plastic called 'Melamine' because it was fashionable. The trend was thankfully shortlived and as a consequence, unfortunately, only one piece survives in the National Collection. There are now signs that British Railways are trying to emulate their forebears in terms of design and the collection at York forms a good reference base for today's designers. For example, the pattern chosen for the crockery on the new 1985 Pullman services is a simplified version of an earlier Pullman design, examples of which are in this collection.

Vast as this collection may appear to the visitor, there are gaps, some more apparent than real. Items from the smaller pre-grouping companies are scarce while items from post-grouping companies, the LMS in particular, are numerous. Other gaps occur because of the nature of the material, silver plate surviving longer than glass or china. This can mean that we have a matching set of cutlery but no crockery to make up a place setting. It is possible to fill gaps with replicas but this can be an expensive process.

The mention of commodities other than silver, china and glass is not meant to confuse but merely to bring the story to a logical conclusion with the advent of plastic, stainless steel and concrete. No museum can terminate its collection at the end of a certain era because that period had more attractive items than later times, unless the subject is a finite one. Artefacts from the railway hotels and ships come into this category and, since their sale to the private sector in the early 1980s no more items will come directly into the National Collection. We can at least now tell the definitive story in each of these two cases. The rest of the collection, by contrast, will hopefully continue to grow.

Saucers showing fashion changes in pattern design and lettering style. The two bowls at the top span roughly a hundred years, from lavishly decorated Victoriana for the GER to British Rail's 'Whispering Grass' pattern of the 1970s. Below these is the Pullman pattern used by British Rail for their new Pullman services, while further down is the stylized coffee pot design of the LMS. Exclusive hotel patterns come next, The Charing Cross, Gleneagles and The Felix. The bottom row shows the designs used to denote railway shipping operations, (left to right) LBSCR's Newhaven–Dieppe service, British Rail's Sealink service and the Caledonian Steam Packet Company's service.

Early railway companies explored every possibility in the field of souvenir production and British Rail still find such items worthwhile today. At the top are items commemorating three Stockton and Darlington celebrations, 1825, 1925 and 1975. The pair of plates (second row) were souvenirs produced by the LNER in the 1920s depicting six cathedrals in their operating area, while the mug (bottom left) was British Rail's commemorative offering for the Queen's Silver Jubilee in 1977. Other items range from a souvenir of the LMS steamship *Duke of Argyll* to two mugs depicting railway scenes in the 1830s.

This display is part of a collection bequeathed to the Museum and shows a variety of unusual catering artefacts. The oval salmon dish (centre right) is 28 in long and is one of the prime pieces in the collection. When made for the Midland Grand Hotel, St Pancras in 1873 it cost £36 11s 4d (£36.56p). Also featured are grape scissors, lobster pick, melon scoop and a large cover marked with the crown and garter of the Midland Hotel, Derby.

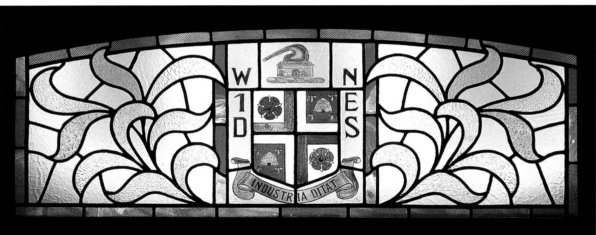

This picture shows two uses of glass outside the field of catering: the stained glass panel from Widnes station was the creation of the Great Central & Midland Joint Railway but is fairly typical of station decoration throughout the land at this time. It is one of a group of five such panels in the collection each depicting a different station. The etched panels are two windows in Queen Victoria's saloon of 1869. Several of its windows depict the various insignia of the orders of chivalry, and the pair in this picture show the Order of the Garter and the Order of St Patrick.

A silver salver presented to David Jones, CME of the Highland Railway, on the occasion of his retirement in 1896.

Art

by Susan Underwood

Situated in the basement of the Museum is the Picture Store, which contains all the NRM's pictorial collections of a non-photographic nature. These consist of the finest collection of railway posters in the country, numbering some 3,500, 2,500 prints (engravings, aquatints, etc.) and 1,000 oil paintings and watercolours, with a small number of pen-and-ink sketches and charcoal drawings.

The subject matter covered by these collections ranges across more than a hundred and fifty years of railway history, from the opening of the Stockton & Darlington Railway in 1825, to the present day. The posters illustrate, besides the expansion of the railway network itself, styles in art, changing patterns of holidaymaking, fashion, urban and rural landscapes, architecture and developments in advertising standards and approaches. The posters were designed to be displayed in waiting rooms, booking offices and railway platforms, and their prime function was to promote the railway companies which issued them.

The prints illustrate all aspects of railway history, in particular the nineteenth-century growth of the railway industry, advances in engineering, the labour force and the physical building of the railways, architecture (with particular reference to stations) and the people and goods which travelled by railway.

The paintings include a collection of well-known Victorian works, like A. Solomon's pair *The Departure* and *The Return*. There are also a number of paintings which concentrate on portraying the technical details of particular locomotives. Pride of place among the paintings must go to the extensive collection of poster originals, including works by R. Jack, M. Griffenhagen and Norman Wilkinson.

At least 85 per cent of the collections can be traced back to the former museums at Clapham and York. Since 1975 current acquisitions come from three sources:

'redundant' items claimed from the British Railways Board (in addition British Rail sends the Museum some of its current posters); the general public, which makes donations to the Museum; and purchases via the auction rooms. Nowadays, the collecting of Railwayana is a popular, if expensive, business, and the Museum must expect to pay for collectable items. As a rough guide the collections increase each year by 250–300 posters, 15–25 paintings, and 30–40 prints. Occasionally the number of additions is inflated by large bequests or donations.

Posters

All the posters collected by the NRM are British, and can be easily subdivided into four main groups: Pre-grouping, the Post-grouping years of the 'Big Four'; Wartime (the Second World War) and British Railways (1948 to the present day). These collections comprise a marvellous pictorial account of railway history, but also serve to illustrate the history of the poster, the poster artist and the advertising industry as a whole.

Although railway companies did advertise their lines before 1923, there was little thought given to persuasive marketing in the modern sense and such policy as there was, seems to have been merely to cram as much information as possible, both pictorial and descriptive, on to the poster. Many of these posters confused potential customers instead of informing or attracting them. The artist N. Wilkinson described them as being 'an uninspired jumble of small views of resorts, frequently arranged in little circular frames, with a good deal of meaningless decoration interwoven between each picture. The effect was a hotchpotch which was quite unintelligible at a distance' (*A brush with life*, N. Wilkinson). The NRM's small collection of pre-grouping posters contains good examples.

The finest posters in the NRM Poster Collection were produced by the 'Big Four' railway companies between the wars, which can be called the 'Golden Age' of the railway poster. In 1924 the LMS took an initiative

Tom Purvis's well-known set of six posters produced in the late 1920s showed various leisure activities available on the East Coast, served by the LNER. These have been reproduced by the NRM for sale as postcards and in poster form.

which one artist described as 'the most significant event ever to have occurred in the British Poster World'. Having reviewed their existing publicity, and with a nervous acknowledgement of the threat posed to their business by road transport, the LMS directors, in an unprecedented move, employed Royal Academicians to produce a series of promotional posters. Dull information sheets were suddenly replaced by works of art which were to have a far more profound impact on the travelling public and which set standards of advertising for others to follow for years to come. Seventeen posters were produced by eminent artists like M. Griffenhagen, D. Y. Cameron, B. Mackennal, W. Orpen and N. Wilkinson. As well as the posters themselves, the NRM has several of the original paintings in its collections.

This campaign by the LMS proved to be highly successful. The newspapers were quick to pick up this new idea and journal-ists wrote of the impetus which this movement would give to pictorial advertising generally. However, there was a backlash, causing the LMS to view the idea of using accomplished artists with some suspicion, because it was felt that the general public remembered the poster and the artist, but not necessarily the railway company. Although it continued using some Royal Academicians and other well-known artists, the LMS changed the emphasis from the artist to itself, but, nevertheless, continued to produce many fine posters.

The Southern Railway concentrated its advertising on the mythical image that the 'Sun always shines in the South'. There are two famous posters in particular, which stand out in the SR's advertising, one being the 'Little Boy' poster – a small boy speaking to the engine driver saying, 'I'm taking an early holiday 'cos I know summer comes soonest in the South'. This poster, or variations of it, were brought out several times. The NRM has several versions, including one issued in about 1940 for the Red Cross Fund, and ones in Italian and German! The other poster which is synonymous with the

ST COAST JOYS
travel by L·N·E·R
TO THE DRIER SIDE OF BRITAIN

EAST COAST JOYS
travel by L·N·E·R
TO THE DRIER SIDE OF BRITAIN

EAST COAST JOYS
travel by L·N·E·R
TO THE DRIER SIDE OF BRITAIN

SR is the 'Sunny South Sam' poster. This was first issued in 1930, and the Sunny South Sam personality continued into the early 1940s. It was generally considered that the SR never reached the same high standards as the LMS and the LNER. Perhaps this is reflected in the fact that, of the four companies, the SR was the only one not to hold any exhibitions of its posters. Their publicity did improve under the guidance of J. B. (later Sir John) Elliot, and the NRM has in its collections some wonderful sunshine scenes from the SR.

The GWR has long been considered to have represented the more traditional view of poster advertising. In some quarters the GWR's advertising was considered almost dull when compared with that of the other companies. One reason for this was that the company had to have each poster agreed, not only by itself, but also by the relevant town council. The NRM has several examples of these posters, such as the one of Bournemouth by C. Buckle. It was by using posters by artists like Buckle and A. Tripp that the company's advertising improved.

Slogans played a major part in the com-

pany's advertising campaign. In the 1920s 'Go Great Western' appeared, followed in the 1930s with 'Speed to the West' and the national theme 'It's Quicker by Rail'. Under the new management of W. H. Fraser, the company's publicity made many strides, one of the most important being the adoption of the GWR monogram in 1934. This new, clear monogram was adopted for use on all posters, folders, rolling stock and uniforms. A number of GWR posters belonging to the NRM are on long-term loan to the GWR Museum at Swindon. There is still a small selection remaining at York, and these illustrate the improvements made by the company over the years.

It was, however, the LNER which seemed to obtain both original and impressive posters from the start of its campaign. Teasdale headed the Advertising Department, and under his direction the LNER stormed ahead. The designs for the posters were not dictated to the artists; Teasdale preferred to choose artists he admired and allow their style to develop. There were five artists who continually produced quality work for the LNER: Fred Taylor, Frank Newbould,

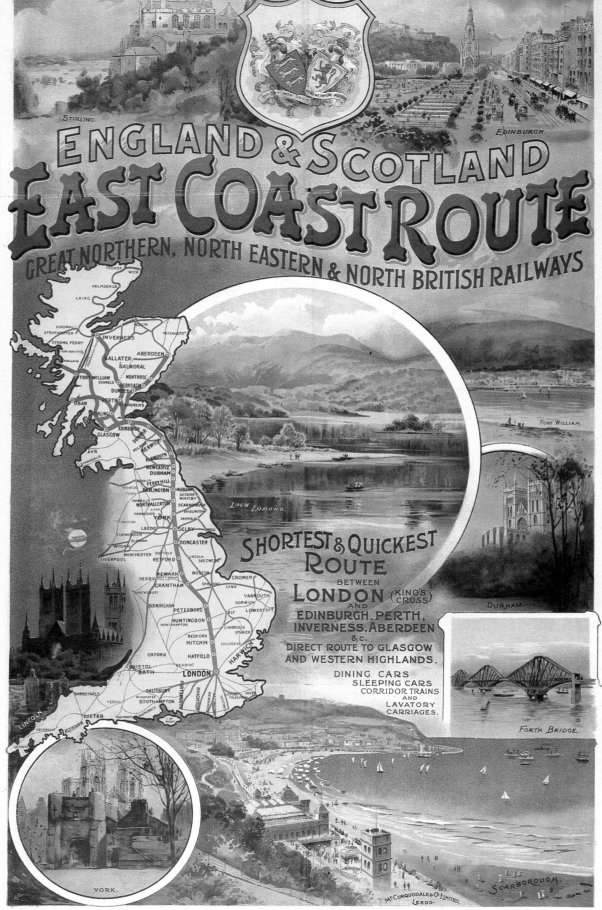

STIRLING.

EDINBURGH.

ENGLAND & SCOTLAND
EAST COAST ROUTE
GREAT NORTHERN, NORTH EASTERN & NORTH BRITISH RAILWAYS

FORT WILLIAM.

LOCH LOMOND.

DURHAM.

SHORTEST & QUICKEST ROUTE
BETWEEN
LONDON (KING'S CROSS)
AND
EDINBURGH, PERTH, INVERNESS, ABERDEEN &c.
DIRECT ROUTE TO GLASGOW AND WESTERN HIGHLANDS.

DINING CARS
SLEEPING CARS
CORRIDOR TRAINS
AND
LAVATORY CARRIAGES.

FORTH BRIDGE.

YORK.

SCARBOROUGH.

McCORQUODALE & CO LIMITED, LEEDS.

CHARLES STEEL, General Manager, G.N.R.   **GEORGE S. GIBB**, General Manager, N.E.R.   **W. F. JACKSON**, General Manager, N.B.R.

IS YOUR JOURNEY REALLY NECESSARY?

BERT THOMAS

RAILWAY EXECUTIVE COMMITTEE

IM TAKING AN EARLY HOLIDAY COS I KNOW SUMMER COMES SOONEST IN THE SOUTH SOUTHERN RAILWAY

Austin Cooper, F. Mason and T. Purvis. Of these, Purvis was particularly significant for two reasons. Firstly, he developed a particular two-dimensional style by using a selection of completely flat colours. It was to be copied throughout the world of advertising. Secondly, he believed that the lettering should be an integral part of the design, as may be seen in the Cleethorpes poster.

This era of railway posters can be seen in relation to the poster world as a whole in which the commercial artist was gradually finding recognition for his/her work. A general awareness that commercial design needed to be taught in art schools alongside fine art was becoming more accepted. Tom Purvis summed it up: 'I am a commercial artist and "Commercial Art" demands exactly the same skills, training, knowledge, genius if you like, as a Royal Academician.'

With the outbreak of the Second World

Civilian travel was very fimly discouraged during the Second World War, and Bert Thomas's famous poster was widely used on railway stations.

One of the most famous of all railway posters. It was based on a photograph taken at Waterloo, but various artistic alterations were made, including the addition of the Southern Railway's name on the tender and the deletion of the little boy's glasses. The Museum also has versions with German and Italian text, and the theme of the poster has been copied several times since.

War, the production of commercial 'Sunshine' style posters ceased, and only a few specifically railway posters were printed. Needless to say, these were pure propaganda, emphasizing the united front of the railways and of the country they served. Few are remembered for their artwork as opposed to their sentiments or message.

In spite of the richness of its company coverage, the bulk of the NRM Poster Collection actually dates from the British Railways era. Here again it is interesting to compare the poster designs with the styles elsewhere. The 1950s railway posters tended to be fairly traditional and to reflect the art of the previous decade. Gradually the style

One of the earliest posters in the collection, dating from the end of the nineteenth century, extolls the advantages of the East Coast Route to Scotland.

changed, reflecting the fashion of the time. Many of the 1960s posters are remarkable for their psychedelic colours and imagery of the 'swinging' young people of that decade.

In and after the 1970s British Rail began using 'personalities' to advertise their services, notably the group ABBA and Jimmy Savile, OBE. Although the NRM has an early poster of Gracie Fields advertising a seaside resort, few living personalities were used before recent decades. Historical romantic figures such as Bonny Prince Charlie had been portrayed, but the use of easily identifiable contemporary personalities was a new idea. Photography was also introduced into the poster world and many British Rail posters are based on photographs. The role of the graphic designer became paramount, and still remains so.

To sum up, the NRM Collection of posters contains a wealth of information about design, fashion trends, the art of photography and the role of the commercial artist. It makes a considerable contribution to our knowledge of international art and British social history.

Prints

The NRM currently owns 2,500 prints (engravings, aquatints, etc.), some of these being the finest examples of their time such as A. F. Tait's *London & North Western Railway* and J. C. Bourne's *The Great Western Railway*. Unfortunately many of these prints are badly foxed, but there is now a conservation programme under way which will help to preserve these items. Many of the individual prints are of marvellous quality, such as T. Rowlandson's *Catch-me-who-Can*, and G. Hawkin's *Britannia Bridge*; but it will be some time before a full catalogue is compiled to cover the print treasures of both the NRM and the Science Museum.

The large set of post-1900 colour prints come from magazines such as the *Railway Gazette*, and are most useful because they portray the technical details of locomotives. These include a large set from the drawing board of F. Moore, the well-known pseudonym of Thomas Rudd, who for over forty years produced painted pictures of locomotive and railway scenes, based on photographs. It is, however, the nineteenth-century prints which deserve pride of place within this part of the collection: the romantic views of the countryside, with the train a blur on the horizon, through to the pictures of the navvies working on the construction of the line. These help to trace the propaganda which the railway companies used, to show on the one hand that the railway was so quiet and peaceful that it blended easily into the countryside; yet on the other the power and strength of this splendid new force, the railway. There are also many delightful engravings showing stations and other buildings, including the late lamented Euston Arch and Gates (the latter being in the NRM Collection).

Paintings

The thousand-odd paintings are an astonishingly varied collection. Clapham Museum collected several hundred poster originals, mostly dating from the 1920s (including works by Stanhope Forbes and G. Clausen) to the 1960s. Some are earlier, including one from 1897 advertising the Ascot races. This collection is important for the quality of its art and for showing the differences between the originals and the actual posters. With artists such as T. Purvis, the difference seems to be minimal, but with others it is more obvious. This collection of original art deserves to be seen in its own right, and many people have studied it.

The Museum also has a small collection of Victorian paintings, some of which are either frequently on display or on loan to other institutions. This collection includes the two Solomon paintings, *The Departure* and *The Return*, which are interesting for the insight they give us into Victorian morality. Other well-known paintings include

The pair of paintings by A. Solomon entitled *The Departure – Second Class* and *The Return – First Class*, are very well known and, as well as having been on display at York, have been lent by the NRM for special exhibitions elsewhere. In the original version, now in Canada, the old man in *The Return* was asleep, and Victorian views about the unchaperoned young people resulted in the second version being painted!

This Post-Impressionist painting by Frederick Spencer Gore was purchased for the Museum in 1983. It forms an artistic record of a significant social and historical development in the life of the time – the development of the Garden City at Letchworth.

Farewell to the Light Brigade and *Seats for Five*. The collection includes a large selection of works by F. Moore, including one which is incomplete and therefore reveals the photograph beneath the painting.

Carriage prints became an integral part of travelling, and as well as the numerous prints in the collection, the Museum has several originals. These show mainly the delights of the countryside, or famous places to be visited such as castles and cathedrals. Among these paintings is a small collection of pen-and-ink sketches by the artist H. McKie which portray daily life at Waterloo station during the Second World War, and include several portraits of women porters, tired soldiers, fond farewells and the hustle and bustle of a station in wartime.

In 1983, the Museum was fortunate to acquire the oil painting of Letchworth station by Frederick Spencer Gore. It was the first Post-Impressionist painting to be refused an Export Licence, and was purchased for the Museum, with financial assistance from the National Heritage Memorial Fund, the National Art-Collections Fund and the Friends of the National Railway Museum. Painted just before the First World War, it forms a contemporary artistic record of a significant social and historical development in the life of the time, and thus complements the well-known Victorian and other railway paintings already in the collection.

Many of the Museum's paintings and prints portray the age of steam, and even the most recently painted tend to look back with nostalgia to that era. However, the Museum has a responsibility to look beyond that to modern times, which is why the NRM, at the same time as filling the more obvious gaps in the collection (for example, pre-grouping posters), must ensure that its collections reflect the scenes of modern railway travel for the benefit of future generations.

Railwayana
by Lilian Hogg

A key fob, a timetable the size of a stamp, a whistle in the shape of a dog's head, a steel penknife ... this brief list reads like the contents of a small boy's pocket, but in fact they are just a few of the items newly acquired by the NRM. All have a railway connection and a story to tell. The timetable, for example, was made in miniature by the LMS railway and presented to Queen Mary for her famous Dolls House at St James's Palace. A copy is still there, kept in a tiny bureau drawer. The whistle in the shape of a dog's head belonged to a station master and had been presented to him by his staff.

Such incidental, ephemeral, items as these form the core of the railwayana collections. Many are pieces of railway equipment discarded and forgotten as invention and science advanced, while others represent railway heirlooms handed down through generations and presented to the nation for posterity. Brought together they provide us with an alternative history of railways, a history that takes us from the ornate company stamp of the self-made Victorian businessman to the slick corporate image of British Rail in the present day. Along the way it gives us a chance to glimpse the times and toils of the millions of lives touched by the passing train.

Railway building in this country reached a peak in the mid nineteenth century. To build a railway, businessmen of like mind joined together and engaged an engineer to produce a survey of the proposed route. This proposal was then presented to Parliament. If the Bill passed, the businessmen, by an Act of Incorporation, were permitted to raise capital and begin their railway. At this juncture, most railway companies produced a seal which could henceforth be used to authenticate documents. The term 'seal' refers to the impression made. This could be in wax but was more often embossed on paper. The item that makes the impression is termed a 'matrix' or 'die'. The collection of dies at the Museum is unique. There are well

This NER clock from the signal box at Durham Viaduct has a smaller dial which is a stop watch actuated by trains crossing the viaduct. The signalman read the stop watch, calculated the speed of the train using tables provided and all drivers exceeding the 30 m.p.h. limit were reported.

Seals were regarded as the company's signature so they were kept under tight security in purpose-made seal boxes. Even the ornate seal presses were kept padlocked for security.

over eight hundred designs, many from obscure, joint or light railways that were in existence for only a few years. The designs chosen were often very like coats of arms: some railway companies chose to use designs based on armorial devices of the towns they served; others felt their company should be represented by designs capturing the spirit of the new age. Hence there is a profusion of coal wagons, locomotives, docks and kilns, most in true Victorian style, surrounded with cherubs, scrolls and lethargic-looking aphrodites.

With the parliamentary hurdle behind them, the next step for the railway directors was to begin construction of the line. But here there was another pause, for no railway 'worth its shares' could let such a momentous occasion pass without a little self-indulgent celebration. Local dignitaries were called on to cut the first sod of earth. To do this they were usually provided with ceremonial spades and matching wheelbarrows. Some of these sets have come into the Museum's collection and are admirable works of craftsmanship and skill. Among our more unusual items from such occasions is a tiny gilt casket, little bigger than a matchbox, from the Hull, Barnsley & West Riding Junction Railway & Dock Company. Inside this little box, wrapped in tissue and silver paper, is a 1 in cube of earth cut as part of the railways' first sod on 15 January 1881. An unspecified number of these caskets were given to VIPs attending the ceremony.

With the coming of the industrial age, work no longer ceased when the sun went down, and railways were expected to respond to the demands for transport after dark. Good lighting, particularly for signalling, was essential for safety. Necessity made development swift. By the 1840s the primitive brazier and bonfires at the lineside had been replaced by policemen holding coloured lamps. Ten years later the lamps were fixed to signal poles. Although the lineside policeman was made redundant, his tri-colour lamp, far from being obsolete, developed swiftly into a standard piece of equipment used by shunters, guards, signalmen and all others with a responsibility to control the movement of trains. The Museum has a rich and varied collection of these lamps. All have a central flame and a magnifying lens, but many different designs were developed for changing the colour of the light. One of the earliest has push buttons on the handle which, when pressed, move coloured glass slides between the flame and lens. The most common type has the coloured glasses fitted in a rotating cylinder inside the lamp body. Although a number of patents was issued for devices to enable the holder of the lamp to change its colour using only one hand, most of these came to nothing when it became common practice among railway workers to snap off the clip locking the inner cylinder and, with a flick of the wrist, change the colour. The basic oil tri-colour lamp remained in exclusive use until the 1960s, when battery-operated Bardic lamps became standard issue on British Rail.

Many other types of railway handlamps were perfected to give the special service required by the user. Carriage & Wagon inspectors, for example, needed bright white light and they often used the carbide or acetylene type. Ticket inspectors' lamps tended to be very simple affairs showing a white light only through flat glass. Railway Police lamps showed only white light, but often had a shutter suddenly to darken the light without extinguishing the flame.

Locomotives and trains normally carried lights showing white at the front and red at the back. Lamps therefore usually showed a white light, but had a means of changing the colour to red. In the collection there are locomotive lamps with hinged shutters of coloured glass that clip over the outside of the lens. Others have coloured glass housed in an internal cylinder like the tri-colour handlamps, but the most common is a bulkier lamp with side pockets to house coloured glass slides that slot in front of the flame, behind the lens. On the footplate, a special lamp was provided to enable the crew to keep their eyes on the all-important level of the water in the boiler.

The main fuel for lamps until the turn of the century was Colza or Rape Seed oil. The lamp worker's job was not a pleasant one, for the oil had a heavy, greasy smell which clung to their clothing, making them often solitary figures going about their duties at stations and railway works. After 1900 paraffin was employed, and that remained in use until battery lamps were introduced.

Apart from lighting, probably the most important activity on the early railways was timekeeping. Before the railways came, each town and village throughout Britain kept to its own local time which could vary considerably depending on the longitude from Greenwich. Like the mail coaches before them, trains had to operate to a timetable to find favour with the public. This and the use of the time-interval system of working, described in Chapter 3, made it important that time was synchronized along the whole line. In 1840 the Board of Trade saw the logic of this and decreed that all trains should run to London time. This became known as 'railway time'. The collection boasts a beautifully preserved wall clock by Avison of York with 'Railway Time' clearly printed on the face. Before 1852, when Greenwich introduced a telegraph signal at noon each day, it was quite difficult to keep clocks synchronized. The railways adopted the system, originally used on mail coaches, of providing guards with a watch locked in a wooden and glass case. The watch was set at the station of departure, then locked in the case and given to the guard to be presented on arrival at the station of destination. The locked case prevented any accusation that the guard had tampered with the mechanism.

Although railway work was not easy, it carried with it, in the beginning and for many years afterwards, a certain prestige, and was considered well paid and secure compared with farm or factory work. Because of its popularity, competition for jobs was stiff and recruitment strict. For all workers, excellent eyesight was essential, but in the late 1830s a large majority of the population was illiterate, so some means other than the alphabet had to be used to test

This gunpowder boot is a massive 13½ in long. It was made with a wooden sole for use in gunpowder vans, where sparks on the metal floors from the usual hobnail boots could have had disastrous consequences.

The Tay Bridge disaster of 1879 left railway companies concerned about using bridges and viaducts in high winds. This indicator was fitted at Staithes Viaduct on the North Yorkshire Coast; when the wind pressure reached 28 lb sq ft, it activated a bell in the signal box and the viaduct was closed.

eyesight. In the collection are two strange-looking batons covered in dots. These are eye testers. The recruit would be expected to count the number of dots in view from a given distance, usually 15 or 19 yd. Stories abound that the recruit often quickly came up with the correct answer, but the testing

This bullion box is a relic of the Great Train Robbery of 1857. It still contains the lead shot used by the robbers to replace the stolen gold while the boxes were carried on the South Eastern Railway.

doctor had to have several attempts before he managed two totals that tallied.

However harsh the conditions, railways became one of the country's major employers. They took all types of skilled and unskilled labour for their engine sheds, workshops, stations, signal boxes and drawing offices, so it is not surprising that the Museum's collection of workmen's equipment is one of the most diverse, ranging from precision drawing instruments acquired from Ashford drawing office to steel shunting poles from Hartlepool. In the Museum store, along with detonator cans and ticket nippers, are several black metal drivers' sandwich, or 'snap', tins. These rather insignificant-looking boxes belie their status as the most sought-after badges of office. No one would have the presumption to carry one except the engine driver, and he could testify to the twenty or so years it had taken him to work his way up from engine cleaner. To be an engine driver was every small boy's dream.

During the days of steam, railway companies traded on this romantic image by giving their locomotives and certain trains glamorous names. This still leads to consid-

erable confusion for it is not always made clear that trains and locomotives are two distinct terms. 'Locomotive' refers to the vehicle that provides the power to pull carriages or wagons, and 'train' is a term describing a locomotive with carriages or wagons attached. Locomotives often had names displayed on a brass plate fixed on both sides of the engine, and in most cases the locomotive kept this name throughout its working life. When trains were named it was, strictly speaking, the service rather than the train that the name referred to, and as such, the train only bore the name for the time it worked that service. The 1920s and '30s saw the heyday of named trains. Many companies provided headboards that fitted on the smokebox door of the locomotive hauling the train, to supplement the name and destination boards on the sides or roofs of the coaches. Probably the most famous train to have a name was the 10 o'clock passenger express service from London King's Cross to Edinburgh – the 'Flying Scotsman'. The Museum sadly does not have any original 'Flying Scotsman' headboards from steam days, but it is the proud owner of the fibre-glass winged thistle which provided the distinctive headboard used at one time on Deltic locomotives when they worked the service. The train still runs, named as such in the timetable, but is now formed from one of today's standard Inter City 125 sets. It is due to be electrically hauled from 1991 and no longer carries a headboard. As if there was not enough confusion between named trains and named locomotives, the LNER in 1927 called one of its locomotives *Flying Scotsman*. This is now preserved in private hands and still carries its nameplates.

Although the Museum has a fair selection of brass locomotive nameplates, the most unusual is the nameplate from the North British Railway locomotive *Glenshiel*. The North British, with true Scottish frugality, spared themselves the expense of casting brass nameplates for their locomotives and simply painted the name on the splasher (the cover for one of its driving wheels). When *Glenshiel* was scrapped, someone

Station name signs – those with the 'hot dog' shape are referred to as 'totems'. Each of the new Regions formed after nationalization used its own distinctive house colour. Top to bottom on the left are Scottish, Southern, North Eastern and London Midland. Top right, Eastern. The Western Region (not displayed) chose brown. The station sign for Cheam is pre-war Southern Railway and the level crossing sign for Malton Road is much older, dating from North Eastern days.

Nameplates from locomotives of the Big Four, from top to bottom: GWR, SR, LMS and LNER. Plates like these were sold off by British Railways in the 1950s for around £5 each. They now fetch thousands of pounds at auction.

bothered to cut out the name and as a roughly cut piece of metal it now hangs proudly in the Museum store.

Many nameplates and headboards adorn the walls of the Museum, but in the days when the main hall was an engine shed the signs displayed would be less glamorous and more cautionary in nature. Similarly at stations passengers were bombarded with warnings, threats and advertisements. The Museum has examples of most of the various types of notice that any traveller from the 1850s to the 1950s was likely to come across. The most common sign visible at stations and throughout the length of the line was the trespass notice. Trespass is normally considered a civil matter, but from earliest times it was recognized that the practice of trespass on railways was sufficiently dangerous to warrant criminal proceedings. Quite a few companies added clauses to their acts to make it a criminal offence, and some made it compulsory for the company to exhibit notices warning against trespass – hence the vast quantities of these signs still to be found. Cast iron was the most popular and durable material for trespass and other warning notices, such as bridge height and weight restrictions. Although a few companies made their trespass signs in enamel, this was more often a medium for commercial advertising.

In the 1950s, after nationalization, British Railways standardized the use of enamel signs for most station names. The majority of these in the past had been wood. After the corporate identity campaign was launched in the sixties, station names began to appear in black-on-white plastic. The typeface was standardized to Helvetica medium. The signs are now clear and precise, but leave little room for alternative interpretations, unlike one of those from the nineteenth century in the Museum which reads, 'None but Company's horses are allowed to drink at this trough', aimed obviously at the literate if delinquent horse.

The horses have now gone and sadly the water trough referred to was not preserved. Indeed, for every item collected, hundreds have been destroyed. There are inevitably omissions in the Museum's railwayana collections, but items are constantly being offered by private collectors, apart from those received from British Rail through the 1968 Transport Act.

The George Cross awarded to Driver John Axon of Stockport on 7 May 1957. John Axon showed devotion to his duty and outstanding courage in attempting to stop his train which went out of control when the steam pipe feeding the brake fractured. He remained at his post despite the scalding high-pressure steam that was filling the cab in the hope of regaining control and avoiding a collision with the preceding train. He instructed his fireman to jump clear and apply as many wagon brakes as possible. Despite his heroic efforts the train overtook another freight train travelling in the same direction and Axon was killed in the resulting collision. The cross is silver and is suspended on a blue ribbon.

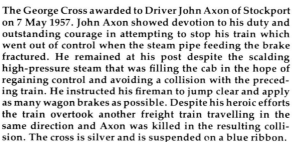

A Collection of Commemorative Medallions:
Obverse of the medallion commemorating the opening of the Liverpool and Manchester Railway on 15 September 1830. The medal is alloy and is of 2in diameter; Obverse of the medallion issued by Barnett & Scott of Hull in commemoration of the opening of the Hull, Barnsley & West Riding Junction Railway & Dock Company by Lt. Col. Gerard Smith, M.P., chairman of the Company on 16 July 1885. This medallion was struck in both gilt and white metal alloy, and in two sizes, 1½in and 1⅛in diameter. It is perhaps surprising that on the larger medallion the manufacturer saved space by substituting an ampersand for the word 'and', whilst the smaller medallion uses the word in full; Obverse of the LNER Centenary medallion issued in 1925; Obverse of the LMSR Centenary medallion, struck in 1938. The reverse of this medallion lists the directors of the LMS at the time of issue. The medallion is bronze and is of 2½in diameter.

Medals and Medallions

by Helen Christian

Almost all museums have some sort of numismatics collection, as medals and medallions have been struck pertaining to every facet of life. The National Railway Museum is no exception, having a varied collection of some four hundred pieces. Through them it is possible to piece together some of the major events in the story of the railways in Britain and of the lives of the men who worked on them.

The majority of the collection consists of commemorative medallions struck to mark some important event and issued for sale or general distribution. J. R. S. Whiting claims, in *Commemorative Medals: A Medallic History of Britain from Tudor Times to the Present Day*, that their production can be traced back as far as the decadrachms given to the winners in the Syracusan games of the fourth century BC, and later to the Roman emperors of the second century AD who issued medallions to distinguished visitors.

In Britain the production of commemorative medallions dates from only Tudor times, when the art was imported from the Continent. Since then their production has never ceased, although the quantity and subject type has varied greatly. The greatest period of medal production was undoubtedly the Victorian era, and as this trend coincided with the development of Britain's railways it is hardly surprising that many commemorative medallions were issued with a railway theme.

The earliest of these medallions were perhaps those issued to celebrate the opening of the Liverpool & Manchester Railway on 15 September 1830. In fact this was so important that it warranted the production of not one but three different designs of medallion, the best known of which is that depicting a goods train crossing the viaduct over the Sankey Canal and Valley, with the entrance to Liverpool station and tunnels on the reverse. Thereafter, many medallions were issued to mark the occasion of cutting the first sod or the official opening of railway lines.

In time, medallions began to commemorate the fiftieth anniversaries and then the centenaries of the railway companies. The most significant of these is the bronze medallion designed by Gilbert Bayes, who was commissioned by the LNER in 1925, to commemorate the centenary of the opening of the Stockton & Darlington Railway. It depicts on one side the busts of Edward Pease and George Stephenson together with the arms of Stockton and Darlington, whilst on the reverse is the figure of Vulcan, holding in his hand *Locomotion No 1* with a Gresley Pacific locomotive in the background. This medallion was issued in two sizes, $1\frac{3}{4}$ in and 3 in diameter, and sold to the public at 5 and 10 shillings respectively. The proceeds were donated to the Railway Benevolent Institution.

The tradition for producing commemorative medallions still continues today. One of the most recent additions to the collection is the limited edition bronze medallion designed by John Mosse and engraved by Robert Lowe to commemorate the sesquicentenary of the incorporation of the Great Western Railway on 31 August 1835. This depicts on the obverse, the broad gauge locomotive *Firefly* surmounted by the arms of the GWR, and on the reverse, the GWR roundel monogram surrounded by the arms of the towns closely associated with the railway: Swindon, Cardiff, Exeter, Plymouth, Truro and Wolverhampton. Only 2,500 of these medallions were struck in bronze, with a further 500 in silver and just 25 in gold. The proceeds of their sale were used to raise funds for the construction of a reproduction *Firefly* locomotive.

Another important section of the numismatics collection consists of gallantry medals. Even in peace-time the railway can be a dangerous place to work, so it is fitting that many railwaymen have been the recipients of awards for outstanding bravery. This type of medal is particularly fascinating as gallantry medals are usually engraved with the name of the recipient and have a citation,

One of the most recent acquisitions in the National Collection: a bronze medallion presented to passengers on the Tees–Tyne Pullman after its record breaking run from Newcastle to London on 27 September 1985.

Medallions awarded by railway companies to their employees for long service and good conduct. Both of these medallions depict the Company crest in brightly coloured enamel on hallmarked gold. The fifty years service on the Southern Railway includes the accumulated service on constituent railway companies prior to the grouping of 1923.

First aid medallions: the Midland was the first railway to institute first aid lessons in 1877. The St. John Ambulance Association formed the same year, was asked to sponsor these classes, which soon caught on amongst the other companies. Depicted here are the British Railways 15 years First Aid Efficiency medal, issued between 1948 and 1958. This medal is silver and enamel, 1¼in diameter; The SECR bronze medal was awarded in recognition of having passed seven annual examinations in succession; The GWR 25 years First Aid Efficiency medal was first instituted in 1928. This medal is of gold and enamel and is 1in diameter, and entitled its holders to an extra two days paid annual leave.

Railway Service Badges awarded in the First and Second World Wars. The circular badge was awarded by all the companies of the pre-grouping era, this particular one being of the NER. The oval badge is the Second World War badge issued by the Big Four Railway Companies.

which enables us to trace accurately the story of the railway employee. The NRM collection includes several interesting examples of this kind of award: an Edward Medal (George V type), issued to Arthur William Lewin in 1928 for risking his own life in an attempt to save an old man from being knocked down on a level crossing, bears the head of George V and hangs on a dark blue ribbon with a narrow yellow stripe on both sides. The reverse of the medal depicts a woman with outstretched arms and the words 'For Courage'.

Perhaps the most famous civil medal of which the NRM holds an example is the George Cross. The medal was instituted in 1940 as a reward for outstanding courage shown at great risk to the life of the recipient, for civilians and for members of the Armed Forces where a military award is not appropriate. All issued crosses are engraved on the reverse with the name of the recipient and the date of the *London Gazette* notification.

Between 1940 and 1947, 105 George Crosses were awarded, and approximately forty since the war. Of these, we know of six which have been awarded for acts of gallantry on the railways:

Norman Tunna, Shunter, GWR, Birkenhead: 24 January 1941

Benjamin Gimbert, Driver, LNER, March: 25 July 1944

James Nightall, Fireman, LNER, March: 25 July 1944

John Axon, Driver, BR(LMR), Stockport: 7 May 1957

Wallace A. Oakes, Driver, BRB, Crewe, Sandbach: 19 October 1965

James Kennedy, Security Officer, BREL Glasgow: 15 August 1975

During the Second World War, when the railways came under severe attack from enemy bombing raids, three of the 'Big Four' companies and the London Passenger Transport Board decided that their employees should be rewarded for their loyalty and devotion to duty in times of grave danger. The LNER, LMSR, SR and LPTB therefore instituted medals to mark gallant and meritorious service to the railways during wartime. These medals were all discontinued at the end of 1947 when the railways were nationalized. The Museum has managed to acquire a few of these awards, and has conducted considerable research in order to obtain citations for all known awards of this type.

Wartime also gave rise to another interesting adornment, which should be mentioned here, although not strictly part of the numismatics collection. This is the Railway Service badge. These badges were issued by the railway companies during both world wars, although for totally different reasons. During the First World War the companies gave their employees a round enamelled badge with the company name on a blue band round the outer edge. The words 'Railway Service' were surmounted by a crown and appeared in the centre on a white background. They were issued to show that the bearer was, in fact, employed on war service by the railway, to avoid them being given white feathers or branded as cowards for not being away on active service. During the Second World War, an oval badge depicting a locomotive and the initials of the railway company, with the words 'Railway

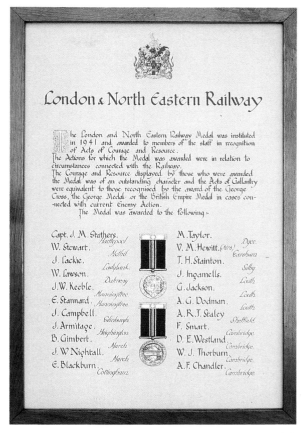

Display board containing two LNER Gallantry medals (unissued), and notes of the twenty-two recipients of the award. Citations for each of these awards are available from the Museum.

Service' on a blue band across the middle, was issued as staff identification.

In peace-time, too, many awards were presented to railwaymen or to railway companies. The Museum has the gold medal won by the Great Western Railway at the Brussels Universal Exhibition in 1910 for their audible cab-signalling apparatus, and the silver one awarded to Joseph H. Moreton, on the same occasion, for his hand-drawn maps of the North Eastern Railway. The LNER and its predecessors were outstanding for several years at the annual Shire Horse Society London Cart Horse Parade, winning a number of silver and bronze medals which are now part of the National Collection. Another award won by the Great Western Railway was a gold medal presented to the locomotive *King George V* which took part in the centenary celebrations of the Baltimore & Ohio Railway in the United States during 1927.

Another achievement often rewarded by medals was long service and good conduct. The medal which features most prominently in the NRM Collection is that issued by the Southern Railway for fifty years' service. This is struck in hallmarked gold with the company crest enamelled on a background of oak leaves. Each medal is inscribed on the reverse with the employee's name and the dates of his employment. It was not only the railway companies themselves who issued long-service medals, but the various branches of the St John Ambulance Association awarded gold and silver medals for different lengths of service, and the railwaymen's unions presented their members with watch-chains and medallions to mark the length of their membership.

Space permits a description of only a small proportion of the collection but it illustrates clearly the pattern of life on the railways, and especially the successes. The collection continues to grow as new medals are struck and old ones are passed on, and the story of the railways and their unknown heroes unfolds before us.

Railway Uniforms

by Helen Christian

With the rapid expansion of the railways, it became necessary for users of the railways to identify the staff in some way. The system of ranking followed a strict hierarchical structure, and military-style uniforms were issued so that passengers could recognize a man's rank at a glance. This also ensured that staff presented themselves at work looking respectable.

In many of the early companies the railway policemen fulfilled a multiplicity of duties, from signalman to booking clerk. Their uniform was based on that worn by the first 'peelers' in London and consisted of leather-crowned top hats, high-stocked tail-coats and tight trousers. The initials of the company and the employee's individual number were embroidered on the constable's stand-up collar.

The relationship of rank with uniforms was extremely clear cut. An engine cleaner was issued only with overalls. Promoted to fireman he was allowed a short serge jacket, and as a driver he was also entitled to an overcoat. The standard headgear was the grease-top cap which had a smooth waterproof crown to allow water and oil to run off rather than soak through.

The grades of staff who were in constant contact with the public were given especially fine uniforms, decorated with ornate brass buttons, gold braid and an assortment of elegant badges and insignia. The guards on the Stockton & Darlington Railway wore splendid red frock-coats with dark brown velvet collars. Later, most of the companies chose serviceable navy blue cloth, which varied in weight and quality according to the grade. At the turn of the century the early frock-coats worn by guards and ticket collectors were replaced by short serge jackets.

By the time of the grouping in 1923, most railway uniforms were fairly similar, consisting of trousers, a waistcoat (sleeveless for public grades, sleeved for outdoor grades such as porter, goods guard, shunter, etc.), with jacket and cap all in navy blue serge, distinguished by the badges and buttons of the company. The same type of uniform was retained by British Railways after 1948, identifiable by the totem-style cap badge and the lion and wheel insignia.

The next major change in the style of railway uniforms was not until 1965 when British Rail developed its 'corporate image', doing away with the regional colours incorporated in the badges. The new uniform moved away from the traditional navy blue serge, and the new grey and blue-grey uniforms that can be seen on stations today were introduced, bearing the British Rail 'double arrow' insignia. The old-style cap was replaced by the straight-sided cap with the turned-up back. Rank is no longer denoted in words but is evident from the

colour and quantity of narrow braid round the cap and badges on the jacket sleeves.

Unfortunately, because of the fragile nature of the fabrics used for the early uniforms, very little has survived from the pre-grouping era. All natural fibres will decay, and start to do so from the moment they are removed from the plant or animal from which they originate. The deterioration rate of fabrics is accelerated by light, dust, dirt, grease, water and various insects such as the clothes moth and carpet beetle. As soon as a garment is worn it is subjected to further hazards: perspiration, dirt, atmospheric pollution, cleaning detergents and, not least of the problems, strain and stress caused by the movement of the wearer. Railway uniforms, especially in the days of steam, were particularly subjected to these hazards, the same uniform being worn daily for at least a year until the next issue.

The National Collection does, however, boast one or two interesting items of early railway uniform, including a jacket and waistcoat from the Maryport & Carlisle Railway dating from about 1890 and a Tottenham & Hampstead Junction Railway guard's cap of about 1870. Most of the uniforms were inherited from the old museums run by British Railways at Clapham and York, and the collection consists mainly of the uniforms of the Big Four railway companies, predominantly the LNER and GWR.

Great Western Railway Stationmaster c.1930. This uniform is made of extra fine blue wool cloth, as befits the rank of the stationmaster. Note the elaborate braiding on the cuffs and the gold decoration on the cap.

A selection of items in the railway uniforms study collection: NER stationmaster's frock coat c.1860, LNER stationmaster's cap c.1940, British Railways Guard's cap c.1950, British Railways Inspector's leggings, railwaymen's armbands. Uniforms in the study collection are stored on hanging rails and individually covered in protective calico bags. Caps are padded with special acid-free tissue paper and stored singly in rigid fibre boxes.

British Railways (Western Region) passenger guard c.1955. The region is denoted by the brown totem badge on the cap. The gilt buttons and the braid on the peak of the cap indicate that this guard worked on passenger services, where he was constantly in the public eye. Goods guards had chrome buttons and no braid on the cap.

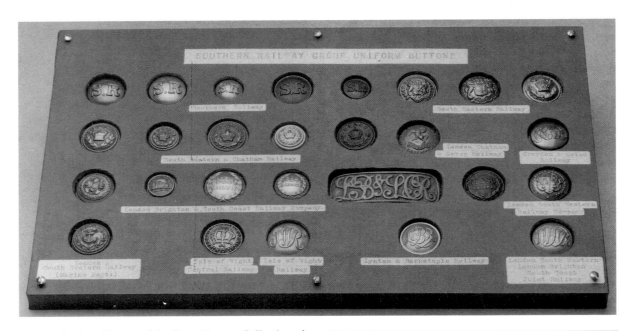

This display board is part of the Great Western Collection of uniform buttons started by David Levein of the GWR Secretary's Office in the early 1920s. It also formed part of a display set up in 1925 for the Railway Centenary celebrations. This particular board contains buttons of the Southern Railway and its constituent companies.

LBSCR staff at Clapham Junction in August 1889. The difference in rank is evident in the different styles of uniform. Note the stationmaster in the centre with his top hat and braided frock-coat, whilst the lower ranking porters have soft caps and canvas-sleeved waistcoats.

The Museum still has an active collecting policy for railway uniforms. The recent setting up of a new Uniforms Store provides the facilities for conserving and storing the uniforms, so we are now able to cope with the growing collection. The Museum is in close contact with British Rail, and the collection has recently benefitted from the acquisition of the standard patterns of many uniforms which are now obsolete. So, whilst we still seek the rarer items of early railway uniforms, we are also attempting to build a comprehensive collection of modern uniforms which will greatly benefit future generations.

Owing to the fragile nature of the collection, it is not practical for original uniforms to be placed on permanent display, so replicas tend to be used to illustrate them to visitors whilst the originals form the basis of a useful study collection which members of the public may visit by appointment. It is an unfortunate fact that, not only have many examples of railway uniform disappeared, but the documentation on the subject is sparse. We rely on snippets of information gleaned here and there from old rule books and other documents, together with photographic evidence, in order to illustrate the history of railway uniforms more clearly and fill the gaps that necessarily exist in the physical collection.

Although few full uniforms have been preserved from the past, their metallic adornments much more frequently survive. The collection is thus supplemented by over 2,500 buttons and badges, including examples from many of the earliest railway companies, right through to the present day.

Railway Heraldry

by Michael Blakemore

In days of old, knights on the battlefield had many hazards to face, not the least of which was the problem of being easily identified and so not being beset by a member of the same side. Encased as they were from head to foot in suits of armour, there was always the risk that in the heat of the moment one would look very much like another; a distinctive symbol, prominently displayed, would reduce that risk, and so the 'coats of arms' came about.

In the Middle Ages heralds were the court functionaries who carried messages between princes and armies, proclaimed tournaments and stage-managed ceremonial occasions. To fulfil these duties they would necessarily have to be able to identify men by their insignia, and eventually the heralds became experts on this particular subject. The passage of time saw the demise of their battlefield role and the genealogical aspects of it became predominant until the term 'heraldry' came to mean the art of armorial bearings.

The usefulness of a unique symbol, especially at a time when illiteracy was commonplace, led to the development of the 'seal' for the purpose of authenticating documents, and in due course civic authorities began to adopt heraldic devices to signify their particular boroughs. The first to do so appears to have been the City of Chester during the early part of the fourteenth century, and the idea was later taken up by commercial institutions, starting with the Guilds. Initially these coats of arms were created locally and were not officially recorded, but as the practice became more widespread so a system of formal organization evolved and by the sixteenth century the issue of arms to individuals or corporate bodies was regulated by the College of Arms. The concept of the identifiable symbol has stood the test of time well and is clearly the forerunner of the modern commercial trademark, typified by the golliwogs, tigers and flour graders of familiar everyday commodites.

The railway revolution of the nineteenth century was accompanied by a proliferation of companies each striving to assert its independence and individuality. On the Royal Assent being given to a company's Act of Incorporation, a seal was designed for legal usage and from this an armorial device derived. These designs often included the

Caledonian Railway

Heraldry in Scotland was supposedly more rigidly control-led than in England and the Lord Lyon King of Arms had drastic powers to act against anyone displaying arms unlawfully. Nevertheless the Caledonian Railway grandly incorporated the full Scottish Royal Arms and the jewel and motto of the Order of the Thistle into its heraldic device without, so far as can be ascertained, ever gaining authority to do so! Supporting the shield and holding the banner of Scotland (left) and the banner of St Andrew (right) are two unicorns, the mythical creature adopted by King James IV to support his coat of arms around 1500.

London & North Eastern Railway

The LNER was the second largest of the four companies created by the Grouping of 1923 and emulated its constituent, the Great Central, in obtaining a full grant of arms, one of only three companies so to do. It further paid the GCR the compliment of adopting its motto 'Forward'. Beneath the figure of Mercury emerging from a cloud of steam, the shield includes the St George Cross and two London griffins, a representation of Edinburgh Castle, and four of the York lions, all signifying the route of the LNER's main line linking the English and Scottish capitals and passing through the ancient capital of Northumbria.

coats of arms (or aspects of them) of the towns which the railway company intended to connect, and they soon came to be applied not just to official documents and stationery but also to locomotives and carriages. The coats of arms thus came to be displayed before a much wider public and the railway companies were amongst the first so to emblazon their individual motifs on their property.

Considering the importance of the railway system, it is strange that the English and Welsh companies devised their own heraldry without seeking official approval (in Scotland matters were more stringently controlled); only three obtained grants of armorial bearings from the College of Arms. The first was the Great Central in 1898; the other two were the London & North Eastern and the Southern, although the state-owned British Transport Commission and Ulster Transport Authority later followed the correct procedure. Furthermore, the additional embellishment of a garter containing the company's name around the crest was also highly irregular – the garter is, strictly speaking, reserved for the order of chivalry of that name which is in the personal gift of the monarch. The railways blithely ignored such conventions.

The NRM holds a collection of over three hundred mounted coats of arms, covering companies from the mighty Big Four, their principal constituents and the nationalized British Railways down to short narrow gauge lines such as the Talyllyn and the Vale of Rheidol. Also represented are railway systems in the farthest corners of Africa, Asia, South America and Australia where British capital and expertise were once so influential. Our own collection has been augmented by a very fine collection of heraldic shields on loan from the Metropolitan-Cammell Carriage & Wagon Co. Ltd, one of the world's best-known manufacturers of railway rolling stock. Its

Rhondda & Swansea Bay Railway
The size of a railway company bore no relation to its ability to concoct an elaborate piece of heraldry, as the Rhondda & Swansea Bay Railway bore witness. The fact that its lines totalled a mere 31 route miles did not deter it from proudly applying its fine armorial transfer to the 27 locomotives and 63 carriages which it handed over to the Great Western Railway in 1906. Most railway heraldry embodied traditional features but the RSBR offered an example of a modern concept adapted to an ancient custom in the form of a representation of one of its 0-6-2 goods tanks, a rare instance of a locomotive appearing in railway heraldry. The ship illustrates the railways' close connections with the Port of Swansea while the device is headed by the arms and supporters of the House of Jersey, marking the fact that the Earl of Jersey was the company's first chairman.

Huddersfield Corporation & LMS Railway Joint Omnibus Services
In 1928 the railway companies obtained powers to operate road services and the LMS subsequently entered into an agreement with Huddersfield Corporation for the joint operation of bus services in that area. The vehicles carried on their sides this device in which the LMS emblem and the arms of the County Borough of Huddersfield were amalgamated. The remarkably modest LMS 'arms' consisted of the dragon's wing of London and a rose and thistle to signify its Anglo-Scottish activities; the Huddersfield arms are based on those of the Ramsden family, holders of the Manor of Huddersfield from Elizabethan times.

collection reflects the range of companies it has supplied; many were overseas customers with names redolent of bygone atlases – whatever became of the Leopoldina Railway, for instance, or the Ottoman Railway? (For the record, the former was the largest British-owned railway in Brazil; the latter originally linked Smyrna and Aidin in Turkey and, until later extensions, proved too short to resist economic competition from camels!)

Possibly the most unusual item in the collection originates not so very far from York and is the coat of arms of the Victoria Hotel, Sheffield, painted on the shell of a turtle. The reason for this curiosity is shrouded in mystery.

The grouping and subsequent nationalization of the railways resulted in the virtual elimination of the private company and so means that we have to look back through history to appreciate the richness of railway heraldry. But not *quite* always, for there *are* still some independent railways, mostly the products of the preservation movement. We have, for example, the crest of the narrow gauge Ffestiniog Railway which has been using its 'Prince of Wales' feathers device since 1863; as the company has remained in continuous existence all this time, it can therefore boast the oldest railway coat of arms still in everyday use. Bringing the heraldry story into more recent times, we have the crest of the Keighley & Worth Valley Railway, a private company formed by a preservation society which reopened the Keighley–Oxenhope branch in 1968. Perhaps other privately operated tourist railways will continue to produce their own attractive armorial devices and so perpetuate the colourful tradition of the escutcheon, the wyvern and the lion rampant.

Chapter 6

Models

by David Jenkinson

Modelmaking is one of the oldest activities known to mankind and from their very inception, railways have proved a fruitful source of inspiration to modelmakers. Not surprisingly, therefore, the National Railway Museum inherited in 1975 a fine, if somewhat randomly classified, collection of models and has continued to add to it since. Railway modelling is a highly diverse 'art' form and there is much specialized literature covering virtually all its various facets. The Museum does not feel obliged to compete in them all and decided, from an early stage, to limit its collecting policy to a few specific categories which, taken with the rest of the collection, seemed best likely to make a positive contribution to the overall story of railways.

The collection acquired in 1975 contained many superb items but also some dross. However, there was a sound basis for a four-fold display and collecting policy to be adopted. These four broad divisions can be summed up as follows:

1   Accurate models of important prototypes which either have not survived in full-size form or, if they have, are not possessed by the Museum.
2   Models of objects which could not, without almost insuperable difficulty be preserved full size – for example a complete 'scene', a full-length train or a ship.
3   The history and development of commercial 'toy' and 'model' railways, preferably with one or two working examples.
4   Special and unique models.

A celebrated 'lost cause' captured in model diorama form – the famous Doric portico at Euston station, much as it was in the mid-nineteenth century.

Before going into detail, one or two general points need to be made. Overriding the above-mentioned divisions are questions of scale and quality. Models can be made at many different linear scales ranging from 1:200 (or smaller) right through to a third or half full size. Larger scales can show, with superb fidelity, every minute detail of the original, whereas small-scale models can paint a three-dimensional picture of a complete scene. For comparative purposes, a *constant* scale between objects is more critical than the specific choice of scale, *per se*. In displaying its model collections, the Museum is attempting to resolve the conflicting problems arising from these differences.

Secondly, the quality factor must be considered. While fairly crude models can possess a degree of 'rustic charm', in the context of Museum interpretation, accuracy must be paramount. Models in the collection can be justified as objects of superb quality in their own right, as well as faithful representations.

It should also be pointed out that clearly defined 'subject parameters' have been drawn as far as future items are concerned. There must, essentially, be a *British* element, however insular this might at first seem. This is not quite as restrictive as might be supposed, since 'Britain' can be prefixed 'bult in or used in' – and this opens up the field considerably. Thus a foreign built model of an object *used* in Britain would qualify as would a British built model of an object used abroad. Without such form of 'restrictive covenant', however, it would be impossible to develop a coherent collecting policy in the context of the Museum's 'National' title.

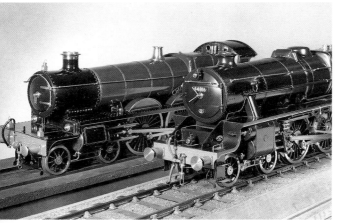

This 1/12 scale locomotive model is typical of those which represent long-vanished prototypes. It depicts a diminutive early 4-4-0 (prototype built in 1866) of the Great North of Scotland Railway.

The advantages of constant scale presentation as revealed by fine 1/16 scale models of a GWR 'Saint' class 4-6-0 (left) and an LMS class 5 4-6-0 (right). These models are used to illustrate locomotive development.

Finally, two special groups of models must be mentioned – civil engineering and ships. The creations of these two areas of railway activity generally cannot be portrayed in three-dimensional form other than by the extensive and almost exclusive use of models. For this reason, the sections of this book dealing with these two topics are based largely on the model collection and therefore will not be considered further here.

The Museum has adopted three main modes of display, usually determined by the scale of the model. In the larger scale category, the prime models are normally displayed in a series of perimeter wall showcases in such a way as to show, with their full-size counterparts in the Main Hall of the Museum, some sort of evolutionary chronology of locomotives, carriages and wagons. If a choice is available, the Museum prefers to display models of 'lost' types, although a chronological display must also include examples of extant as well as extinct types; the Museum generally endeavours not to duplicate in model form any full-size locomotive which is on display.

Because of the richness of the locomotive model collection it has been possible to develop a constant-scale presentation of more than one aspect of this subject. In terms of locomotive development, for example, the chosen scale is one-sixteenth for models representing prototypes built before the end of the company period (1947–8) and one-twenty-fourth for the British Rail years. It would have been more desirable had one scale been possible throughout, but the choice of two was determined by the inherited collection. Fortunately the break in scale occurs at the period of nationalization of the British network. A further collection of constant one-twelfth scale models is used to augment aspects of the railway companies themselves.

In the carriage and wagon field, the smaller number of models available has meant more variable scales which is unfortunate. Nevertheless many of them make up in sheer quality what they may lack in scale comparability.

Those very large models which are either too big to be presented chronologically or, in the case of locomotive models, would destroy the constant-scale approach, are displayed in a variety of appropriate contexts. Some are regarded as exemplary illustrations of craftsmanship, such as the quarter-scale carriage models of King Edward VII's Saloon and an LNWR dining car; others are used to augment the theme of the 'Travelling by Train' gallery, such as the eighth-scale model of GWR *King George V* and a typical carriage; while a third use is to emphasize a specific feature of a subject, such as a simple wallcase treatment introducing the principles of the steam locomotive. In another case, a one-sixth-scale North London Railway 4-4-0 tank engine has a specific design relationship, in the person of William Adams, to the LSWR 4-4-0 No 563 and is displayed alongside it.

The largest single group of vanished species is found in the small-scale (one-forty-third) collection associated with the Museum's working gauge 0 model railway. This scale has attracted many fine craftsmen and the Museum has been able to assemble a growing collection. Some are seen in operation, others are in associated showcases. This scale of model links neatly with the second major division of the collection – that of the conceptual model of scenes and activities which could never be presented full size.

The most obvious of these is the 'train in motion'. A train may be a quarter of a mile long and the only effective way to show this crucial aspect of the railway in a Museum environment is to make a working model. The Museum has chosen gauge 0 for this purpose because it is larger than most 'domestic' model railways which usually adopt smaller scales for space reasons. The objective has been to represent as accurately as possible the theme of 'Trains through the Ages', with the models operating at something like scale speeds.

Another form of model in this smaller scale category is the static 'scenic diorama' which encapsulates one specific place, theme or activity. Combining these two threads is a third category of model, exemplified at the moment solely by the Heckmondwike display in 1/76 scale, which was donated by its builders in 1982. This diorama-like presentation has, as its centre-piece, a typical but imaginary station scene, portrayed as a specific railway at a particular point in time. It is also, like the gauge 0 display, a working model in that representative trains can move through the scene from time to time. Its prime virtue, however, lies in the superb accuracy and

A pair of exquisite carriage models showing something of the evolution of the British four-wheeler. The North Union model, quarter full size, is contemporary with the original vehicle, having been built in the railway shops at Preston in 1842; the GER model (scale 1/12) was built by William Coney (a GER employee) for the sheer joy of it. Everything is of wooden construction, including the track and it took six years to make, early in the twentieth century.

A superb late 19th century 1/6 scale model of a contemporary North London 4-4-0 tank. The paintwork is original.

authenticity of modelling from track level upwards. Correct operation of such a system, with all possible train movements reproduced, would demand manpower resources beyond the Museum's current capability, as would the gauge 0 display. This is essentially the field of the many specialized model railway shows, so the Museum sees no purpose in duplication of such activity, even were it possible.

Another interesting subject area, wholly stimulated by the general interest in railways, is that of the commercial 'toy' and 'model' trains. This is a whole sub-culture in its own right and several collections of international repute have been assembled by 'afficionados' of the genre. Although the National Railway Museum does not feel obliged to rival these, the growth of railway modelling is an important strand in the whole story. This side of the story was not featured at all when the Museum opened in 1975, but a representative collection of models is now on display in showcases, arranged in historical sequence of model evolution. Some of these items can by no means be dignified by the word 'model' in its purest sense; but they often have great charm and clearly stimulate considerable nostalgia amongst visitors. They reveal, however, a growing sophistication and discrimination on the part of the customer as one era succeeded another – and in one particular respect, these 'toys' (for many of them, in their time, were no more than that), have considerable historical value, their colour schemes.

Although the early (c. 1900–25) manufacturers generally adopted a somewhat cavalier attitude to the shape and proportion of the model, they often went to extraordi-

A view of the 4mm scale (1:76) Heckmondwike layout, an attempt to produce, in model form, the railway scene of the mid 1930s with all its hustle and bustle. The attention to detail on the part of its builders is formidable.

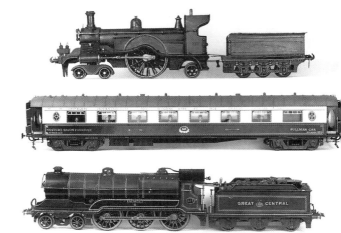

This 'fine-scale' Gauge '0' (Scale 1/43) model of a SECR Stirling 4-4-0 No 241 shows the superb quality which can be achieved in this popular smaller size. It is a working model driven by a 12 volt DC motor and was built and painted in the early 1950s by the late Bernard Miller, one of the finest craftsmen of his time.

A small scene from the Museum's working Gauge '0' layout. The trains featured are a typical branch line operation of the mid 1930s and a characteristic British Railways express of the mid 1950s.

The evolution of the commercial model from early Edwardian times to the present day in the form of a Gauge 3 (roughly 24:1) Carette model of a GNR 4-2-2 (c.1902), a Gauge 1 (30:1) Bing model of a GCR 4-6-0 (c.1914) and a 1982-built British made Gauge 1 model of a French Wagons-Lits Pullman car of the 1930s. The progressive increase in accuracy and authenticity is self-evident; yet such is the strange nature of model collecting that their market value is in totally inverse proportion to their date and accuracy!

The Museum's definitive 1/8 scale model of the Anglo-Chilean Nitrate Company Kitson-Meyer 0-6-6-0 tank locomotive of 1903. The prototype ran on metre gauge and the model was built by Mr. J. A. Hartrup of Lancaster.

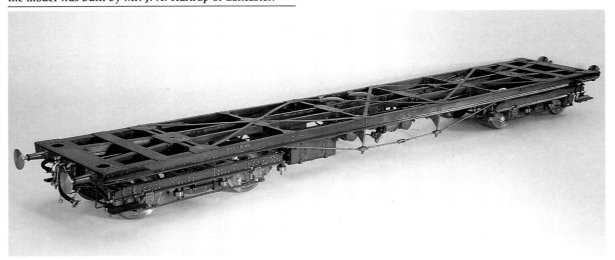

North Eastern Railway carriage underframe to a scale of 1/10. The builder is unknown.

Close-ups of the fine quarter-scale, apprentice-made dining car model, built at Wolverton Carriage Works c.1910. For many years this model graced the shareholders' meeting room at the old Euston Station.

nary lengths to capture the many and varied colour schemes which were then displayed by the railway companies. If a model from this period has survived unscathed, it can sometimes represent one of the best possible contemporary sources for a livery style.

It would be wrong to leave this subject without a further word about the model itself and the reasons for its existence. Most of the really great models were built because of the sheer dedication of the original craftsman and usually reflect his knowledge and love of his subject matter. The Museum is blessed with many such items, for example an exquisite fully working model of a Kitson-Meyer articulated steam locomotive. This model, acquired at auction, was of interest to the Museum because it represented a peculiar and little-known British contribution to railway operation overseas, in this case South America. The amazing thing is that, as far as the Museum is aware, this beautiful creation was the first such model built by its maker.

Fascinating, too, are the instructive, or 'test piece' models. In the first category the NER carriage underframe is possibly the best way to comprehend the construction of a typical British carriage chassis at the turn of the century. Similarly, 'Apprentice' locomotive models are often the only evidence we can display of the lineaments of particular classes; outstanding examples are the aforementioned NLR 4-4-0 tank engine and a fine eighth-scale Great Eastern Railway 4-4-0 *Claud Hamilton*. However, perhaps the most superb example of the apprentice piece exists in the shape of the already mentioned quarter-scale carriage model of a 1910 LNWR dining car. This model, and others like it, were made by apprentices to prove to their supervisors that they were equally capable of making the real thing. The model weighs more than a ton!

The Museum itself modestly tries to continue this great tradition of model making in its own workshops; the whole of the working gauge 0 display has been developed by a team of Museum craftsmen and, at the other end of the spectrum, the passenger-hauling $7\frac{1}{4}$ in gauge steam locomotive *Margaret* was built entirely in the Museum workshops.

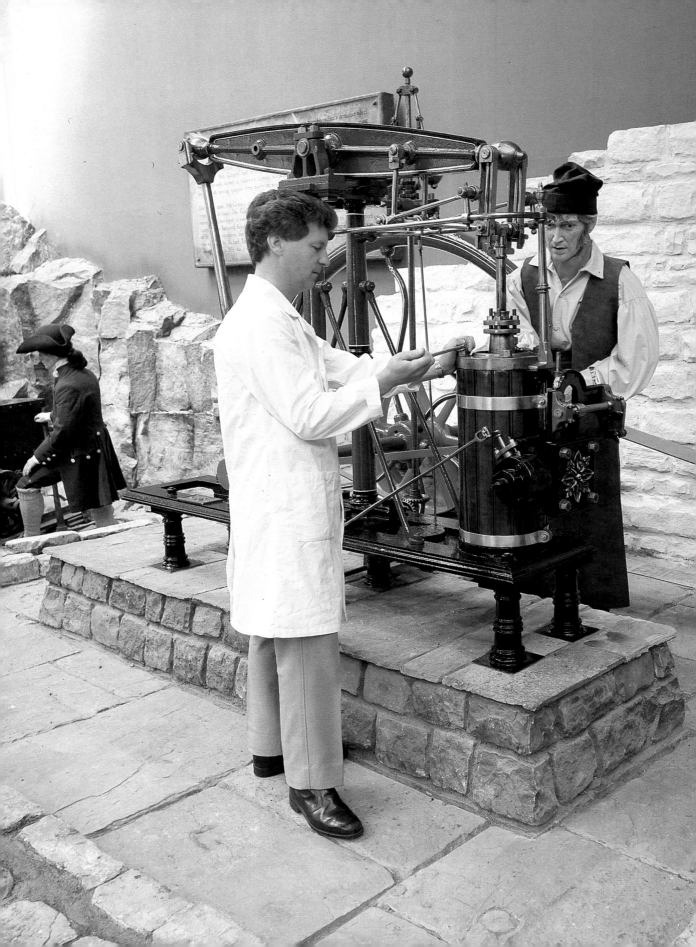

Chapter 7

Behind the Scenes

A museum, like an iceberg, has much of its essential character hidden from direct public view, but the analogy quickly breaks down. There is, of course, the inevitable proliferation of store rooms, material awaiting classification and conservation, 'reserve' collections perhaps awaiting more display space and items on loan to other institutions. But there is a second 'behind the scenes' element which, while not manifesting itself in the form of overt public exhibition is, nevertheless, very much a part of a museum's work with the public.

The unexplained presentation of a museum's treasures, whilst giving a short-lived satisfaction to the onlooker, might well arouse in many people the desire to know more, and a museum must try to satisfy this. The fashionable word is 'interpretation', but there are limits to what can be done in the way of presentation techniques. For one thing, there is a finite limit to the amount of information which a visitor is able or willing to absorb on a single visit. It therefore behoves a museum, especially one funded by the taxpayer, to provide some form of back-up educational and research services for the public, should they be sufficiently stimulated on first acquaintance, to wish to pursue the interest at greater depth.

It is not merely sufficient to set up a research facility, however simple, if the various items in the collection as a whole do not reveal, in their 'as presented' characteristics, those significant aspects which, presumably, were the cause of their saving in the first place. Thus it is that there must always be a close liaison between those whose task it is to 'interpret and explain' and the skilled craftsmen whose role is to restore, repair or even make work again the artefacts of a by-gone age. For this reason, both aspects are included in this chapter.

Education Service

by David Mosley

When the National Railway Museum first opened its doors in 1975, one of the priorities was the setting up of an Education Service. In the cloistered calm of the museum world, 'education' has taken many varied forms and there are almost as many different interpretations of the art as there are museum education services. Within the National Railway Museum, education is a much wider parish than the simple instructing of students of all ages. The formal session still has an important part to play, but the interpretation of the whole museum environment is now of equal importance. The criterion for success is probably enjoyment; a pleasurable visit is soon repeated.

The NRM Education Service, as constituted in 1975, was closely based on the system then operated by the Museum's parent body, the Science Museum. A well-appointed 78-seat Lecture Theatre with provision for cine, video and slide presentations and a display bench for experiments formed the basis. Time was allocated for gallery tours and a former British Railways Mk I coach was provided as a study centre. It was envisaged that the principal work of the Head of Education and, by 1976, his Assistant, would be giving lectures and gallery

Craftsmanship lives on – the finishing touches to a stationary steam engine (from an old railway workshop) now completely restored by Museum technicians. The character costumed display figure is already in position behind the engine.

tours with an underlying scientific emphasis, not always featuring railways. The practice has been different. Lectures were rarely requested outside the railway field and tended to concentrate on the social and historical aspects of railways whilst still taking note of the underlying technology. The study-centre coach has seen a more practical use as a place for eating packed lunches! This forms a much appreciated service to schools, unique in York, and formidable numbers of packed lunches – over 21,000 in 1984–5 – are consumed in the coach.

In an average year the Education Service will deal with about four hundred school and organized parties, but this apparently high number represents only about one-eighth of the organized parties coming to the Museum. The Education Service tries to respond to the needs of school teachers; sessions can be as long or short as required and on topics to suit the teacher's course of study. In the Lecture Theatre, where 'informal formality' is the order of the day, topics

The lecture theatre – centre of the Education Service's activities. Prominent on the bench are models of a Newcomen steam pump of the 18th century and a typical 19th century locomotive.

range from railway history and travelling by train to how locomotives work and a straightforward introduction to the Museum.

'Hands-on' experience is today's watchword in many museum education services. The NRM suffers here by the very size of its objects and their original uses. One can see considerable parental objection to the consequences of arming their offspring with cleaning rag or oil can upon their arrival at the Museum. There can, however, be a limited amount of 'hands-on' experience, and more access to locomotives and coaches under the supervision of the Education Officer can be given during a gallery tour than can be permitted to an unsupervised 'ordinary' visitor. To say that a school party is usually joined on its way around the Museum by many casual visitors is perhaps to give some idea of the popularity of the tour!

It is hoped, within the foreseeable future, to add a classroom-cum-study centre to the facilities that the Education Service can offer. This will supersede the 'study coach' as such, having the advantage of the correct shape! It is envisaged that this new centre will further the modern trends in 'hands on' experience through the use of real objects – uniforms, models and the like – as well as allowing students to solve problems such as signalling and shunting by practical experience, probably aided by models.

One area where the formal lecture still reigns supreme is that of visits made to railway societies and other learned bodies up and down the country. Here the Education Service co-operates with the Keeper of the Museum and the Chief Engineer, and on average one lecture per week is given throughout the year in locations as far apart as Carlisle and Canterbury, Newquay and Newcastle. These outside lectures are seen as an excellent form of publicity for the Museum and also a way of letting the enthusiast fraternity in particular know the thinking which goes into the Museum's policies and what is happening behind the scenes.

A piece of the equipment used in lecture theatre demonstrations on the power of steam, a beautifully detailed coal fired boiler and beam engine, no more than one foot high.

'Learning by Experience', in this case the rather uncomfortable experience of the second-class carriage of the 1840s.

In the footsteps of the Stephensons, young visitors explore the footplate of the Museum's replica *Rocket*.

As the Education Service uses slides and films as its day-to-day stock in trade, it is appropriate that it should co-ordinate the wider Museum development of audio-visual techniques. Three areas are worthy of note. A small tape-slide theatre has proved a popular attraction on the Long Gallery of the Main Hall. Here the 'information through entertainment' theme is pursued as images and music combine to show such varied topics as 'The Changing Colour Scene', 'Carrying the Freight', 'The Story of Steam' and 'The life and times of George Stephenson'. These and other programmes are made 'in-house' – but to a standard indistinguishable from that of outside professional bodies. Further programmes are in constant production, and for the technically minded the basis of the system is the Kodak Carousel projector controlled by Electrosonic a-v equipment. With the opening of the new gallery of the Museum, further a-v techniques will be explored.

In a more archival context is the collection of 16mm films which is being built up by the Museum. These films can be grouped into three principal categories and date back, in any quantity, to the 1930s. The bulk of the films are those acquired from the former British Transport Films organization. These cover many aspects of railway and associated working from nationalization until the demise of the organization in its archival form in the early 1980s. British Transport Films productions of the immediate post-nationalization period seem to capture a world which has gone for ever. The vibrant, resourceful railway world of *Elizabethan Express*, *This is York* and *Train Time* are light years away from today's sector-conscious operation, and it is to the great credit of the film producers that they caught the mood of the time so exactly.

In recent years, the Museum, or items from it, have featured in many films and TV programmes, both fact and fiction, and copies of some of the non-fiction contributions are held in the collection. One series is particularly worthy of note, *Great Railway Journeys of the World*, produced by the BBC in

1980. On the dramatic side, Museum artefacts have featured in the oscar-winning *Chariots of Fire* and the ITV epic *Wagner* to mention but two.

The final category is the most disparate, containing films acquired from all sorts of sources. The East Coat main line at Hadley Wood in the late thirties, in colour, contrasts well with the rural ramblings of the Lynton & Barnstaple line in somewhat grainy black and white. Narrow gauge in the fifties can be compared at Towyn (a transatlantic view in this case) and on the Tralee & Dingle in the far west of Ireland. Main line steam of the sixties can often be seen in colour, sometimes through the lens of Ivo Peters, while perhaps the most evocative footage of this period is the collection of *Railway Roundabout* films produced by John Adams and Patrick Whitehouse for the BBC. Fond memories are evoked of 'trainspotting at teatime' by these splendid films. Three main uses are seen for the film collection: for use in public film shows at holiday times, as sources of reference and as raw material for conversion to 'video-labels', and by showing Museum locomotives and carriages in their former state.

For reference purposes the Museum is also building up an aural archive. This comprises tape recordings of memories and recollections by former railwaymen, hopefully giving an idea of what it was like to be involved in the railway industry. This archive is in its infancy at present, but already the scope of people interviewed ranges from footplate staff to the former Chief Mechanical Engineer of British Railways, R. A. Riddles, who designed Britain's last main line steam locomotive *Evening Star*, one of the Museum's most precious possessions.

It has already been stated that the Education Service is fully involved in the widest context of the Museum and does not simply restrict itself to formal contact sessions with school groups. No better example of this wider involvement can be given than the recent (1987) reorganization of the Main Hall of the Museum and the development of the

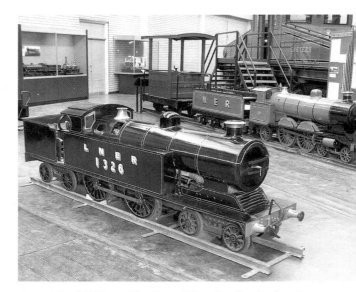

A special exhibition with a large Education Service input, 'Minimum Gauge Railways 1881–1981'. The two Bassett-Lowke 15in gauge locomotives are excellent for explaining the principles without the overbearing size of the real thing.

new gallery during 1987–9. Both displays are the result of sometimes lively discussions between Education Service staff, other curators and the Museum's Engineering Department. The result, in the Main Hall, is an organized display, not overtly didactic, which incorporates most of the salient points in the railway story, both technical and historical. It is now possible to follow a logical and informative course through the development of railways, or simply to enjoy the size and elegance of the locomotives and carriages on a gentle amble. Similar principles have been followed in the development of the new gallery; whilst there is no direct attempt to instruct visitors or go into too much detail, the labels try to sum up the important features of the objects on display. There is no reason to suspect that displays developed in this way will be any less attractive; the objects themselves will retain their own intrinsic attractiveness and their more logical interpretation should enhance the whole Museum's atmosphere and purpose.

Although the special temporary exhibitions held by the Museum to celebrate significant railway anniversaries or social occasions are explored in more detail in the next chapter, it is worth mentioning that several of them were inspired and largely undertaken by the Education Service. Several centenaries and other landmarks have been celebrated, including the 1976 centenary of the opening of the Settle & Carlisle line with the 'Wheels in the Wilderness' exhibition, 'Royal Trains' in 1977 (Jubilee Year), 'Grand Hotels' in 1978 and in 1981 'Minimum Gauge Railways', commemorating one hundred years of the ideas of Sir Arthur Heywood and railways on the 15 in gauge. Also in 1981 'Palaces on Wheels' was the Museum's contribution to the celebrations for the marriage of the Prince and Princess of Wales. In all these special exhibitions, as with permanent displays, the aim has been to present a coherent and interesting story without being dogmatic.

It can thus be concluded that the Museum's Education Service holds a much wider brief than the formal instruction of school parties. 'Education', in whatever form, is seen as one of, if not *the* primary role of the Museum and yet it should be borne in mind that most visitors are at the Museum to enjoy themselves. The two concepts are not mutually exclusive and 'education through enjoyment' would be as fine a phrase to finish on as any.

Library
by C. P. Atkins

The NRM Library is small when compared with its counterparts in other national museums, but its greatest strength is undoubtedly its ever-growing photographic collection. It is important to appreciate that it is primarily a library rather than an archive in that most primary sources, such as board and committee minutes and staff records of English and Welsh railway companies, are deposited with the Public Record Office at Kew. Those for Scottish lines are with the Scottish Record Office in Edinburgh. Parliamentary plans for railways, actual and proposed, are deposited in the House of Lords Library. Copies of the relevant catalogues are held at York.

The NRM Library was originally established to provide internal research facilities for the Museum staff, but it has proved possible to admit the public, strictly by prior appointment only, to the Reading Room which receives around five hundred such visitors annually. The subject coverage of the library is distinctly patchy, being extremely strong on some aspects and certain railways, and weak on others, notably civil engineering. But the situation is continually improving and the research facilities and information resources today bear little resemblance to those of 1975. The reading room contains the main catalogues, general reference material and some seven hundred and fifty photographic reference binders on open access. The library also deals with numerous telephone and letter enquiries, including a number from overseas, and often provides guidance to alternative sources of information when it is unable to help directly.

Published Works

Because of its unique status, *A Bibliography of British Railway History* by George Ottley, originally published in 1965, was taken as the basis for the cataloguing system used at York, in preference to more conventional library practices. This bibliography, to which a supplement has been long awaited, contains about 8,000 entries, many of which will be found on the shelves of the NRM Library.

Since 1965 the number of railway publications has increased markedly, and many have been purchased by the NRM Library. They include works devoted to a number of previously neglected subjects, such as railway architecture, signalling and rolling stock as well as locomotives which have always received much attention in railway literature.

Although the NRM is primarily concerned with railways and railway engineering in the British Isles, railway development here cannot be viewed in total isolation; for this reason the library collection contains a number of items published in North

Although for more than a century, the railways predominantly derived their revenue from freight haulage, they were always anxious to exploit the tourist potential of the areas which they served. In Scotland much was made of the golfing and angling facilities; elsewhere the very different countryside offered by the Yorkshire Dales, North Devon, and the Chilterns was encapsulated in attractive booklets: North British Railway, 1921; North Eastern Railway, 1896; Metropolitan Railway, 1927; Southern Railway, 1938.

Locomotive manufacturer's brochures. That centre top is translated into Russian and describes the unique and exceptionally large 4-8-2 + 2-8-4 Beyer Garratt locomotive built by Beyer Peacock & Co in 1932 for service in Siberia. Locomotives for rather warmer climates are described in the North British Locomotive Company brochure (bottom right) and Armstrong Whitworth & Co (top left).

America, East and West Europe, Australia and the Far East. British railway influence overseas was formerly very extensive, both with regard to British imperial possessions and other countries largely dependent upon British manufacturers for the supply of their locomotives, rolling stock and other equipment. This is reflected in such highly informative directories as the *Railway Year Book*, published from 1899, and *Bradshaw's Shareholder's Guide*, published annually from 1848 until 1923. The latter gave retrospective historical and financial particulars, and identified all current directors and senior officers of every railway enterprise in the British Isles, and many abroad, especially in countries of the former British Empire.

For promotional purposes, manufacturers, especially of locomotives, produced lavish brochures, copies of many being available for consultation; while the railways themselves produced attractive booklets extolling the delights of the more scenic areas which they served. The Furness Railway, for example, capitalized on its close proximity to the Lake District, while the short-lived Lancashire, Derbyshire & East Coast Railway – the self-styled 'Dukeries

Route' – made much of the Robin Hood legend. Also popular were the *On Either Side* (LMS and LNER) and *Through the Carriage Window* (GWR) publications which meticulously detailed every landmark visible during a long main line railway journey, an idea recently revived by British Rail.

By definition the library contains mainly printed material but it does contain a small number of truly unique items: its own 'Book of Kells' is the pocket notebook of Sir Daniel Gooch which measures only 4 in by 5½ in by 1¼ in (10 cm by 13 cm by 3 cm) yet contains about six hundred pages which bear exquisitely executed scale drawings of GWR broad gauge locomotives and rolling stock, both complete and their detailed components. Regrettably Sir Daniel's notorious handwriting has precluded the possibility that he was personally responsible for the excellent draughtsmanship in his own notebook!

A typical double page from Sir Daniel Gooch's notebook. Note the detailed calculation of the boiler heating surfaces on the left, the lower half of which relates to the superbly drawn locomotive on the right. Ten broad gauge 4-4-0s of the 'Waverley' class were built by Robert Stephenson & Co in Newcastle-upon-Tyne in 1855 for the GWR.

A fine drawing of a locomotive safety valve from Gooch's notebook. The accompanying scale (Imperial) shows the almost incredible precision of these minuscule drawings.

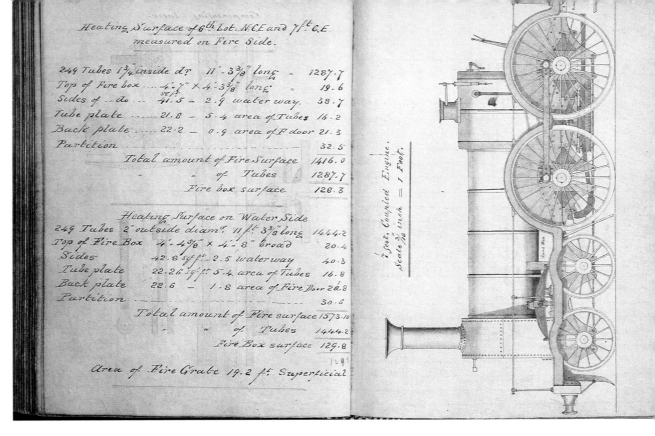

Heating Surface of 6th Lot. N.C.E and 7th C.E.
measured on Fire Side.

249 Tubes 1¾ inside d? 11'- 3⅜" long	=	1287.7
Top of Fire box .... 4'.7" × 4'-3⅜" long		19.6
Sides of ― do ― 41.5 ― 2.9 water way		38.7
Tube plate ...... 21.8 ― 5.4 area of Tubes	16.2	
Back plate ...... 22.2 ― 0.9 area of F door	21.3	
Partition		32.5
Total amount of Fire Surface		1416.0
" " of Tubes		1287.7
Fire box surface		128.3

Heating Surface on Water Side
249 Tubes 2" outside diam? 11ft. 3⅜" long		1444.2
Top of Fire Box 4'-4⅝" × 4".8" broad		20.4
Sides 42.8 sq ft 2.5 water way		40.3
Tube plate 22.26 sq ft 5.4 area of Tubes	16.8	
Back plate 22.6 ― 1.8 area of Fire Door	20.8	
Partition		30.6
Total amount of Fire surface		1573.10
" " of Tubes		1444.2
Fire Box surface		129.8

Area of Fire Grate 19.2 ft. Superficial

6 feet Coupled Engine.
Scale 3/16 inch = 1 Foot.

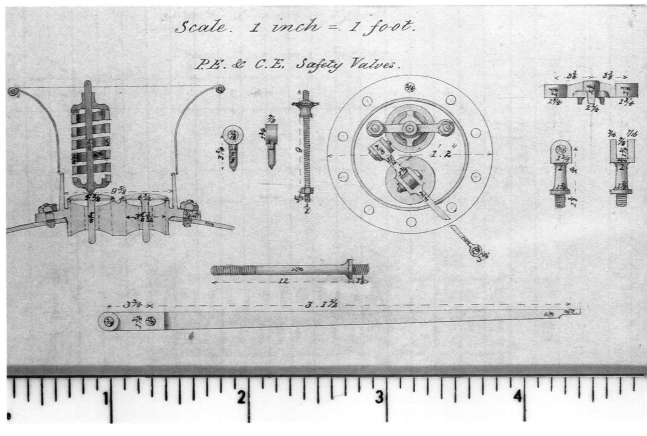

Scale. 1 inch = 1 foot.

P.E. & C.E. Safety Valves.

The library subscribes annually to around three hundred periodicals, and contains many others which have long ceased publication. It is interesting to note that the *Railway Magazine* and the *Locomotive Magazine* (which ceased publication in 1959) both first appeared during the mid 1890s which undoubtedly reflected the increasing popular interest in railways. However, even when railways had begun to appear sixty years earlier, a host of related journals were born (analogous to the spate of electronics and computer periodicals today) concerned primarily with the financial and political aspects of railway promotion and development. The *Railway Times* ran from 1839 until 1914, the noticeably thick twin volumes for the years 1845 and 1846 reflecting the height of the Railway Mania, when large numbers of sometimes ludicrous railway enterprises were projected.

Specialized branches of railway engineering produced technical papers in their various fields. Much of relevance also appeared in the published proceedings of the respective institutions of the Civil and Mechanical engineers. The 'Mechanicals' was founded in 1847 by George Stephenson who was its first president, followed in that office by his son Robert, who later was also president of the 'Civils'.

Railways have long attracted an enthusiast following, often manifested by specialized societies. One of the oldest of these, the Stephenson Locomotive Society, was founded in 1909, and the once rival Railway Correspondence and Travel Society in 1928. In recent years a surprisingly large additional number of societies of amateur status have become established, devoted to the in-depth study of all aspects of individual railway companies, or particular aspects of railways in general. Many of the larger pre-1923 railway companies, the Big Four and BR itself are the subject of societies which produce highly informative publications, copies of all of which are obtained by the NRM. Other societies specialize in railway ephemera, philately, branch lines, and at one time, tunnels!

Railway and Government Publications

In addition to orthodox publications, the library holds many official and quasi-official printed books and papers. For example, a surprisingly large number of railway companies, including each of the Big Four after 1923, produced house journals for the benefit of their staff. By the standard of the day the quality of these was quite lavish, as were one or two similar publications produced by some locomotive manufacturers for limited periods.

From the outset the railways of Britain enjoyed an enviable safety record, largely because their construction and operating procedures were closely scrutinized by the Board of Trade. From an early date all accidents which resulted in the deaths of fare-paying passengers were the subject of detailed and sometimes profusely illustrated reports which were often published with commendable speed, and a full set of these is maintained in the library. Such accidents resulted from derailments, collisions and, in earlier years, locomotive boiler explosions. The great majority could be ascribed to 'human error', as in the case of the worst accident of all, that at Quintinshill on the Caledonian Railway in May 1915 with over 220 fatalities. Tragically large numbers of railwaymen were killed every year whilst on duty, not infrequently during permanent way work or shunting operations. Even such relatively minor injuries as bruised hips and cut fingers were dutifully investigated by the BoT inspectors whose findings were published in quarterly returns, and whose recommendations not infrequently improved the lot of the working man.

By statute every railway enterprise in the United Kingdom and Ireland (well over two hundred) was required to render detailed annual statistics to the Board of Trade. This consisted of financial data in terms of expenditure and receipts under various headings, and traffic statistics concerning mileage run, number and classes of passengers carried, merchandise tonnage and totals of locomotives, carriages and wagons in stock at the year end. All this data was systematically tabulated, with grand totals, in ponderous annual Board of Trade Railway Returns. Referring to these one can determine in a matter of seconds that 16,624 first-class passengers travelled on the Maryport & Carlisle Railway during 1885, whilst in 1913 the Neath & Brecon conveyed 15,284 sheep and 322 pigs. In the same year 3084 London & North Western locomotives covered a computed total of 76,535,989 miles, as against 16,250 miles run by the North Sunderland Railway's solitary tank locomotive over the $4\frac{3}{4}$ miles between Chathill and Seahouses in Northumberland. Astonishingly, such information for the whole period 1858–1922 occupies only 2 ft of shelf space.

With so many privately owned railway companies operating in fierce competition with each other in almost every part of the country, with their rolling stock (and sometimes locomotives) working over other companies' lines, which were themselves sometimes jointly owned, the British railway network prior to the amalgamation of 1923 was of bewildering complexity. This resulted in the establishment of the Railway Clearing House, or RCH, as early as 1842 to apportion joint receipts and expenditure. The RCH issued a succession of beautifully coloured folding maps which covered most, but for some strange reason by no means all, parts of the country. These were frequently updated and the last was issued as late as 1960 for Scotland, shortly before the RCH was disbanded. An almost complete set of these, together with the RCH Junction Diagram Books, which covered every railway junction in the country where two or more different railways were involved, are held for consultation in the library.

Essentially ephemeral by their very nature, surviving railway timetables are unwitting social documents. When viewed in retrospect, these unconsciously speak volumes concerning contemporary aspects of railway operation and social conventions, quite apart from details of the trains them-

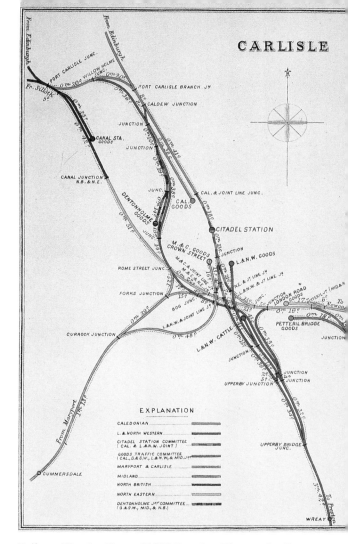

Railway Clearing House (RCH) Junction Diagram for Carlisle. No fewer than seven different companies, four English and three Scottish, entered the city prior to 1923.

A selection of railway public timetables encountered during the early twentieth century. The oldest shown is the first issue by the then newly opened Hull & Barnsley Railway (1885) covering its limited passenger service. The two Bradshaws are separated in date by almost a century.

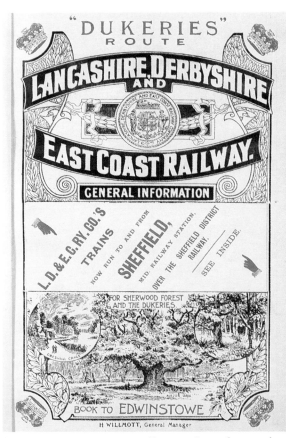

The last entirely new major railway project to be conceived in Britain, the Lancashire, Derbyshire & East Coast Railway, sought to span England from Warrington to Sutton-on-Sea. Only the central 38 miles between Chesterfield and Lincoln were ever constructed. Here is the cover of a rare LD&ECR promotional publication of c.1902.

The LNER introduced the first British high speed streamlined express train between London and Newcastle-upon-Tyne on 30 September 1935. This album contains the signatures of many of those on board the inaugural run.

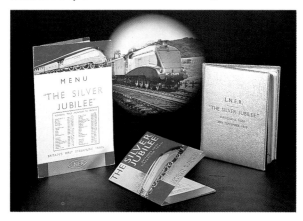

selves. The more familiar public timetables were attractively produced items giving full details of the passenger services and how these interconnected with those of adjoining railways. They were often published quarterly, but the famous *Bradshaw* was issued every month from October 1839 until May 1961. This achieved the virtually impossible task of tabulating the passenger services of every railway in the British Isles, and examples are held for almost every decade of its publication. Using standard quoted rates per mile, it is often possible to determine the approximate cost of rail travel from A to B.

Working timetables were purely internal railway documents covering the operation of both passenger and freight services on the railway, which were sometimes issued separately, and close study of earlier examples can reveal the extremely long hours engine crews could be expected to work prior to the institution of the eight-hour working day in 1919. Periodically Appendixes to the working timetable would be issued, which would contain a mass of information, generally in the form of strict rules and regulations, together with such sundry data as, for example, which signal boxes were closed on Sundays, the diameter of locomotive turntables or the amounts to be charged to passengers found guilty of breaking carriage windows! Such publications were often complementary to the Rule Books issued to every member of the railway staff. Almost every contingency was anticipated and an appropriate course of action prescribed. Train loading tables, passenger train marshalling circulars and gradient profiles were also issued, all of which were essential if efficient operation was to be achieved.

Private Collections

As stated earlier, much more information is available now concerning locomotive history than was the case fifty years ago. Published lists were almost non-existent regarding the locomotive stock, not least because it was continually changing with new construction and scrappings. Such information was hard won by a small band of dedicated enthusiasts, some of whose meticulous notebooks are now preserved at York. Since coming into being in 1975, the NRM has acquired quite a number that might be broadly termed 'private collections'. Many of these tend to be wholly or partially photographic in nature, but all are the result of a close study of a particular railway or railways or aspects thereof.

One of the earliest thus acquired was that of the late Eric Mason, on the Lancashire & Yorkshire Railway. Mason possessed an unrivalled knowledge of LYR locomotives and he has left detailed notebooks and a series of photographic albums concerning them. For instance, one such album is devoted entirely to the Aspinall 'High Flyer' 4-4-2s and contains several photographs of every member of this forty-strong class at each stage of its development. Many of the photographs, not necessarily of Mason's own taking, will now be unique, as it is doubtful if the corresponding negatives still exist.

Several collections comprise locomotive and train performance logs, including the notebooks of the late Cecil J. Allen. Regrettably, most of the runs he recorded are undated but the work of other less renowned recorders is meticulously presented.

The late H. B. Oliver spent a great deal of time in the 1950s photographing all surviving traces of the former North Staffordshire Railway, particularly its distinctive stations but even level-crossing gates and minor sidings. His records are now at York.

The T. Beckett Collection comprises photograph albums, official reports, tickets and other ephemera relating to the railways in the Isle of Man, a lifetime's work and a collection which it would be impossible to compile today.

The largest such collection is that of the late Selwyn Pearce Higgins, whose special interest was the smallest of minor British railways, including the Bishop's Castle, Snailbeach District and Wantage Tramway.

He personally photographed the BCR in its last years, including its dismantling in 1936, secured some rare photographs of wartime activities on the Shropshire & Montgomeryshire Railway when it was under military control, and wrote a definitive history of the Wantage Tramway.

Many of these collections were the products of a very different age, compiled despite limited financial resources and undoubtedly more restricted leisure time. They provide fascinating contemporary records of a vanished era now fast receding beyond the range of human recollection.

Photographs

The science of photography evolved c. 1840, soon after the first appearance of main line railways in the landscape. The earliest known railway photograph is generally considered to be that of the South Eastern Railway 4-2-0 Crampton locomotive *Folkestone* on display at the Great Exhibition of 1851. The oldest negative in the NRM collection dates from April 1866 and depicts a brand new Ramsbottom LNWR 2-4-0 No 1480 *Newton* at Crewe Works.

This is the earliest of approximately 100,000 official negatives, almost entirely glass plates, which vary in size from quarter plate ($4\frac{1}{4}$ in by $3\frac{1}{4}$ in) to 16 in by 18 in, the predominant format being wholeplate ($8\frac{1}{2}$ in by $6\frac{1}{2}$ in). These range in date from 1866 to 1967, with a concentration in the 1890–1950 period. Almost all the larger railway companies are covered in this respect with the notable exception of the Great Western, whose negatives are presently still under the control of British Rail and are promoted commercially. In due course, they are expected to come to the NRM.

The larger railway works, such as Crewe, Derby and Doncaster, employed permanent resident photographers, who primarily recorded new locomotives, carriages and wagons. Sometimes they would record these under construction, then an everyday sight. Despite the encumberance of a heavy plate camera and associated equipment,

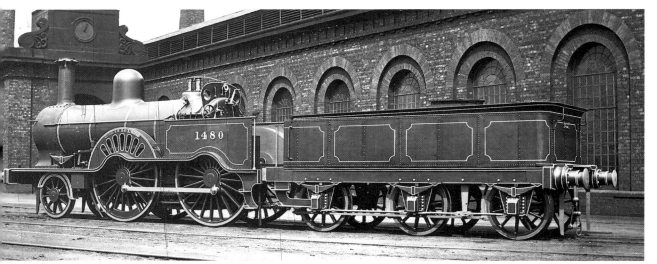

these men would sometimes travel beyond the confines of the works and record delightful contemporary railway scenes. During the exceptionally hot summer of 1911, the Derby (MR) photographer set up his equipment adjacent to the Lickey Incline, and a few days later on the Settle–Carlisle line. Unfortunately, views of railway staff are comparatively rare, although the employment of female labour during the First World War was clearly such a novelty as to attract the attention of both the Derby and Horwich (LYR) photographers! It is sometimes forgotten that in addition to running trains, the railways were also major operators of self-propelled road vehicles, ships and even aircraft, many examples of which are portrayed in the official negatives.

LNWR 2-4-0 No 1480 *Newton* poses for the camera when new outside Crewe Works in April 1866. The building date, inscribed on the brass nameplate of the driving wheel splasher is discernible on the original negative. It is the oldest negative in the National Railway Museum Collection of which the date is known and measures 12in by 10in. The practice of painting up new locomotives in matt grey, often fully lined out, for photographic purposes persisted for almost a century (LNWR official).

Where the photographic archives of the once numerous private locomotive, carriage and wagon builders still exist, these are very often deposited with a local major library or county archive. In consequence, the NRM's holdings in this area are limited and the only

In the major railway towns, the railways as major employers played a dominant role in the male-orientated social life. Here is the LYR Horwich Works Prize Silver Band in April 1921 (LYR official).

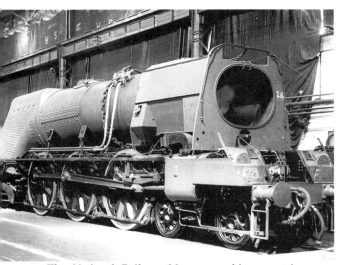

The National Railway Museum archives contain many views of steam locomotives under construction in various railway works which can often provide valuable information, not always discernible from working drawings. Here is a Bulleid Southern Railway 'Light' Pacific (4-6-2) under construction at Brighton Works in 1945 (SR official).

An official view of the Midland Railway's Avonside Wharf at Bristol, as seen from nearby Temple Meads. The date is 30 May 1922 and the photograph contains much of interest to industrial archaeologists, quite apart from recording an often overlooked aspect of railway operations. To the left of centre are two early road vehicles, one steam and the other petrol driven (MR official).

major collection of negatives of industrial origin held by the NRM is that of Charles Roberts & Co of Horbury, near Wakefield. This firm specialized in building wagons of Railway Clearing House-approved design for the numerous pre-1947 privately owned collieries. Serving as mobile advertisements for their owners, such wagons were often brightly and boldly painted and could impart a remarkably variegated appearance to a humble goods train.

By the end of the nineteenth century, photography was becoming a leisure pursuit and the contemporary railway scene was an obvious target at which to aim one's camera. The kaleidoscopic array of locomotive types then extant attracted particular attention with the result that only very few variations on the theme are known totally to have escaped the lens. In terms of subject matter the golden years of railway photography were probably the 1920s and 1930s,

and many of the people who were active during that period have died only recently. The Museum has been fortunate in being able to obtain (by purchase or bequest) the negative collections of many of them. In their field, Maurice Earley and Pat Ransome-Wallis were household names, being active for fifty years or so, the latter travelling extensively abroad and photographing locomotives overseas long before there was appreciable interest in Britain in what ran beyond the English Channel. Other lesser-known photographers operated for more limited periods and were associated with particular geographical areas: R. D. Stephen, a son of the manse at Inverkeithing in the shadow of the Forth Bridge, when aged only thirteen or fourteen, began to photograph the locomotives and trains of the North British Railway and to a lesser extent those of the other still independent Scottish railway companies on the eve of the railway amalgamations of 1923. Another was G. H. Soole, who in the early 1930s during vacations from Cambridge University took spectacular scenic photographs of the Canadian Pacific Railway in the Canadian Rockies, including views of trains double-headed by 2-10-4 steam locomotives. Later in that decade he took numerous photographs of GWR operations in the Bristol area. The results have proved fascinating to rolling stock specialists,

A very mundane scene when photographed at Scours near Reading in early 1953, yet almost every major ingredient of it has now disappeared – a steam locomotive on pilot trip working (ex-GWR 0-6-0PT No 7708), semaphore signals and shunting truck, not to mention the general atmosphere of the steam railway (M. W. Earley Collection).

R. D. Stephen (d.1980) had lived and taken photographs in the shadow of the Forth Railway Bridge for several years before he was able with permission to scale its heights and take some striking photographs. North Queensferry is seen from the highest point (360ft) on the centre span in 1928 (R. D. Stephen Collection).

although Soole himself was probably only consciously photographing locomotives.

Such is the enormous extent of this legacy that many of these negatives can never have been printed, but in most instances the originators, both professional and amateur, kept records of what lies within the negative cabinets. It is the Museum's policy, as time and funds permit, to print selectively for reference purposes from these collections, from which copies can be ordered for private study or use in publications and display. It is an exciting prospect – who can tell what visual treasures wait to be discovered in this rich source of material?

A Yorkshireman born in Halifax, G. H. Soole is now best remembered for his photographs of the GWR in the Bristol area in the later 1930s. A little earlier he recorded a series of views of Canadian Pacific Railway trains amid the spectacular scenery of the Canadian Rockies in high summer (G. H. Soole Collection).

Private industry probably operated collectively as large a fleet of small locomotives as did the main line railways between the wars. A draughtsman in the Drawing Office at Derby Locomotive Works, the late F. G. Carrier secured this view of an immaculate 0-4-0ST (Hudswell Clark 452 of 1896) at the Worthington Brewery at Stoke on Trent, illuminated by the setting sun (F. G. Carrier Collection).

Archive Collections

by Richard Durack

In addition to what might be called purely library material, the Museum has large collections of engineering drawings and papers relating to the technical development of locomotives, carriages and wagons, not to mention such items as printed maps and notices. The Museum has always collected official material of this type even though it is the Public Record Office that is the main custodian of the historical records of the British Railways Board in England and Wales. The reason for this division of custody can be traced back to 1951 when separate departments dealing with Historical Records and Historical Relics were established by the British Transport Commission. The distinction between records and relics was never adequately defined and the engineering drawings and papers were housed with the locomotives, rolling stock and other relics at the former Museum of British Transport at Clapham. They were transferred to York in 1975 and have been greatly added to since then. In Scotland all railway records are held at the Scottish Record Office. Recent concern over the danger to historic records has seen the establishment by the BRB of an Advisory Panel on the Disposal of Historic Records, on which the Museum is represented, and the appointment of a Records Officer. Surveys are now carried out on a regular basis to ensure that no drawings or papers of historic importance are lost.

Over twenty different railway works are represented in the collections, ranging from the major establishments of Crewe, Swindon, Derby, Doncaster and Eastleigh to the small and now largely forgotten works of Highbridge and Melton Constable. Records from private sources include material from independent locomotive and carriage and wagon builders as well as the papers of former railway employees who played a major role in mechanical engineering development. The variety of material within the collections includes diagram books, instruction manuals, specifications, repair files and history cards as well as test reports, research papers and project sketches. They enable the large-scale introduction of diesel and electric traction and other major developments of recent years to be traced in great detail. The papers also cast light on some of the more interesting technical experiments, including the use of gas-turbine locomotives and the attempt to introduce double-deck coaches. But most of the material consists of engineering drawings, now estimated to number over 200,000 in total and ranging in date from the early stages of steam locomotive development to the advent of the experimental version of the Advanced Passenger Train. The engineering drawings are sufficiently important to justify special consideration (below).

Another category of archive material is railway maps which range from the sets of construction plans prepared by promoters to the attractive and often colourful products of commercial publishers and railway companies. The Museum also has good collections of early notices and handbills.

Before a railway company could acquire land and construct its line, it had to promote its own Bill and obtain the approval of Parliament. Plans showing the course of the line, its major features and property affected, had to accompany each Bill, and these Parliamentary Plans provide a unique record of all major lines both proposed and constructed. The original plans are held at the House of Lords Record Office, and copies are also to be found in local record offices. The Museum has copies of several of these plans, including a set of eight volumes showing lines built by the Manchester, Sheffield & Lincolnshire Railway. The first volume, drawn to a scale of one inch to two

Drawing of the proposed Locomotive Testing Station at Rugby, October 1938. Building ceased at the outbreak of the Second World War and the station was not completed until 1948.

Part of the engine history card for preserved 4-6-2 *Duchess of Hamilton.* **The original card is double-sided and contains four times the amount of information shown on this extract.**

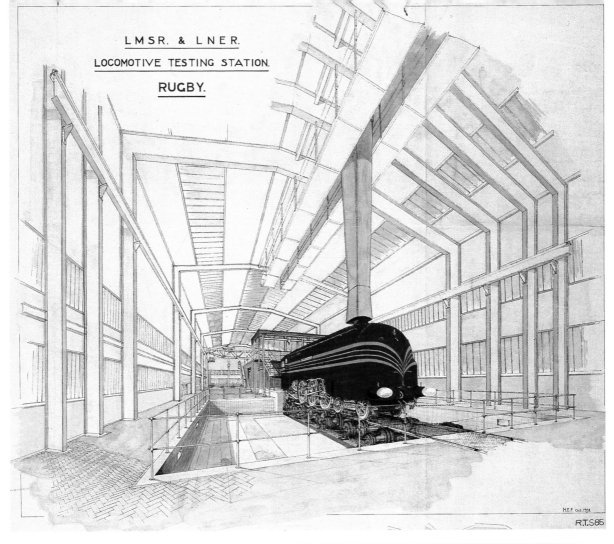

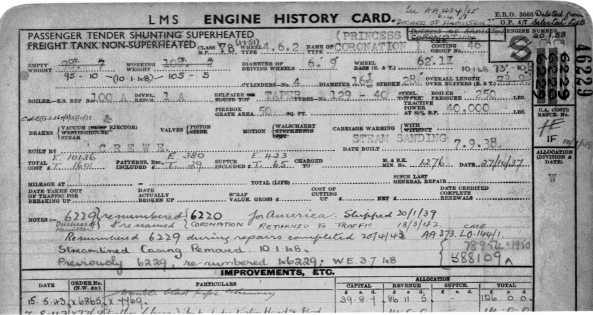

chains, contains coloured plans of the line opened between Manchester and Sheffield in 1845 and shows cuttings, embankments, crossings and track and station layouts in great detail. Subsequent volumes include lines in Lincolnshire and Yorkshire as well as plans of the ambitious London Extension which was built to the new terminus at Marylebone and opened in 1899.

As the number of railway travellers grew after 1830, so the first commercially produced maps began to appear. Early publishers included Charles Cheffin, James Wyld and George Bradshaw, and all three produced useful maps of the growing network. More specialized maps were also issued with both Cheffin and Wyld producing attractive maps of the London & Birmingham Railway, opened in 1837, and 'Mogg's Railway Map of Great Britain' of 1846 offering full details of the 'steam navigation to the continent'. As the century progressed more information began to appear. Zachary Macauley published his 'Station Map of the Railways of Great Britain' in 1851, followed by John Airey with the first in his series of junction diagrams. 'Bradshaw's New Railway Map' of 1854 included stations, distances and plans of towns, while 'Cheffin's Map of the Railways of England and Wales' of 1865 even distinguished between track of broad and narrow gauge. Maps were regularly updated and new editions continued to appear until well into the present century: several very attractive folding maps were published showing the 'New Grouping Railway Companies' of 1923.

The railway companies, too, began to produce distance tables and maps of their own systems. These were originally for the use of their own officials, but the advantages of developing them for advertising purposes soon became apparent. Many companies produced maps of the collieries or 'manufacturing districts' within their territory, or plans of their docks and freight facilities, to give to customers. Diagrammatic maps of their network began to appear on stations and in carriages. Pocket maps were printed and sold cheaply to customers. The LNER produced a folding map of its lines in 1924 to coincide with the British Empire Exhibition at Wembley, and used the reverse to boast of its 'non-stop trains right into the grounds in 12 minutes from London Marylebone'.

Railway notices and handbills date from the opening of the very first lines to passengers. Cheap to print, easy to display and with a large captive audience, they were the ideal means for the directors of the new companies to communicate with their passengers and keep them in order. A study of early notices reveals the fascinating range of subjects covered. Details of station openings, train services and fares alternate with warnings of dire penalties should the passenger smoke, spit, trespass, cross the line (other than where allowed), join the train while in motion or in any other way disobey company regulations. Fraud and theft were of particular concern; imprisonment and even transportation could be the result of travelling without a ticket or stealing company property.

An interesting feature of early railway operation that is well illustrated by notices and handbills is the development of the excursion train. It was not until the Great Exhibition of 1851 that many companies realized the potential of excursion traffic, but several had run trains in the years before this and notable among these was the Newcastle & Carlisle Railway. Excursions 'at greatly reduced fares' were offered regularly and included such attractions as Newcastle Races, the Grand Tyne Regatta and the 'celebrated and highly picturesque grounds of Corby Castle'. Many of these special trains were run on Sundays and the Newcastle & Carlisle soon found itself in conflict with Sabbatarian interests. In August 1841 the Rev. W. C. Burns, later to become a missionary in China, distributed handbills to passengers at Newcastle station warning them of the dangers of boarding a Sunday excursion to Carlisle:

A Reward for Sabbath breaking.
People taken safely and swiftly to Hell!
Next Lord's Day by the Carlisle Railway for 7s 6d
It is a Pleasure Trip

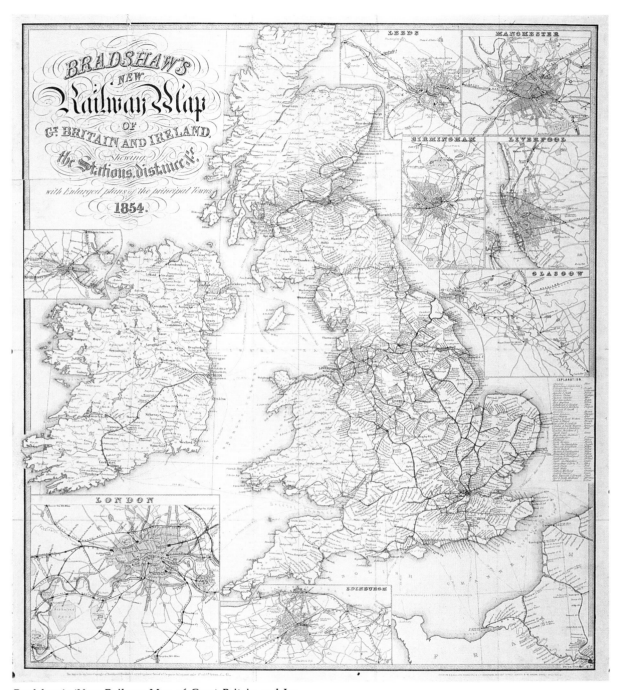

Bradshaw's 'New Railway Map of Great Britain and Ireland', 1854.

Excursion notice, Midland & North Eastern Railways, 1864.

On and from MONDAY, 13th JUNE, 1955, the passenger and freight service on the line between EAST GRINSTEAD and LEWES, via SHEFFIELD PARK, will be withdrawn and the following stations closed:—

KINGSCOTE	SHEFFIELD PARK
WEST HOATHLY	NEWICK & CHAILEY
	BARCOMBE

HORSTED KEYNES which will remain open for passenger and freight traffic, will in future be served by trains to and from HAYWARDS HEATH only.

British Railways will continue to provide collection and delivery services throughout the area for parcels and freight traffic. Facilities for truck load traffic and small consignments to be handed in or collected at the station are available at surrounding stations including EAST GRINSTEAD, HORSTED KEYNES, HAYWARDS HEATH, BARCOMBE MILLS, UCKFIELD, COOKSBRIDGE and PLUMPTON.

Further information may be obtained from the Station Masters at EAST GRINSTEAD (Telephone East Grinstead 85), HORSTED KEYNES (Telephone Dane Hill 242) and LEWES (Telephone Lewes 167) or from the District Traffic Superintendent, Redhill, whose address is British Railways, Redhill, Surrey (Telephone Redhill 3361).

Alternative bus facilities in the area are provided by Southdown Motor Services Ltd. and (subject to the approval of the Licensing Authority), additional and extended journeys on certain routes will be introduced on the closure of the line. The London Transport Executive also provide bus services between EAST GRINSTEAD and THREE BRIDGES via KINGSCOTE.

Enquiries regarding bus services should be addressed to:—

London Transport, East Grinstead Garage, Garland Road (Telephone 308).
Southdown Motor Services Ltd., 33, High Street, East Grinstead (Telephone 798).
Bus Station, Lewes (Telephone 250).

Closure notice, East Grinstead to Lewes, 1955. The line had to be reopened the following year but was finally closed in 1958. Services are now operated over part of the line by the Bluebell Railway.

There is no evidence that passengers were deterred, despite the threat to their spiritual welfare, but opposition to the running of Sunday trains was persistent and widespread. The Anti-Sunday Travel Union had branches throughout the country and was well supported.

In the present century the notice has tended to lose ground to the pictorial poster, but it continues to play an important role and many comparatively recent examples are not without interest: 'No man who does his duty loyally to the Company in the present crisis will be left unprotected by the State from subsequent reprisals' was the promise made by the LMS to its employees during the General Strike of 1926. 'Look out for any unattended packages or bags' warns of new dangers, while 'Fog Service and Your Train' reminds us that less than thirty years ago the Southern Region of British Railways was still having to run curtailed services because of the infamous London 'smogs'. And the closure notice, an unwelcome feature of any station platform, provides graphic evidence of the contraction of the railway network in the years since the Second World War.

Engineering Drawings

by Michael Rutherford

Technical drawing, in a formal sense, developed during and after the Renaissance in Europe. The main feature of this type of drawing was the depiction of solid objects through a single view which exhibited *apparent* shapes. This was done using geometric techniques and ideas of perspective, and these ideas later appeared in much of the technical illustration and 'exploded' views found in maintenance and instruction manuals. It was not until the complexities of dieselization that such drawings became familiar in a British railway mechanical engineering context but they can be found in the diesel locomotive manuals.

There was, however, an alternative method of drawing; this was to feature a three-dimensional object through a number of views each of which portrayed *true* shapes. These views are known as plans and elevations and are known to date back to more than 2100 BC and a Sumerian engineer named Gudea. Drawings of this sort remained typical in building work. However, each view was usually done on a separate piece of parchment so the relationship between them was not obvious and had to be established by captions. Such drawings contained basically scaled-down marking-out information, and architect's plans have retained this characteristic. They became more sophisticated from about the late sixteenth century with the draughts prepared for ships, and some measure of standardization in presentation developed.

In the early days of railways, few individual drawings were prepared for a locomotive or a piece of rolling stock. Much of the final product depended on the men in the workshops who had blacksmith or coachbuilders' traditions of which they were fiercely proud. This often led to many early builders supplying equipment to the railway companies that was neither to their specification nor to their required dimensions, although it must be said that the early companies were often very vague about their requirements. Many early builders, too, especially of locomotives, were ill-equipped to do the work, and both materials and workmanship were often poor as demand outpaced supply. Even the very first of the purpose-built locomotive factories, that of Robert Stephenson & Co, which was established in 1823, did not purchase a drawing board until about four years later, and it was not until May 1828 that the company engaged the services of a full-time draughtsman, one George Phipps. His appointment was undoubtedly due to Robert Stephenson himself who appreciated the value of the drawing board as a design tool. On Robert's return to the firm in November 1827, after a period in South America, he instigated a fundamental review of locomotive design, and seven locomotives were then built, each incorporating different design changes. Although there is nothing of this nature from that period in the collection at York, quite a large amount of primary design work has survived, although inevitably it is in need of considerable conservation work and is often incomplete, especially with regard to corresponding written documents.

It was problems with early locomotive builders that made Daniel Gooch of the GWR supply complete sets of lithographed drawings, plus many full-sized iron templates for critical components, to the seven firms that built his first express locomotives, the 'Firefly' class, between 1840 and 1842. This was to be little more than an interim measure, and in 1843 the GWR opened its own factory at Swindon under the managership of Archibald Sturrock. He left in 1850 and joined the Great Northern Railway for whom he supervised the layout and construction of a new locomotive works at Doncaster, first occupied in 1853.

The new towns that grew up round locomotive works became tightly knit railway communities where every boy's ambition was to enter the drawing office and help to design new locomotives. It was also in the railway towns that a new kind of man rose to fame, a man of God-like authority and inflexible demands, the British locomotive superintendent. Many of these Victorian autocrats became legends in their own lifetime and were unique to the larger British companies which built their own locomotives and rolling stock; in other countries where private builders supplied the railways with their equipment either from 'stock' or to their own design (to a specification drawn up by the company), idiosyncrasies soon died out, if they ever appeared. In Britain they became virtues of the relevant locomotive superintendent and then traditions of the company, to be changed at any newcomer's peril. This legacy, of quickly developed traditions and fiercely held company loyalty has meant

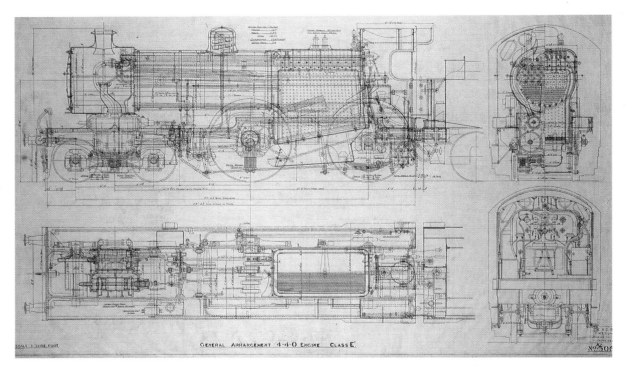

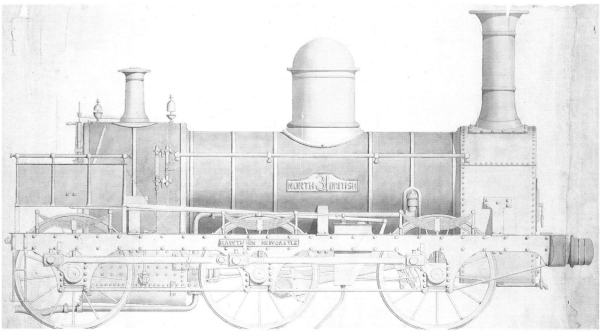

A very typical 'General Arrangement' locomotive drawing. It depicts SECR 4-4-0 Class E1 as rebuilt in 1919–20 by Maunsell from Wainwright's original Class E, itself a belpaire-boilered development of SECR No 737 in the National Collection.

North British Railway 0-6-0 No 31 buit by R. & W. Hawthorn of Newcastle in 1846 and one of six known as 'Dalkeith Coal Engines'. The drawing itself is probably contemporary but there is no indication that it was actually executed by the builders.

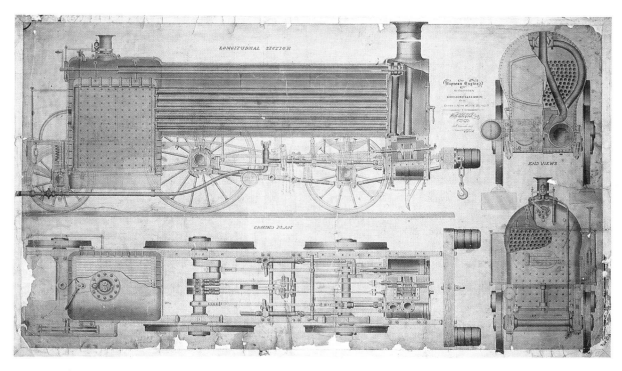

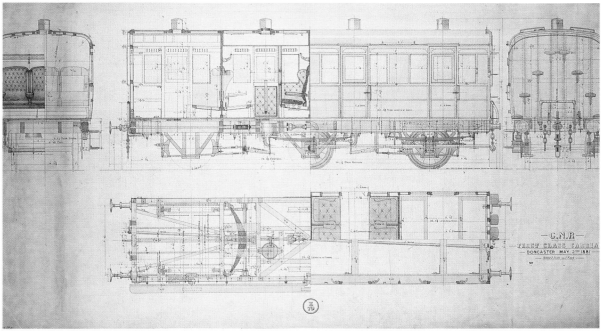

A beautifully prepared sectioned and shaded drawing of the Bury, Curtis and Kennedy 2-2-2 *Liverpool* built in 1848 for the LNWR. This more conventionally framed locomotive took the name of the original bar-framed 'Liverpool' – see Chapter 2.

GNR six-wheeled first-class carriage of 1881. The drawing reveals virtually the whole construction, inside and out, and may be compared with the luggage van of the same style shown in Chapter 1.

that the drawings and records held in those works have survived in whole or part for a considerable length of time. Together with material held in the Science Museum and elsewhere, including various engineering institutions, this British heritage is, on an international scale, unique.

The collections at York, however, do not contain solely drawings prepared by the railway companies. In the case of smaller companies (and some not so small) which bought locomotives from outside, a set of drawings was supplied with each order and in a number of cases these have survived intact. In general, however, drawings for locomotives do not come in complete sets. The use of many small standard parts, as well as specialized equipment from outside suppliers, obviate this, and as numbers for each sheet were usually taken from a consecutive drawing office series, drawings were stored by numerical sequence and size of sheet. This practice has considerably complicated the classification of large parts of our collection.

A recent acquisition by the NRM was the collection of drawings and papers of Peckett & Sons Ltd of Bristol, who built, together with their predecessors Fox, Walker & Co, nearly two thousand small industrial steam locomotives between 1864 and 1958. The Museum also houses the collection of the Industrial Railway Society which consists mainly of drawings of Baguley industrial locomotives. GEC Traction has donated a substantial amount of locomotive material from their Robert Stephenson & Hawthorn holdings, while the collections of drawings of rolling stock from railway company drawing offices were considerably enhanced with the donation of the drawings and order books from Charles Roberts & Co of Horbury near Wakefield (now trading as Procor Ltd), who supplied carriages and wagons to railways at home and abroad from 1856 to the present day.

One of the limits of the usefulness and efficiency of drawings to the workshops was the problem of supplying copies of the original drawings for actual use. For many years

it was necessary to redraw the original; there were short cuts, like pricking through the most prominent points and intersections with the original drawing laid on top of a blank sheet, but copying by hand increased the probability of error enormously. It was possible to use tracing paper, but that was very fragile and it was not until the near universal use of tracing cloth, following a great reduction in its cost, that this problem receded. The development of the blue print process enabled any number of copies to be made from one tracing. This process, using light-sensitive chemicals, produced a white-lined print on a deep blue background. It was described by Sir John Herschel to the Royal Society in 1842, but it was not until the end of the 1860s that the process began to be used for copying engineering drawings. It was not long before this system was improved upon by the dyeline process, which produced a black or blue line on a white background, but the blueprint lingered on. An appreciable number are in the collection, covering information on equipment bought in by railway companies, such as injectors, lubricators and brake gear, as well as drawings supplied with quotations for complete locomotives.

It was usual to glue the original drawings to a cloth backing, for strength when handled, and to use these drawings for reference in the drawing office. It has long been the practice to colour various parts of assembly and arrangement drawings to indicate different materials used and this became standardized. Run-of-the-mill engineering drawings were transformed into highly attractive illustrations; by the time of the railway grouping in 1923, this practice had all but ceased as far as mechanical engineering was concerned.

Not all drawings were either dimensioned component drawings or assemblies of such components. Drawings of a schematic nature were also prepared, to illustrate systems of piping or wiring, to be used for maintenance purposes (grease and oiling points, for example) or to summarize information in chart form. One of the best-known non-constructional drawings was the weight diagram. It was in the later Victorian years that the diagram system became universal, and was especially needed by the larger railway companies. All locomotive, carriage and wagon types (as well as station barrows and road vehicles) and their variations were included on a unique diagram consisting of an outside elevation and end view, to quite a small scale. These diagrams included dimensions such as length, width, height, wheelbases and weights, and, in the case of locomotives, a table of other technical dimensions. Copies of these diagrams were issued to other departments of the company (Civil Engineering, Operating, Accountants, etc.), and continually updated with new information. A diagram was also usually the first step in proposing a new design of locomotive or vehicle.

In order to gain raw data for design improvements, small groups of specialists began working in most of the larger drawing offices, and it was these draughtsmen who worked in the dynamometer cars and who took indicator diagrams of cylinder pressure while the locomotives were moving. A considerable amount of test material in the form of drawings, charts and graphs has survived as well as much material, including plans of the plant and equipment, from the Rugby Locomotive Testing Station.

An engineering drawing is produced in order to communicate information and may be systematic or symbolic rather than pictorial. The 'redundancy', or duplication of information, in such pictures can be likened to the reduction of melody content in much serious modern music, or representative likeness in modern sculpture, and for the same reasons cause some alarm to the layman. The current advances in computer-aided design means that, before much longer, additions to the drawings collection at the NRM may be computer programs and perhaps in later years these programs will be regarded as 'elegant' and even poetic by new generations brought up to learn and understand the languages used to communicate with machines.

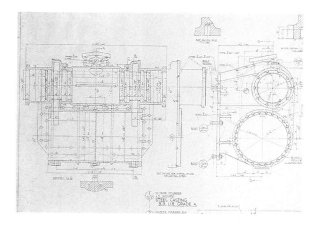

Part of the original drawing and the final product: one of the first pair of cylinders destined for the prototype BR standard Class 7 4-6-2 locomotive No 70000 *Britannia*. The intermediate casting process in the pattern shop and foundry would necessitate numerous 'repeats' of the original drawing.

Restoration and the Museum Workshops

by John Bellwood

The duties of the workshop at the National Railway Museum can be briefly summarized as 'wood/metal/paint technicians working in connection with the repair, maintenance, restoration, conservation, display and interpretation of the National Collection of railway relics'. When that collection is the largest in the world covering the subject of railways, in all its diverse aspects, it will be appreciated that the workshop technicians, few in number, not only have no shortage of work but that the skills required and materials worked on are far more extensive than the basic divisions of wood, metal and paint may suggest. There is no doubt that their skill and ingenuity has enabled them to meet virtually every challenge.

The workshops were set up at a fairly early stage in the run up to opening the Museum and played a substantial part in the preparation for opening. The equipment provided was specified by, and based on long experience of activities at our parent body, the Science Museum at South Kensington. Although well equipped for a staff of six technicians, it was not really geared to the heavy engineering associated with the operation and maintenance of railway traction units and rolling stock, and this has posed its own problems. Over the years, much has been achieved in making up this shortcoming.

A particular breakthrough was the unexpected early acquisition of the former diesel traction maintenance depot, complete with operating wheel drop and overhead cranes. With modest supplementary provisioning, it should soon be possible to tackle, in house, most engineering tasks like to arise. Before looking in some detail at a selection of specific workshop activities undertaken in the last decade, it may be as well to outline some of the problems associated with the development and maintenance of the National Collection.

Margaret **at work on the Museum's 7¼in gauge railway.**

In engineering and transport terms, railway equipment has an exceptionally long working life. Much of the infrastructure is still in daily use over a century and a half after being built. That bridges, for example, are now able to carry rail vehicles of twenty times the weight and at twenty-five times the speed of those for which they were designed, can be put down to either remarkable foresight, over-caution, lack of knowledge of strength of materials or a desire to build long-lasting monuments. Whatever the reason, present-day railway engineers and conservationists should be grateful! Until relatively recently, dating particularly from the impact of the 1955 British Railways Modernization Plan, much of the operating equipment of the railway had a working life of fifty years or more.

Amongst other factors, this long working life gives rise to two basic questions concerning selection, restoration and preservation: how much of the item under consideration is original, and to what period of its long service should it be restored and displayed? This is, of course, a curatorial problem, but it has inevitable workshops implications. For example, the desire to preserve the pioneer member of the LNER V2 class, *Green Arrow*,

Margaret **and the workshop staff responsible for her construction.**

Basic trackwork laid and scenery under construction on the Gauge '0' model railway.

resulted in the now sole-surviving example of this outstanding design having a badly cracked mono-block cylinder casting, which, whilst not preventing the locomotive from being a regular performer on the main line, is a continued source of anxiety to the Museum. It can be argued that at the time of selection for preservation, there was no thought that the locomotive would ever steam again, but where there is a choice of examples, it is at least arguable that overall mechanical condition should be a major deciding factor. Another difficult to justify selection based on workshop criteria, was the LNWR G2 class 0-8-0 No 485 (LMS No 9395), which had suffered a major failure resulting in its withdrawal from service with a fractured cylinder block and motion bracket, amongst other damage. These were excellent engines and their historical justification is mentioned in Chapter 2, but, given that there were many examples to choose from, it might have been wiser to choose a better one in the mechanical sense! The reason for preserving No 485 was that it was the first of the final series of these engines to be built.

The opposite is true of BR Class 9F No 92220 *Evening Star* which, having had a

working life of only five years and being destined for preservation from the day it was built, is probably as near to an original as possible. Conversely, it is questionable how much, if any, of the locomotive now restored to working order as LNER No 4468 *Mallard* actually ran at 126 m.p.h. on 3 July 1938. It should, therefore, be obvious that striving for strict originality in historical terms has to be of much less importance than suitability for restoration and preservation, if working operation is contemplated. Without the 'operational' factor, strict originality assumes greater significance.

What other factors should be taken into account? Artefacts are mainly preserved to illustrate the continuing story of railways in all its aspects, and again the curatorial input is paramount. But it can affect the workshop's response. Take, for example, the two GNR Atlantics in the National Collection, analysed in Chapter 2: *Henry Oakley* was the first example of the 4-4-2 wheel arrangement to be built in this country. Four years later, the design was developed to include an even larger boiler with wide firebox on the same chassis, as exemplified by the pioneer No 251. However, it was the fitting of thirty-two-element superheaters from

1918 which transformed the performance of the large wide firebox examples. Ironically, *Henry Oakley*, the pioneer Atlantic, has been preserved in its later superheated condition, while No 251 is in pseudo-original non-superheated form. Should a curatorial decision be made to rectify these anomalies, it would be a costly workshop exercise to resuperheat No 251. As stated in Chapter 2, *Henry Oakley* has been given early LNER livery as more typical of its superheated condition; this posed no great technical problem.

Given our overall constraints, the NRM's 'period of restoration' policy has generally been to select that which was of most significance during the object's working life, taking into account the practicalities of undertaking the restoration work required. These practicalities include the physical condition of the object as received, availability of data (including engineering drawings, records, photographs, etc.), the desire to illustrate a particular feature or development using the object as an example, the need to fill a gap in a particular period, or perhaps just to improve the overall presentation of the collection by including a different livery style.

Even within this fairly wide range of options, there can still be problems. Queen Victoria's Saloon is one of the most popular exhibits with visitors to the Museum. It is displayed in the condition when last used by Her Majesty at the turn of the century. Or is it? The internal fabric is mostly the actual material *in situ* in 1900, but the obvious ravages of time are such that they would never have been retained in a vehicle 'fit for a Queen'. To restore or not to restore, that is the question! The decision cannot be deferred indefinitely and something will have to be done before complete disintegration occurs. Probably a traditional British compromise will result, with a major refurbishing still retaining some examples of the better condition nineteenth-century material wherever practical or appropriate.

Since 1975, following participation in the Stockton & Darlington Railway 150th Anniversary celebrations, the Museum has had a policy of maintaining a significant proportion of the locomotive and rolling stock collection in working order. The locomotives and carriages which have been operated in the period 1975-86 are annotated in Appendices I/II from which it can be seen that the number is considerable. It must be made clear from the outset that restoration to operational condition is a very different matter to 'cosmetic' restoration wherein authentic appearance is likely to be the prime consideration. This inevitably affects the workshop's response in a way probably quite unknown to many other museums.

Nowhere is this more important than in the maintenance and operation of preserved locomotives. The heart of the steam locomotive is the boiler; as a pressure vessel, major failure can result in disaster so strict safety measures are laid down. The Board of Trade issue statutory regulations, the Department of Transport produces guidance notes on boiler maintenance and operation, insurance company surveyors regularly inspect boilers covered by their policies and British Rail lay down their own additional requirements for locomotives running on the main line.

As will be appreciated, the Museum's activities in the operational field have been far from minimal; but perhaps surprisingly, the biggest and most expensive locomotive restoration project undertaken to date has been on one which is not even a part of the National Collection! The former LMS Pacific *Duchess of Hamilton*, after withdrawal from BR service in 1964, was purchased by Butlins Ltd, repainted in pseudo-LMS livery and for the next eleven years exhibited at the owner's Minehead Holiday Camp. When the loan to the NRM had been negotiated, the engine was moved, in 1975, to the BREL Swindon Works for a £20,000 cosmetic restoration at NRM expense. So far, everything was much in accordance with normal Museum practice, but when operational status was desired, the situation changed. The initial cost was sponsored by a fund-raising appeal carried out under the banner of the Friends of the National Railway

Typical small tube removed from the boiler of No 46229, *Duchess of Hamilton*.

Collapsed main internal steam pipe as seen from the front tube plate of *Duchess of Hamilton*.

Museum, largely because it was deemed inappropriate to expend public funds on an item only 'on loan'. In due course, the engine was steamed early in 1980, and in 1981 the Friends of the National Railway Museum took over from the Museum responsibility for the costs, both running and maintenance. As a regular and favourite performer on steam-hauled charter trains, the big red four-cylinder Pacific eventually worked itself into a 'profit-making' situation, thus creating a financial reserve for its further extensive overhaul, at an estimated cost of £75,000 or more, to enable it to run on the main line for a further five years after its mandatory stoppage in 1985. It is important that the enthusiasts for operating steam locomotives have some appreciation of the costs involved: in the case of No 46229, they will approach £150,000 since departure from Minehead when the current work is completed.

By contrast, the cheapest and most straightforward restoration undertaken to those steam locomotives currently operational is also the oldest. The Stirling 8 ft single-wheeler No 1 was built at Doncaster in 1870, withdrawn from active service in 1907, reinstated in 1925 for the Stockton &

Darlington Railway centenary and again for special exhibition purposes in 1938, returning to a static museum existence the following year. After an abortive effort to have the locomotive accepted by British Rail as a working exhibit in the S&D 150 parade on 31 August 1975, it was subsequently decided to look at the practicality of non-British Rail operation. The Engineering Insurance Co, which had 'cleared' *Henry Oakley* for operation on the Keighley & Worth Valley Railway in the late 1970s, was asked to look at the boiler of No 1. The workmanship of the large 'window' patches on firebox crown and sides was admired, rather than looked upon as a cause for concern, and removal of a sample of tubes for examination revealed them to be in almost 'as new' condition. Considering they had been fitted in 1938 and were over twenty years older than those removed from *Duchess of Hamilton*, which had literally disintegrated, it was a remarkable tribute to the care given to conservation back in 1939 and subsequently. It also confirmed the view that age alone should not be the determining factor in tube renewal, despite current British Rail policy! The tubes sampled were reusable if re-ended, but it was a simpler operation to fit replacements and this was done. The hydraulic and subsequent static steam tests confirmed all was well with the steam producer, but in deference to the uncertain age of the boiler, the safety valves were set to blow-off at 110 lb/sq in, 20 lb/sq in less than in 1870. On 19 June 1981 No 1 moved again under its own power for the first time since 1939. Everything seemed in good order, but after a few applications of the vacuum brake, the ageing of the canvas-reinforced rubber diaphragm brake cylinder 'piston' took its toll and the fastening to the rod tore away.

In due course, on the private Great Central Railway at Loughborough on 2 December 1981, No 1 was back in passenger traffic running like the proverbial sewing machine. All those concerned with the operation commented most favourably on the beautiful ride, free steaming and overall excellent performance of the 112-year-old veteran. Since returning to York, the locomotive has had two outings on the North Yorkshire Moors Railway for filming purposes and was in steam at the Museum's tenth anniversary celebrations.

These two examples, at opposite ends of the preserved operational spectrum, must needs suffice to illustrate the type of problems faced by Museum staff in trying to reconcile the demands of the present-day with the obligation to posterity. We could have chosen many more, such as *Hardwicke*, *Green Arrow*, MR No 1000 and, perhaps most spectacularly, *Mallard*, but there is another solution in some cases – the working reproduction. In Chapter 2, a fairly comprehensive analysis was given of the reasons behind, and some of the compromises arising from, the building of *Iron Duke*; but at the time of compilation of this account, the Museum itself has had most experience in this field from the operation of its now world-famous *Rocket* replica.

Rocket was commissioned for the NRM and has since become almost as famous as the original in consequence of its worldwide travels. After participation in the 1979–80 150th anniversary celebrations of the Liverpool & Manchester Railway, it was never intended to be steamed other than for occasional demonstrations within the Museum complex. Even so, a number of alterations, including a welded boiler and modern brake equipment, had to be made to the original design to comply with present-day safety requirements.

In operating service, the reasons for the substantial differences between the original as built and as finally withdrawn soon became patently obvious. A study of the sectioned replica and remains of the original *Rocket* at the Science Museum revealed what was done in the 1830s and 1840s to keep this truly historic locomotive operational. These same deficiencies were in need of rectification if the 1979 version was to be a practical regular operating locomotive.

A major rebuilding on the scale applied to the original could have been undertaken, but this would have destroyed the outline and character of the 1829 as-built form. The main differences between the original and rebuilt *Rocket* were the subsequent lowering to an almost horizontal position of the steeply inclined cylinders, fitting a proper smokebox and the provision of front and rear firebox water spaces. It had been generally thought that the repositioning of the cylinders was undertaken to improve the riding quality of the locomotive. Experience with the working reproduction tends to discount this theory. When given its head on the Amersfoort to Woudenburg branch line in Holland in 1981, our *Rocket* rode remarkably well at a recorded speed of 27 m.p.h. What was noticeable, however, was the considerable deflection of the driving wheel springs which, coupled with the 1830s state of the spring making art, probably resulted in frequent breakages. It is now thought most likely that the cylinders of the original were moved to overcome this particular problem rather than improve the riding characteristics. To date, the inclined cylinders have not caused any problems on the 1979 version and no spring breakages have occurred.

The lack of a proper smokebox made routine tube cleaning an awkward and

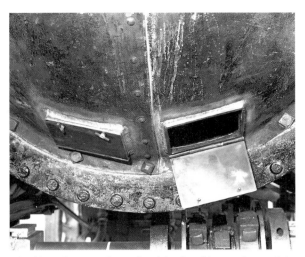

The hinged access doors fitted in the chimney base of the *Rocket* reproduction to facilitate soot removal after tube cleaning.

On the first stage of *Rocket*'s journey to Japan in 1983, the hinged chimney is evident in this view.

time-consuming operation. Although a suitably flexible brush could clean the tubes from the firebox end, the soot removed built up in the curved base of the chimney. To remove it from there it was necessary to dismantle the whole chimney unit and unbolt the base from the boiler barrel front. Burning a good quality, relatively smoke-less, Welsh steam coal, this operation was only necessary after about seven days' steaming, but with the fuel generally avail-able, tube cleaning is an almost daily requirement. The problem was neatly and inexpensively solved by the Museum tech-nicians fitting two unobtrusive hinged doors to the chimney base, through which the accumulation of soot and ash could be read-ily raked out.

The third problem area was dramatically brought to our attention when, on the sec-ond day of public operation, the fireman's trousers caught fire! The 'dry' firebox back plate was at this stage glowing red hot. A fire cement lining had been applied as protec-tion to both front and back firebox plates, but quickly failed. The problem was subse-quently solved with the application by specialist contractors of a special and expen-sive ceramic-based thicker lining of the type used on molten metal carriers. Although this resulted in a marked reduction in fire grate area, the excellent steaming qualities of the locomotive have not been marred and the lining continues to give good service.

The original and reproduction locomo-tives delivered feed-water to the boiler via a crosshead-driven pump. It follows that the boiler could only be topped up when the driving wheels were turning. The inevitable long periods of waiting followed by demands for instant action when making the TV documentary film *The Grand British Experimental Railway*, highlighted the short-comings of such an arrangement in circums-tances the Stephensons could never have visualized. Only the threat of an imminent boiler explosion caused the producer to relent in his refusal to allow a few trips up and down the line to put some water in the boiler! A temporary hand-pump, subse-quently replaced by a more effective version manufactured in the Museum workshop, was fitted to alleviate the situation.

Contemporary records do not reveal how often the original *Rocket* became derailed, but our version came off the road at the slightest hint of gauge widening on a curve, whether in the UK, California or Germany. Frequent derailment of the driving wheels at Bold Colliery on the first day of the Rocket 150 celebrations prevented the star of the show from leading the grand cavalcade.

Equally embarrassing were the results of the derailment which caused deformation, subsequent re-trueing and general drying-out of the wood; this ultimately resulted in the wheels finally 'collapsing' as the locomotive ran on to the 'A' turntable in the Museum after being host to the Prime Minister! To avoid any further possible embarrassment, the decision was taken to replace the 'wooden' driving wheels with a cast-steel pair to standard tread dimensions, prior to the locomotive appearing at Nuremburg in connection with the Deutsche Bundesbahn 150 celebrations in 1985. One of the 'original' wooden wheels, suitably modified, was used as a pattern when casting the new pair.

Although conceived to fulfil rather different criteria, our *Rocket* has taught us much about the problems which must have faced those early pioneers. It is an unexpected bonus, and the resolution of these problems has required considerable skill and ingenuity on the part of the workshop staff. To that work-load has now been added the much larger reproduction, the broad gauge *Iron Duke*. At the time of writing, it remains to be seen what further insights may be gained into nineteenth-century operating practice!

Another major commitment is the restoration and maintenance, sometimes in operational order, of the carriage collection. The carriage is the piece of railway equipment with which the travelling public are most intimately associated, yet it does not always attract the same degree of interest as the locomotive. However, if most carriages are regarded as so commonplace as to be taken for granted, the Royal Saloons are noteworthy exceptions.

The York collection of Royal Saloons is the finest and largest in the world. By their specialized nature and exclusive use, they have generally had an above average length of service, care and attention. As a result it is usual to find only minimal restoration work necessary to make them fit for public exhibition. Of those taken into the collection sinced 1975, an external repaint has been the major requirement in most cases. However,

one area which tends to be overlooked and yet is of vital importance to the ultimate safety and conservation of the older wooden-bodied vehicle, whether Royal or not, is the electric lighting system. Until relatively recently, carriage lighting was based on the 24V DC system, with relatively high current, a corollary of the low voltage. Coupled with the finite life of the natural rubber insulation of the contemporary wiring, there is a real danger of fire risk in such vehicles. For the most effective display, the interior illumination of carriages should use the existing fittings. This can be readily achieved by using a transformer to reduce the voltage of the mains 'shore' supply from 240 to 24. Alternatively, the 24V bulbs can often be replaced with 240V and the system fed direct from the mains. In both cases it is essential to ensure the integrity of the vehicle wiring system. Rewiring any carriage is a difficult proposition at any time (other than at major internal restoration, refurbishing, overhaul or rebuild) by nature of the desire to hide, cover and protect the vulnerable electrical arteries. The Museum policy is now to include in the specification for major carriage restoration work a thorough check of the electrics, with complete rewiring if in any doubt. An interim arrangement, applied particularly in the case of the Royal Saloons, is to fit discreetly a general illumination system utilizing fluorescent tubes. Whilst not providing quite the same atmospheric and authentic glow, there are bonuses: a generally higher lighting intensity, allowing a better view of the interior fittings when seen from the 'platform', reduced generation of heat and the easy fixing of ultra-violet light filters. The latter two are important conservation advantages.

Another hidden and worrying problem is asbestos. Until recently, this material was extensively used in carriage construction as both a noise and temperature insulator. In particular, the later carriages of BR standard MK1 design incorporated sprayed-on blue asbestos over all the internal surfaces of the body shell during construction. The harmful effects of inhaling asbestos fibres are now widely known and stringent regulations are enforced whenever such a hazard is likely to exist. Exposure of the unsealed material or disturbance of asbestos in any form is a potential hazard and gives rise to expensive means of resolving problems when restoring such vehicles, a number of which are included in the National Collection. The ultimate aim is to eliminate this material from items in the collection by a rolling programme of removal by specialist contractors when major restoration is undertaken, and ensuring that, so far as possible, no new additions are made which include this substance. In the meantime, both the public and working areas of the Museum are regularly monitored to ensure that neither visitors nor staff are at any risk from this cause. In some cases, the presence of asbestos may prevent the acquisition of an important item for the collection, the cost of removing the asbestos being prohibitive.

Mention is made elsewhere of some of the factors for consideration in determining a period of restoration. With coaching stock there is a further option; a different period for the interior and exterior, or even further variations between compartments or sections of the interior. From a practical viewpoint, this can have a significant advantage in restoration cost and work-load terms if, for example, it is possible to avoid re-upholstering seats in an earlier style material which probably has to be specially woven. There are a number of examples in the collection where this policy has been adopted, including ECJS exterior/LNER interior of third-class corridor No 12, LMS exterior/BR 1960s interior of the class 502 EMU and LSWR exterior/late SR interior of tri-composite No 3598.

Some vehicles, on acquisition, are in such a poor state that they require thorough restoration, rather than a general 'tidy up'; the first major project undertaken on Museum premises was the LNER buffet car No 9135. Built in York Works in 1937 and the last wooden-bodied passenger vehicle in revenue-earning service on British Rail, it became part of the collection on withdrawal

Gresley buffet car No 9135 after removal of soft and plywood panels.

Repanelled Gresley buffet car, to enable varnished teak style to be reinstated.

in late 1977. Forty years on, the character of the vehicle had been materially changed: the varnished teak exterior had given way to the standard British Rail blue-grey livery; and the 1930s interior rexine wall finish, long bar, and chromium-plated tubular-framed seats and fittings had been replaced by formica, a sales counter and fully upholstered bucket chairs. Worse was revealed when, on stripping off the exterior paint, it was found that many of the original teak panels had been patch repaired or replaced by softwood or plywood – not a problem with a painted livery, but very much so with the intention to restore to a varnished teak finish.

The vehicle was to be part of the 'Centenary of Rail Catering' touring train in 1979. The time-scale and availability of resources necessitated some compromises, and it was decided that a joint Museum staff and contractor input was necessary to achieve an 'impression of the period' rather than strictly accurate 1937 restoration. In this respect, the North Norfolk Railway's similar vehicle is a much more accurate and thorough restoration, albeit at the cost of as many years' work as the Museum took months! The Museum staff undertook the main bodywork repairs, including repanelling with specially formed, extra thick, teak-faced marine plywood as necessary, and reinstatement of windows blanked-off during the years in service. Internally, local shopfitters stripped out the modern counter, manufactured and fitted the distinctive curved-end long bar which was such a feature of the original décor. Rexine is no longer manufactured, now being considered an unacceptable fire risk, but a substitute was found and used. A real find was a set of original tubular steel-framed chairs in a store room at the York Railway Institute; we were able to do a deal with the caretaker by exchanging a like number of the modern chairs received with the vehicle! The 'new' chairs needed replating, but at least they are authentic. The kitchen was left unaltered to comply with modern hygiene regulations and allow food to still be prepared therein, as also was the false ceiling in the saloon area. Despite the compromises, the vehicle now has an authentic look and feel, and has been transformed from its as-received 1960s style to an earlier period, with minimal effort and expenditure. Moreover, the option to go the 'one step further' to complete reinstatement of the 1937 condition is still available.

A further example of a major restoration undertaken in-house is the LSWR tri-composite built in 1903. A complete train in

Evidence of dry rot in the roof of LSWR tri-composite No 3598.

itself, this interesting non-vestibuled wooden-bodied vehicle features accommodation for first-, second- and third-class passengers (including a separate toilet for each compartment), luggage and the guard. Superficially restored to LSWR livery for display at the centenary of Waterloo station in 1948, the vehicle was subsequently stored. Intended for display with the Drummond class M7 0-4-4T No 245, a start was made on stripping the body side panels which over the years in service had had galvanized sheet steel substituted for the original wood. The structural wooden framework was found to be in remarkably good condition until, near the cant line at the roof edge, clear evidence of dry rot was discovered. To ensure complete eradication, it was recommended that all affected material, plus a further metre beyond the last visible evidence, be cut out and burned. The most badly affected area was in the centre of the vehicle, and the illustrations show the extent of renewal work necessary. The body has been completely repanelled in wood, with new mouldings manufactured by the Museum's 'coachbuilder'.

The carriage restoration work-load is far beyond the capacity of the Museum work-

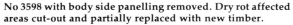

No 3598 with body side panelling removed. Dry rot affected areas cut-out and partially replaced with new timber.

Mallard **stripped down in the NRM Workshops.**

shop technicians, and a number of major projects have been undertaken outside. Prior to the Museum opening in September 1975, the MR six-wheeled composite carriage No 901 was completely restored at the Wolverton BREL Carriage Works, whilst the York establishment dealt with GNR passenger luggage van No 948. Wolverton has made the major input with much vital work, particularly with the Royal Train vehicles, while Doncaster and Derby have undertaken similar work on a lesser scale to both LNER and LMSR stock. In each case, excepting some of the Derby work used as an apprentice-training exercise, the Museum has paid commercial rates for the work carried out – contrary to popular belief, we are not part of the British Rail system and do not qualify even for departmental rates!

Outside, non-BREL contractors have also played a major part. Resco restored the pioneer GWR diesel-mechanical railcar of 1934, with Steamtown, Carnforth, undertaking work on Pullman *Topaz* and Midland diner No 3463, both of which included the manufacture and reinstatement of saloon furniture and fittings, and ECJS third-class corridor No 12. The last restoration included the electrification of the original gas-lighting

fittings. In all such outside work, the necessary initial research, work specification and supervision is undertaken by Museum staff.

So far, wagon restoration has been something of a 'Cinderella' in the restoration programme. None the less an appreciable amount of sponsorship has been received from some of the original private owners and a fair number of the less modified wagons have lent themselves to fairly speedy overhaul prior to paintshop attention.

Mention of the latter brings the discussion logically to the question of livery and painting in general. To some enthusiasts, ensuring the livery is correct in every detail is the most important part of restoration – it is, after all, the first thing to be seen; but at the other end of the scale is the practical view that the paintwork is only applied to protect the material so covered, and if the result is decorative that is a bonus. Whilst every effort is made by the Museum staff to ensure both viewpoints are met, it can be very difficult to ensure absolute accuracy. This is particularly the case with older colour schemes, when the use of natural pigments, together with the variations in skill at paint mixing and matching by the individual

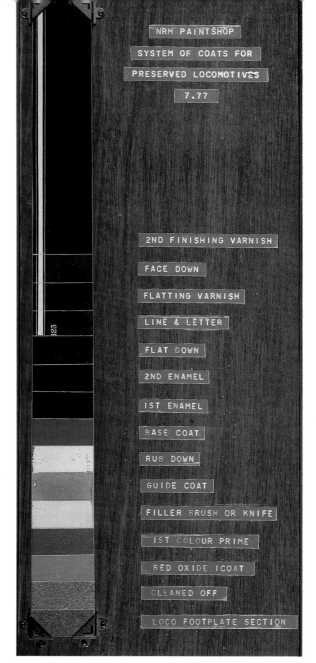

NRM paint specification for locomotive restoration.

covered being lost, it does have the benefit that careful rubbing down can reveal the colour, lining and lettering details of much earlier coatings. It was this facility that enabled the Museum staff to ascertain the chocolate-brown livery formerly applied to the 1898-built electric locomotive of the Waterloo & City Railway, when all other sources of information had failed. However, whether discovered 'by accident' or found by means of contemporary colour panels (in the case of GNR locomotive livery), the colours themselves are often such as to necessitate special 'mixes' being made by commercial paint firms.

Painting specifications applied by the Museum follow those specified by the railway companies, or as drawn up by our paint technician to meet particular circumstances or requirements. Many full specifications raised by the old companies are held in the Museum library and this has enabled a fairly standard 'Museum' specification to be evolved, although not every stage may be required in each case.

The sheer size of some of the objects and the volume of work necessitates a fair amount of painting to be contracted out. A number of locomotives and carriages have been given such attention at BREL workshops, often, particularly in the case of Royal Train vehicles, at the works formerly responsible for their painting before they became Museum objects. When contractors are utilized on-site, the general practice is for the final lining and lettering to be undertaken by the Museum painter/signwriter.

Although railway rolling stock spends most of its working life outdoors, such items in the collection likely to be displayed in a similar environment are given additional or modified attention to prolong the period between repaints. Visitors to a Museum also seem to expect objects to be displayed in a much more pristine state than was the case during normal service! Thus, for example, wooden wagons have been treated with pre-coloured preservative stain as an alternative to paint, whilst others have been given a protective coat of varnish.

painter, was the order of the day. Even in relatively recent times, it was possible to discern the marked variations in shade and style of interpretation of a railway company's standard livery depending at which works the vehicle had been painted. The effects of time, heat, varnish and general environment can also all affect the colour.

Traditional railway painting practice is to put paint on paint. Although this in time can result in the finer detail of the material

Much of the painting undertaken in the Museum is less glamorous than that associated with Royal Saloons or nineteenth-century steam locomotives. It can and does cover just about the full range of such activities, from applying emulsion paint to a display board, painting a scenic backcloth to the model railways or decorating a post-box, to producing an elaborately lettered sign for the tape-slide presentation. With the possible exception of producing, from scratch, the elaborate heraldic devices on a Royal Saloon, the Museum itself has always been able to meet the challenge.

Although much less spectacular than some of the activities outlined, the day-to-day servicing and maintenance of the collection on public display is vital to the well being of the Museum. It tends to be forgotten that the Museum is open to the public 361 days each year, during which some one million or more visitors contribute their share to general wear and tear. Special exhibitions invariably call for the workshops to produce display material in the form of boards, screens, stands, cases, brackets, notices, etc., involving all three 'branches'; travelling exhibitions not only require proper cases and packing to prevent damage

Final Synthesis: *Green Arrow* **hauls the catering on rail 'Centenary Express' on the last lap of a 2500-mile tour of England, Wales and Scotland in 1979.**

in transit, but also workshop expertise to set up the display in foreign locations.

The number of bodies in the Main Hall can make a significant difference to the temperature and humidity of the environment, which in turn can affect the condition of the objects on display. An increase in humidity speeds up the rusting of iron-based components, whilst a decrease can cause timber panels to dry out and split. The number of visitors also has a direct relationship to the wear rate suffered by the working models, although with the regular fixed-time demonstrations the need for maintenance attention is on an elapsed-time basis. Keeping the track and locomotive power pick-up gear clean on the model railway is a constant requirement to maintain efficient operation. With a changing display there is an on-going need to produce or modify label boards and stands. New acquisitions, whether permanent additions to the collection or on loan, usually require the skilled attention of the workshop technician before being put on display. And so it goes on . . .

Chapter 8

The Live Museum

by P. W. B. Semmens

Every curator of a transport museum faces a fundamental quandary. Transport is all about movement of people and goods, whereas a museum's first responsibility is the preservation and conservation of its objects which are essentially static responsibilities. For many people, the traditional idea of a museum conjures up an image of infrequently changing displays of preserved items, with the staff just being involved in historical research behind the scenes.

Over the last few decades, however, museums generally have adopted a much more dynamic approach to their subjects, with more interpretive displays and special exhibitions, while those with exhibits that are capable of being operated frequently restore them to working condition, so that visitors can obtain their own impressions of what they were like in their heyday. Throughout its first ten years, the National Railway Museum has been very active in these fields, arranging numerous special exhibitions, and operating some of its original and reproduction rolling stock, not only in this country, but as far afield as Japan, California and Australia.

During the NRM's first decade, there have been numerous important anniversaries which have been suitably celebrated by special exhibitions of various sorts. Some of these have been national in scope, such as the 150th anniversaries of the opening of the Stockton & Darlington and Liverpool & Manchester Railways in 1975 and 1980, as well as that of the formation of the Great Western Railway in 1985. Such events have

LMS third-class sleeping car, LMS Class 5 4-6-0 No 5000 and LNER Class V2 2-6-2 *Green Arrow* preparing to take part in the *Rocket 150* cavalcade, Bold colliery, May 1980 (D. Jenkinson).

particularly involved the museum in the operation of its rolling stock and other external activities.

The latter half of the 1870s saw the railways of this country moving into their own *belle époque*, and the centenaries of some of these events have provided opportunities for notable exhibitions: the year 1976 marked the centenary of the opening of the Midland Railway's Settle & Carlisle line and provided the theme for the museum's first major special exhibition 'Wheels in the Wilderness', which was supplemented by the use of preserved rolling stock over the line during British Rail's celebrations, as well as the joint production with them of a commemorative booklet.

In 1977, the centenary being celebrated was that of the present York station. The museum co-operated with the Eastern Region of British Rail to present an exhibition of historic and present-day rolling stock in the station. A few months earlier the NRM was host to the international touring exhibition 'Towards the Future by Rail'. This had been organized jointly by the *Union Internationale des Chemins de Fer* (UIC) and the International Association of Transport Museums (IATM). To supplement the touring exhibition, a display of freight rolling stock was arranged in the museum car park. These were all specialized vehicles used on the train-ferry services across the Channel. The international display material appropriately arrived in York by train from Germany and left again for Spain in one of the 'Transfesa' ferry vans whose axles can be changed to accommodate the different rail gauges involved.

Both the UIC and IATM were to feature again in the NRM's contacts during the subsequent decade. The former celebrated its own sixtieth anniversary in 1982, with one of their rooms in its Paris headquarters being dedicated to the name of Stephenson. To mark the occasion, the NRM was asked to assist in arranging a small exhibition there. The museum's involvement with IATM has been considerably greater, with the NRM's Keeper becoming the organization's president in 1983–6. The association held its annual meeting in York in 1975 to coincide with the Stockton & Darlington Railway celebrations that year, and the delegates were able to see the work in progress for the final run-up to the museum's opening a month later.

The centenary celebrated in 1978 was that of the museum's neighbour in York, the Royal Station Hotel. From their earliest days, the railways of this country had been involved in the provision of hotel accommo-

dation for their passengers. The exhibition concentrated on the period when they were at their most opulent, being entitled 'Grand Hotels', and covered the whole spectrum on this facet of railway activity. It is indicative of the changed economic climate that all the British Transport Hotels have since been sold by British Rail. The museum was nevertheless able to acquire some of their more outstanding relics before the sale was completed, while the records of the company have been transferred to the Public Record Office.

The centenary was marked in 1979 of the first successful use of electric traction on the railways, when Werner von Siemens hauled passengers around a Berlin exhibition behind his 150-volt locomotive. Since then

Midland Compound No 1000 in York station at the head of a special train organised by British Railways. The leading vehicle is also part of the NRM's collection.

railway electrification has spread throughout the world, and it was considered appropriate to devote the NRM's 1979 special exhibition to this theme. Not only was there a display of small exhibits but the full-size rolling stock on exhibition in the Main Hall was rearranged to fit in with the same theme. Several of the electrically-powered units in the collection were specially restored, and, in co-operation with the manufacturers and owners, one of the Metro-Cammell units for the Tyne & Wear Metro was put on display, being side-tracked in the course of its delivery journey from Birmingham to Newcastle. Throughout its existence, the Museum has considered that it has a duty to display, whenever possible, current railway activities.

For the BBC TV film *Races to the North*, a line-up of East Coast motive power was staged in York station and involved four of the Museum's steam locomotives (P. W. B. Semmens).

Since 1975 numerous special exhibitions of modern railway activities have therefore been held in the museum, many of them provided by British Rail. These have covered a wide spectrum of subjects, and have included such themes as 'Journey by Design', 'Creating a Diversion' (covering the new line that was built south of York to take the East Coast Route around the Selby coalfield), and the development of the Advanced Passenger and High Speed trains. These exhibitions only involved small exhibits or displays, but others have featured full-sized rolling stock, such as one of the three remaining British Rail steam locomotives, from the Vale of Rheidol in Mid-Wales. An exhibition of vehicles with new types of brakes was displayed in conjunction with an international braking conference held at York University in 1979, and there was similarly a special display of mod-

The Museum's working reproduction of *Rocket* on a 30-metre length of track outside the Palais des Festivals at Cannes (P. W. B. Semmens).

ern 'On Track' engineering equipment to coincide with the visit of the Permanent Way Institution during their centenary celebrations in 1984.

British Rail's architectural heritage and its preservation have featured on more than one occasion, the most recent exhibition providing an example of how the facilities of the NRM can be used co-operatively to enhance the original concept of an exhibition. In 1984, the Royal Institution of British Architects (RIBA) was holding its 150th anniversary celebrations in York, which included an evening reception in the Museum. British Rail approached the NRM to see whether it would be possible to put up a small panel exhibition on the night concerned, but it was quickly decided to make it a full-scale special exhibition, which could

also be included in the York Festival programme that year. The exhibition was opened by the President of the RIBA, and drew extensively on the NRM photographic archives. It was also shown subsequently at a number of other locations, and finally produced by British Rail in book form as well.

Another example of a co-operative exhibition was the one opened in 1984, following the spectacular collision staged by British Rail and the Central Electricity Generating Board (CEGB) between a diesel locomotive and one of the nuclear flasks that have been used to transport used fuel rods safely by rail for over twenty years. By arrangement with the CEGB, the 46-ton flask concerned was put on display outside the north end of the Main Hall, the story of the whole testing programme being explained in a short continuously playing video inside the Museum. It proved very popular with the visiting public, providing an example of the way in which museums can create interest by displaying the actual artefacts seen on television.

The relative ease with which the NRM can rearrange the full-size exhibits in the Main Hall has also assisted with the generation of the 'living museum' image. There have undeniably been visitors who have been disappointed to find their favourite item was not currently on display, but they have been more than matched by the thousands who have made return visits knowing there will be something new to see in the way of full-size rolling stock. The museum is always sympathetic to advance requests for information on the whereabouts of a particular exhibit, especially when the would-be visitor is one of the 9 per cent of those who come from overseas countries.

This flexibility enabled the NRM to present its 1981 tribute to the Royal Wedding that year, with the special exhibition 'Palaces on Wheels'. All the royal coaches in the collection which were then at York were put on display, and the Museum was subsequently honoured by a visit from their Royal Highnesses, the Prince and Princess of Wales, during the course of the exhibition.

Railway art and photography have not been neglected when it comes to the arranging of special exhibitions. Not only have opportunities been taken to display some of the Museum's own material normally in reserve, but various visiting exhibitions have been staged. Notable among the former was the 'Weston Collection', the series of specially commissioned paintings by David Weston which depicts the story of steam locomotives in Britain, which was shown in 1979–80, and the annual exhibition of the Guild of Railway Artists, which was held in York in 1982.

Several exhibitions of railway posters have been arranged, culminating in 1985 with the museum mounting a major poster exhibition that was shown in several countries on the Continent, before becoming a touring exhibition in Britain. It was prepared primarily to form part of the long-standing exchange arrangements between the Sci-

The Museum's 7¼in gauge locomotive *Taw* giving rides at the Science Museum Open Day at Wroughton.

ence Museum (and its outstations) with the National Technical Museum in Prague. The opportunity was taken to invite other museums on the Continent to show it as well, and it was at Mulhouse, Munich, Utrecht and Odense before returning to Britain. Representing the other side of the Anglo-Czech exchanges, an exhibition of model locomotives from the Prague museum has been held in York, and was opened by the Czech ambassador.

Photography has inevitably been involved with most special exhibitions, as well as the Museum's ordinary displays, but there have been occasions when the work of a particular individual has been marked, such as the memorial exhibition for the late Bishop Eric Treacy in 1978, who died while photographing one of the Museum's

Evening Star **heads 'The Bishop Treacy' memorial steam train at Dent station in September 1978 (J. A. Coiley).**

locomotives in action on the Settle & Carlisle line.

Another way the Museum has developed its living image has been with television and film-makers. Most of the openings of special exhibitions in the Museum have been covered by the local television news on one or both channels, while other activities have similarly been shown to wider audiences in their own homes, encouraging them to visit the Museum. The steam trials of any locomotive at the Museum are likely to attract similar coverage, and on many occasions a member of the Museum staff is invited to speak 'to camera', which provides a direct opportunity to put over some of the Museum's aims and policies.

Other television involvements have been the recording of two of the heats of the 1985 series of the popular BBC TV *Mastermind* programme. For the invited audience in the Main Hall, it was fascinating to see the recordings being made, while the viewers were given a short visual tour of the Museum, which provided much valuable publicity. Anneka Rice has also descended by helicopter into the car park to find one of her Channel Four *Treasure Hunt* clues in the cab of the Chinese 4-8-4 locomotive.

The increase in the number of local radio stations, including the opening of BBC Radio York, has also provided the opportunity to give news about the Museum to the listening, as distinct from the viewing, public. Railways have a widespread fascination for the British, as the NRM's attendances show, and it is not just the local radio stations in the immediate vicinity of York which have requested recording sessions, particularly as the ease of travelling to York from many parts of the country has mar-

'Deltic' No 55002 *The King's Own Yorkshire Light Infantry* is greeted by a fanfare from the trumpeters of the Light Infantry Brigade as it enters the NRM. For its final year's service, the locomotive was painted in its original green livery, with a grant from the Friends of the National Railway Museum, and carried a plaque to record that it was due to join the Museum's collection when it was withdrawn. It briefly visited the Museum after being overhauled and repainted at Doncaster, and was on the 14.15 train from York to King's Cross the same afternoon.

kedly improved over the last decade.

Sound is always highly evocative as far as steam locomotives are concerned, and, as part of the creation of the 'living museum', recordings of steam locomotives at work are played automatically at intervals over special loudspeakers in the Main Hall. Records and tapes of many different locomotives at work are also popular sales items in the shop.

Live music is also at times featured in the Main Hall. On the occasion of the Royal Opening in September 1975, the York Railway Institute Silver Band played in the pit of the 'A' turntable. The reception this received has prompted subsequent visits by the same band on other special occasions, such as the evening reception held for the Anglo-French Railway Conference, when the British members of the party were to be seen teaching their French visitors how to do the 'Gay Gordons' in front of the statue of George Stephenson. Other bands have appeared on an *ad hoc* basis, but in recent years a pre-announced programme of weekend concerts by school bands and orchestras has been arranged. More recently still the provision of a brass band is one of the options offered to organizations now being invited to hold their evening functions in the Museum.

As part of the 1976 York Festival, a promenade concert of railway music was held on the 'B' turntable, at the other end of the Main Hall. The main work was a contemporary choral one by the conductor, Arthur Butterworth, entitled *Trains in the Distance*. Other pieces included Honegger's *Pacific 231*, two railway polkas by Eduard Strauss, and the *Railway Song* for choir and orchestra, written by Berlioz for the opening of the *Chemins de Fer du Nord* in 1846, and rarely performed since. The concert was recorded, and an edited cassette of it has since been selling steadily in the shop.

In the run-up to the opening in 1975, the Museum was involved in three major documentary television films, two of which were devoted entirely to the new National Museum itself. The process has continued ever since, with assistance being sought by film crews from Britain and overseas. One French production was subsequently given Japanese sub-titles, and shown shortly before the arrival of the reproduction *Rocket* in that country, while Queen Victoria's saloon featured in the BBC *Royal Heritage* series. The most recent documentary films that have involved the Museum included some made in 1985 for the BBC2 series 'Steam Days', while Yorkshire TV, one of the companies involved at the time of the opening, returned to make a further film covering the Museum's first ten years.

Making the film depicting the life of Richard Wagner in the reserve collection building in 1982, with Richard Burton and Vanessa Redgrave. The anglicized version of the station nameboard is amusing, as it would only appear as 'München' in real life.

A scene from the closing sequences of *Chariots of Fire*. As the hero supposedly arrives back from the Olympic Games in Paris, the driver of the SECR 4-4-0 No 737 inspects his locomotive after it had worked its boat train into 'Victoria' Station, actually York in disguise!

In some of these ventures, the Museum has co-operated closely with British Rail, an example being the BBC TV film *Races to the North*, produced just before the introduction of the Inter City 125 services on the East Coast route. Several of the locomotives involved in the races of 1895 are preserved in the National Collection, and appropriate use was made of these in the film. An idea of the time involved in the production of such documentaries is provided by the fact that the celebrated three and a half minute

'Palaces on Wheels' was the NRM's contribution to the Royal Wedding year of 1981. On 12 November, the Prince and Princess of Wales visited the exhibition and are seen here descending from Queen Victoria's saloon.

locomotive change that took place on the racing special in York station on one August night that year took no less than four hours to record on film. A copy of the resulting film is often requested as part of such deals which has assisted the Museum to build up its film archives.

Ordinary feature films have also included the Museum's rolling stock, as the companies involved have sought to produce more authentic portrayals of the past. It is not always possible to recreate all the correct rolling stock involved, and the 'props' departments have developed numerous ingenious techniques to make up for this. The application of specially painted wall-

paper to the exterior of a coach, using vaseline instead of paste, can prove very convincing, and not only just in the background. After the filming is over, the vehicle can be restored to its normal condition very easily and without damage.

While some of these filming sessions have involved the steaming of locomotives, it is remarkable what the special-effects departments can manage in the way of producing 'steam'. The photograph showing a scene that occurs in the closing sequence of *Chariots of Fire* gives some idea of what can be achieved with a locomotive that is not in steam. The great success of this British film at the box office, and in gaining Oscars, prompted the editor of the Friends' Newsletter to wonder if there might be an award for the 'Best Supporting Locomotive'!

On other occasions the film company may be less interested in exact authenticity rather than the ability to take a number of dramatic, scene-setting, railway shots at minimum cost. The film made about the life of Wagner some years ago provided an example of this, with the interior of the reserve collection building being transformed in the course of a single day into representations of Munich and Venice. There have also been opportunities for stock to be used in 'commercials', the resulting revenue on all such occasions being an important consideration. In the present economic climate, museums are being encouraged to develop other sources of finance by offering their services in this way in addition to seeking sponsorship.

For the many thousands of individuals who spend so much of their time each year on one of the numerous preserved railways throughout the country, it is the actual operation of their rolling stock that is vitally important. Many of these enthusiasts have thus expected the NRM to operate its locomotives on a comparable scale, and it has taken a considerable amount of effort to convey the NRM's operating philosophy to the public. Fundamentally, the Museum does not have the resources to operate full-sized locomotives on more than a limited number of occasions each year. The staffing

and security arrangements in a national museum limit the use that can be made of volunteers, although the support team of the Museum's Friends has provided valuable assistance when locomotives have been operating away from York on special occasions. There is also the need to ensure that, if rolling stock from the National Collection is operated, it will not be to the detriment of its long-term conservation, a constraint that is not so severe for the average railway preservation society. Nevertheless an appreciable proportion of the Museum's locomotive stock has been steamed under carefully controlled conditions since 1975.

The major national celebrations in 1975 and 1980, already mentioned, involved the NRM in the provision of many working items. The main Stockton & Darlington event took place just before the Museum opened, but there were nevertheless eight locomotives from the National Collection amongst those that participated in the cavalcade from Shildon to Heighington on 31 August 1975. Not all were in steam, and, with the Museum's preoccupation with its own opening a month later, much of the preparation work on the locomotives was carried out on its behalf by certain preservation societies. For example, the former Wantage Tramway 0-4-0 tank, *Shannon*, on long-term loan to the Great Western Society at Didcot, was restored by them to steaming condition for the occasion, and it returned south after the celebrations.

Hardwicke, the famous LNWR contender in the 1895 races, and *Green Arrow* went to the North East from Steamtown, Carnforth, while *Evening Star* was similarly prepared for the occasion on the Keighley & Worth Valley Railway, where it had also been used to operate some of their normal services over the previous months. These three locomotives thus made their way to their new permanent home at York by way of the Shildon cavalcade, returning south from Darlington on the Sunday night. So, when the Museum staff came to work on the following Monday morning, there were seven more locomotives than there had been when they went home on the Friday evening, and five of these were still warm.

As a result of the experience gained in 1975, a very different, and much more ambitious, format was adopted for the 150th anniversary celebrations of the Liverpool & Manchester Railway five years later. The main event was spread over three days, and also included many more items of rolling stock, carriages and wagons being involved on this occasion, in addition to the operating locomotives. The NRM contributed more than thirty items from the National Collection, not all of them going direct from York, although, on the other hand, the Museum prepared the Welshpool & Llanfair narrow gauge locomotive *Earl* which was at that time on loan from the preservation society that owns it. The whole operation involved considerable co-ordination by the Museum staff, and representatives from various preservation societies assisted with the preparation of the locomotives for the three cavalcades. There was nevertheless still an opportunity for the Museum staff to assist BBC TV with the production of two programmes about the event, which were subsequently combined into a single one for a repeat showing, while help was also provided with the on-site commentary.

Another notable anniversary during the period under review was the centenary of the introduction of restaurant cars in Britain,

which took place in 1979. In conjunction with Travellers Fare, British Rail's subsidiary responsible for restaurant-car and station catering, a special train of seven vintage catering vehicles (plus two service ones for the staff) was assembled from the Museum's collection. It made an extensive tour of Britain lasting for two and a half weeks, during which it travelled 2500 miles and was inspected by thousands of visitors during its station stops. It provided an opportunity for passengers to be fed on the move (from a modern kitchen car) amidst the luxurious surroundings of past eras of rail travel.

The open weekend held in York at the end of September 1985 to mark the Museum's tenth birthday was also an occasion when several locomotives were steamed, with rides being given to the public behind some of them. This special occasion saw three locomotives operating at the rear of the Peter Allen Building, with another two performing alongside the British Rail main line outside the former diesel depot. In addition to these full-sized examples, the Museum's miniature-gauge locomotive *Margaret* was

Two earlier East Coast Route record-breakers, GNR No 1 and *Mallard*, salute the InterCity 125 'Tees-Tyne Pullman' as it passes the Museum on 27 September 1985 in the course of establishing a world record of 115.4 m.p.h. between Newcastle and King's Cross.

Young visitors admire one of the model locomotives in a visiting exhibition from the Czech National Technical Museum at Prague in 1981.

giving rides on the length of $7\frac{1}{4}$ in track adjoining the museum car park. This engine was constructed in the museum's workshops; amongst those who have ridden behind it is the Prince of Wales.

The full-sized locomotives operating from the former BR diesel depot included the world record-holder *Mallard*, making its first movements under steam for over twenty years, in preparation for the celebrations being planned for 1988 to mark the fiftieth anniversary of its record. Together with the Stirling Single, it was able to salute the record-breaking InterCity 125 as it passed York in the course of its 115.4 m.p.h. dash from Newcastle to London. It came into the Museum car park on the following day for a ceremony when one of its power cars was named *The National Railway Museum – The first ten years – 1975–1985*.

When British Rail completed the dieselization and electrification of their main line services in 1968, they banned the operation of privately owned steam locomotives over their tracks, with the exception of *Flying Scotsman* whose owner had an agreement with some years still to run. From a management point of view this decision made sense, forcing everyone to concentrate on getting the best out of the new forms of motive power, commercially as well as operationally. As the years passed, increasing pressure from the public encouraged British Rail to relax the ban, and it was finally agreed that a limited number of charter specials could be operated from 1972 onwards, with the prospect of good revenue to be made from such operations.

A number of different factors have to be

The entrance to the special exhibition 'Grand Hotels' in 1978.

A mercury-arc rectifier was one of the exhibits in the Railway Electrification exhibition in 1979, and visitors could make it work by pressing a button.

taken into account if steam-hauled charter trains are to make a profit, and the formula has been continually revised during the past fifteen years to increase their appeal to the fare-paying public. One of the important factors is the attractiveness of the locomotive concerned; a unique Pacific, for example, may be much more likely to attract custom than a smaller locomotive from a class that is represented in several other steam centres. It is also important for the locomotive to be capable of hauling a long enough train to contain an economic load of passengers. The large preserved locomotives in the National Collection meet both these requirements, and many of them have been called on to undertake main-line operations since the Museum has been open.

The Museum's staff resources at York are only sufficient to support a limited number of steaming operations in the year, but these have been supplemented by locomotives that have been restored to steaming condition by other preserved railways and steam centres on the Museum's behalf. In certain cases the locomotives may be on long-term loan to the organization concerned, and appear in ordinary service on their own tracks, but others, such as *King George V* at Hereford or *Sir Lamiel* at Hull, can only haul public passenger trains on the main lines, since their custodians do not possess running lines of their own. The National Railway Museum has to ensure that all the organizations looking after one of its locomotives possess the required technical skills and other resources to restore, house and operate it to the required standards. It is therefore necessary for any society requesting the loan of a National Collection locomotive to have a proven track record.

It is not possible to mention all the different locomotives from the National Collection that have operated revenue-earning trains during the last twelve years, although all the working examples are listed in Appendices I and II. The following review is therefore highly selective. The Settle & Carlisle line has proved one of the most popular routes for these specials, although, on the

occasion of its centenary in 1976, the only concession to steam was to allow two light engines to visit Settle one afternoon. Two years later steam haulage over this route was permitted, and it was one of the Museum's locomotives, *Green Arrow*, which hauled the first special train.

The same locomotive was used to inaugurate the Eastern Region's public steam excursions when they commenced in the following year. These were operated over a circular route from York, travelling via Leeds and Harrogate, and were thus fairly closely associated with the Museum itself from the point of view of visitors and passengers. Even so, the NRM was only able to provide the motive power on a limited number of occasions. Indeed, in the second of the two years when this service operated, its locomotives only appeared on two occasions. The close co-operation between the Museum, the locomotive owners and British Rail demonstrated by these workings is reflected in the use of the Museum's facilities to prepare and service the visiting locomotives which have sometimes been exhibited in the Main Hall between operations.

At the time the Museum was opened, the route from York to Scarborough was a popular destination for steam-hauled specials but, with the closing of the Filey Holiday Camp station in 1977, it was no longer possible to turn locomotives there. In 1981, however, a turntable was specially installed at Scarborough, with financial assistance from the resort, to enable a new series of operations to commence during the tourist season. Scarborough's great interest in such operations has also resulted in them sponsoring the restoration of *Mallard* to steaming condition.

Another operating locomotive that has become very popular with the public and crews alike has been *Duchess of Hamilton*, in spite of prior doubts by British Rail. The Friends appointed a retired British Rail engineer to take over the responsibility of operating the locomotive, by agreement with Butlins and the NRM, and this has enabled it to appear in action far more frequently than any other Museum locomotive. In 1985, during its last season before its statutory boiler overhaul, it was one of the locomotives heavily involved in operating the services from Marylebone to Stratford-on-Avon. Previously British Rail had not operated steam specials out of London, but these premium-fare workings proved popular with overseas tourists. Together with two other locomotives involved, the *Duchess of Hamilton* and her 'minders' were recipients of the 1985 award from the Association of Railway Preservation Societies.

The National Railway Museum has also operated certain of its historic locomotives which are not normally large enough to haul economic-sized charter trains. Such activities are virtually unique in this country, and it has enabled such notable locomotives as *Henry Oakley*, the Midland Compound No 1000, the Stirling Single and *Hardwicke* to be seen in action. In addition to

being used for filming purposes, there have been instances when one of them has been hired by British Rail for a special promotional event, sometimes in conjunction with the Museum's pair of 1960 Pullman cars *Emerald* and *Eagle*. Although British Rail does not allow preserved diesels to operate over their tracks as yet, some of ours have seen action on preserved railways. No D5500 has worked on the North Yorkshire Moors Railway, while the diesel-hydraulic *Western Fusilier* has appeared on the Torbay & Kingswear line in Devon. The Museum's preserved 2-BIL unit from the Southern Railway has also helped to pioneer rail tours and other passenger-carrying operations using vintage *electric* rolling stock, providing a Museum 'presence' in the south of Eng-

The 'live museum' concept well and truly came alive on the 'Centenary Express' of 1979, when some of the passengers elected to travel in period costume. This scene was taken inside Midland dining car No 3463 at the start of the inaugural trip from Leeds to London on 13 September.

The Great Northern 4-2-2 No 1 operating tender-first on the Great Central Railway at Loughborough in December 1981 (G. Wignall).

land, where steam activities are not possible on the main lines.

By far the most widely travelled locomotive in the world is the Museum's working reproduction of *Rocket*. The idea of these working reproductions started with *Locomotion*, built by Locomotion Enterprises for the Beamish Open Air Museum, as part of the activities for the 1975 anniversary of the Stockton & Darlington Railway. For the Liverpool & Manchester celebrations five years later, the same builders constructed the much more complicated working reproduction of *Rocket* for the NRM, which made its first public appearance in Kensington Gardens in August 1979. As well as taking part in the Rainhill cavalcade of 1980, in March that year it was steamed into St Pancras station in London to help publicize the commemorative postage stamps then being issued. The event made every news broadcast on all the three television channels that day between midday and midnight.

Since then, the locomotive has been in great demand for numerous special events up and down the country. Weighing only 8 tons with its tender, it is easily transported and can be quickly unloaded and steamed. It has also made a number of appearances abroad, the first of these being on the sea front at Cannes, its arrival beside an anything-but-blue Mediterranean coincid-

ing with what the local press referred to as a 'tempest'. The following year it became the first full-sized steam locomotive to fly the Atlantic, being sponsored by Midland Bank International to represent Britain at the opening of the California State Railroad Museum at Sacramento. It helped perform the actual inauguration, being driven through the ceremonial tape in the opposite direction to the Southern Pacific 'Daylight' 4-8-4 on the adjacent line. *Rocket* has also visited Australia, Czechoslovakia, Holland, Canada and Japan.

As this account has shown, the National Railway Museum's activities during its first decade have fully lived up to the standards it set itself to become a 'living museum'. Surveys have shown that the million or so visitors who flock through its doors every year are not just an elite minority, but a fairly wide cross-section of the population of the country that invented the steam locomotive and gave railways to the world. The visiting public, as well as the thousands who have experienced what the Museum can offer at a distance, will undoubtedly want the process to continue as long as there are railway tracks on which it can operate its working exhibits, be they steam, diesel or electric.

Appendix I – Locomotives and Rolling Stock based at York

This information is correct as at January 1988, but locations do vary from time to time. Locomotives and rolling stock which have been operated under the auspices of the NRM since 1975 are marked *.

Locomotives – Steam

Date built	Company	Wheel arrangement	Number	Name
1829	Shutt End Colliery	0-4-0		Agenoria
1845	LNWR (ex-Grand Junction Railway)	2-2-2	1868	formerly No 49 Columbine
1846	Furness Railway	0-4-0	3	'Coppernob'
1847	LNWR	2-2-2	3020	Cornwall
1866	MR	2-4-0	158A	
1869	NER	2-2-4T	66	Aerolite
*1870	GNR	4-2-2	1	
1874	NER	0-6-0	1275	
1875	NER	2-4-0	910	
1880	LBSCR	0-6-0T	82	Boxhill
1882	LBSCR	0-4-2	214	Gladstone
1887	LYR	0-4-0ST (narrow gauge)		Wren
1889	LYR	2-4-2T	1008	
*1892	LNWR	2-4-0	790	Hardwicke
1893	LSWR	4-4-0	563	
1893	NER	4-4-0	1621	
1897	LSWR	0-4-4T	245	
*1898	GNR	4-4-2	LNER No 3990	Henry Oakley
*1899	MR	4-2-2	673	
*1899	GNR	0-6-0ST	1247	
1901	SECR	4-4-0	737	
*1902	MR	4-4-0	1000	
1902	GNR	4-4-2	251	
1904	GER	0-6-0T	87	
1905	GER	0-6-0	1217	
1905	GWR	2-8-0	2818	
1921	LNWR	0-8-0	LMS 9395	
1926	LMSR	2-6-0	2700	
*1926	SR	4-6-0	BR 30850	Lord Nelson
*1934	SR	4-4-0	925	Cheltenham
*1934	LMS	2-6-4T	2500	
1935	Chinese Gvt Railways	4-8-4	(607)	KF7
*1936	LNER	2-6-2	4771	Green Arrow
*1938	LNER	4-6-2	4468	Mallard
*1938	LMS	4-6-2	BR 46229	Duchess of Hamilton (on loan from Butlin's Ltd)
1946	SR	4-6-2	BR 34051	Winston Churchill
1949	BR(SR)	4-6-2	35029	Ellerman Lines (sectioned)
1956	Imperial Paper Mills	0-4-0 (Fireless)	1	(Andrew Barclay Works No 2373
1957	Tees-Side Bridge & Engineering Co	4WTG	H 5	(Sentinel Works No 9629)
*1960	BR	2-10-0	92220	Evening Star
*1979	'L&MR'	0-2-2		Rocket (reproduction)
*1985	'GWR'	4-2-2		Iron Duke (broad gauge reproduction)

Locomotives – Electric

1898	Waterloo & City	Bo (third rail)	75S	
1904	NER	Bo-Bo (third rail & overhead)	1	
1917	NSR	Bo (battery)	1	
1951	BR	Bo-Bo (overhead)	26020	BR class 76
1958	BR	Bo-Bo (third rail & overhead)	E5001	BR class 71
1960	BR	Bo-Bo (25kV overhead)	E3036	BR class 84 (on loan from BR Board)

Locomotives – Internal Combustion

Date built	Company	Wheel arrangement	Number	Name
1918	War Dept/ Yorks Water Authority	4-wheel p Simplex 60 cm gauge		
1937	Yorks Water Authority	4-wheel dm (2ft gauge)		(Ruston-Hornsby Works No 187105)
*1953	BR	0-6-0 de	08064	
1954	CEGB	0-6-0 dm	3	(Robert Stephenson & Hawthorns No 7746)
1957	BR	Bo-Bo de	D8000	(20 050)
*1958	BR	A1A–A1A de	D5500	
*1960	BR	0-6-0 dm	03 090	
*1960	BR	0-4-0 dh	D2860	
*1961	BR	Co-Co de	55 002	'Deltic' The King's Own Yorkshire Light Infantry
1972	BR		41 001	Prototype HST Power Car

p =petrol
dm =diesel-mechanical
de =diesel-electric
dh =diesel-hydraulic

Rolling Stock – Powered Units

Electric

Date built	Company	Type	Number
1915	LNWR	Motor open third brake	LMS 28249
1925	SR	Motor third brake	8143
1937	SR	Motor open third brake	11179

Diesel

1934	GWR	Railcar (with buffet)	4

Gas Turbine

1972	BR	Advanced Passenger Train PC1 & 2 – Experimental	

Rolling Stock – Departmental

Date built	Company	Type	Number
1850	GNR	Four-wheel hand crane	112
		Match truck	DE 942114
c.1890	GNR	Loco tender	1002
1891	NER	Snowplough	DE900566
1899	GWR	Hand crane	537
1904	MR	Officers' saloon (formerly steam railmotor)	2234
1906	NER	Dynamometer car	902502
1907	NER	Steam breakdown crane	CME 13
1926	LNER	Match truck	DE320952
1931-2	LNER	Platelayers powered trolley (petrol)	960209
1932	LMS	Ballast plough brake	197266
1936	GWR	Ballast wagon	80659
1938	LMS	Mobile Test Unit No 1	45053

1949	LMS/BR	Dynamometer car No 3	45049
1949	BR	Inspection saloon (GWR design)	80790
1957	BR	Track recording trolley	DX 50002
c.1963/4	BR	Matisa tamping machine	74/007
1969	BR	Plasser tamping & lining machine	73/010

Rolling Stock – Passenger

Date	Company	Type	Number/Name
c. 1834	Bodmin & Wadebridge	Second	
c. 1834	Bodmin & Wadebridge	Third	
c. 1834	Bodmin & Wadebridge	First & second composite	
1838	GJR	TPO (replica) on wagon frame	
1842	London & Birmingham	Queen Adelaide's saloon	2
1845	S&DR	First & second composite	59
1851	Eastern Counties Rly	Four-wheel first	1
1861	NBR	Dandy Car (Port Carlisle branch)	1
1869	LNWR	Queen Victoria's saloon	(LMS 802)
1872	NLR	Directors' saloon	1032
*1885	WCJS	Postal sorting van	186
1885	MR	Six-wheel luggage/composite coach	901
1887	GNR	Six-wheel brake van (passenger)	948
1897	Lynton & Barnstaple Rly	Brake composite/Observation saloon(L&B2)	SR 6992
1895	Cambrian Rly	Luggage composite	238
1898	ECJS	Third corridor	12
*1899	Privately owned	Duke of Sutherland's saloon	57A
*1900	LNWR (ex-WCJS)	Dining car	LMS 76
1902	LNWR	King Edward's saloon	LMS 800
1902	LNWR	Queen Alexandra's saloon	LMS 801
1903	LSWR	Tri-composite lavatory brake	3598
*1905	LNWR	Corridor First Brakes (rebuilt 1923–4)	LMS 5154 & 5155
1908	ECJS	Royal saloon	395
1909	ECJS	Royal saloon	396
*1908	ECJS	Passenger brake van	LNER 109
*1913	Pullman Car Co	First-class parlour car	Topaz
*1914	MR	Dining car	3463
1925	LMS	Third vestibules	7828 & 7863
1927	LMS	Third vestibule	8207
*1928	LMS	Third sleeping car	14241
*1930	L&MR	First	Huskisson
	Reproductions	First	Traveller
		Third (two)	
1936	LNER	Third opens	13251 & 13254
*1936	CIWL	'Night-Ferry' Sleeping car	3792
*1937	LNER	Buffet car	9135
1937	LMS	Corridor third brake	5987
1941	LMS	Royal saloon	799
1945	GWR	Royal saloons	9006 & 9007
1950	BR (LMS design)	Corridor third brake	27093
*1955	BR	Lavatory composite	E43046
1956	BR	Second open (used as study coach)	E4286
*1960	BR	Griddle car	Sc1100
*1960	Pullman Car Co	First-class Kitchen Car	311 Eagle
*1960	Pullman Car Co	First-class Parlour Car	326 Emerald

Rolling Stock – Freight and Non-Passenger Carrying

Date built	Company	Type	Number
1797	Peak Forest Canal	Quarry truck	
1816	Grantham Canal	Tramway truck	

c.1826		Chaldron wagon	
c. 1828		Dandy cart (replica)	
		Chaldron wagon replicas	
		Chaldron wagon	
c.1850	South Hetton Colliery	Chaldron wagon	1155
c.1870	Seaham Harbour (Londonderry Rly)	Chaldron wagon	31
1889	Shell-Mex	BP oil tank wagon	512
1894	LSWR	'Road' van	99
1894	LSWR	Open carriage truck	5830
1902	NER	20 ton wooden hopper wagon	
1908	LNWR	Open carriage truck	
1912	LSWR	Gunpowder van	KDS61209
1912	LBSCR	Open wagon	3537
1912	NER	Sand wagon	DE14974
1912	GNR	8 ton van	E432764
1914	GWR	Shunters truck	W94988
1914	MR	8 ton open wagon	
1914	GCR	Van	
1914	LNWR	Van	
1914	NER	Van	
1914	Shell	Tank wagon	3171
1928	ICI	Nitric acid tank wagon	14
1924	LMS	Van	
1924	LNER	Fitted tube wagon	181358
1926	GWR	Fitted open wagon	108246
1931	GWR	Goods van, Mink G	112884
1931	Stanton Iron Works	12 ton mineral wagon	
1933(?)	LMS	Gunpowder van	288824
1933-4	LMS	20 ton goods brake-van	295987
1935	SR	Bogie goods brake-van	56297
1935	GWR	Motor car van (Mogo)	126438
1935	PLM	Train ferry van	475014
1936	LNER	20 ton goods brake-van	187774
1936	LMS	Fitted 3-plank open	472867
1936	LMS	Tube wagon	499254
1937	GWR	Siphon (bogie milk van)	2775
1937	LMS	Milk tank (United Dairies)	44057
1938	LMS	Single bolster wagon	722702
1940	WD	Warflat (Flat WC)	161042
1944	LMS	Lowmac MO	M700728
1944	GWR	13 ton open wagon	DW143698
1945	GWR	25 ton machine truck (Loriot P)	42367
1946	ex-SNCF	16 ton mineral wagon	ADB192437
1946	LNER	20 ton hopper wagon	B270919
1948	SR design	12 ton shock absorbing wagon	14036
*1949	BR	40 ton Flatrol MHH	B900402
1949	BR	Bogie bolster D	B941000
1950	BR	24 ton iron ore hopper	B436275
1950	BR	12 ton cattle wagon	B892156
*1950	BR	20 ton Weltrol MC	B900805
1951	BR	8 ton cattle wagon	B893343
1951	ICI	Liquid chlorine tank wagon	47484
1951	BR	Special cattle van (SCV)	S3733S
1952	BR	30 ton bogie bolster wagon	B943139
1954	BR	27 ton iron ore tippler	B383560
1954	BR	National Benzole oil tank wagon	2022
1955	BR	16 ton mineral	B234830
1955	BR	16 ton mineral	B227009
1957	BR	Horse-box (HB)	S96369
1959	BR	Fish van	B87905
1959	BR	Conflat	B737725
1960	BR	Banana van	B882593
1961	BR	Presflo cement wagon	B873368
1962	BR	Speedfreight container	BA4324B
1970	Phillips Petroleum	100T GLW tank wagon	PP85209

At the time of compliation, many of the above vehicles are unrestored and not on public view. Those for which no running number can be ascertained will be given appropriate numbers for the type concerned when restoration takes place.

Appendix II – Locomotives and Rolling Stock based at other locations

This information is correct as at January 1988, but note that locations do vary from time to time. Locomotives and rolling stock which have been operated under the auspices of the NRM since 1975 are marked*.

Locomotives – Steam

Date built	Company	Wheel arrangement	Number	Name
1813	Wylam Colliery	0-4-0		Puffing Billy

Location: Science Museum, South Kensington, London

| 1822 | Hetton Colliery | 0-4-0 | | |

Location: Beamish – North of England Open Air Museum, Stanley, Tyne & Wear

| 1825 | S&D | 0-4-0 | | Locomotion |

Location: Darlington Railway Museum, North Road Station, Darlington, Co. Durham

| 1829 | L&MR | 0-2-2 | | Rocket (remains of original, much rebuilt, and full-size sectioned reproduction) |

Location: Science Museum, South Kensington, London

| 1829 | L&MR | 0-4-0 | | Sans Pareil |

Location: Science Museum, South Kensington, London

| 1829 | | 0-2-2 | | Novelty (replica incorporating parts of the original) |

Location: Greater Manchester Museum of Science & Industry, Liverpool Road Station, Lower Byron Street Entrance, Manchester

| 1837 | GWR | 2-2-2 (broad gauge) | | North Star (replica) |

Location: Great Western Railway Museum, Swindon, Wiltshire

| 1845 | S&D | 0-6-0 | 25 | Derwent |

Location: Darlington Railway Museum, North Road Station, Darlington, Co. Durham

| *1857 | Wantage Tramway | 0-4-0WT | 5 | Shannon |

Location: Great Western Society Ltd, Didcot Railway Centre, Didcot, Oxfordshire

| 1865 | LNWR | 0-4-0ST (narrow gauge) | | Pet |

Location: Narrow Gauge Railway Museum, Tywyn, Gwynedd

| 1865 | LNWR | 0-4-0ST | 1439 | |

Location: Ironbridge Gorge Museum, Ironbridge, Telford, Shropshire

| 1868 | SDR | 0-4-0T (broad gauge) | 151 | Tiny |

Location: Dart Valley Railway, Buckfastleigh Station, Devon

| 1874 | LSWR | 2-4-0WT | 298 | |

Location: Dart Valley Railway, Buckfastleigh Station, Devon

| 1874 | Hebburn Works | 0-4-0ST | 2 | Bauxite |

Location: Science Museum, South Kensington, London

| 1885 | NER | 2-4-0 | 1463 | |

Location: Darlington Railway Museum, North Road Station, Darlington, Co. Durham

| 1886 | MBR&O | 0-4-0 | 84 | (Tram engine) |

Location: In store (dismantled)

| 1893 | S&MR | 0-4-2WT | | Gazelle |

Location: Museum of Army Transport, Beverley, East Yorkshire

| 1894 | GER | 2-4-0 | 490 | |

Location: Bressingham Steam Museum & Gardens, Bressingham Hall, Diss, Norfolk

| 1897 | GWR | 0-6-0 | 2516 | |

Location: Great Western Railway Museum, Swindon, Wiltshire

| 1897 | TVR | 0-6-2T | 28 | |

Location: Caerphilly Railway Society Ltd, Harold Wilson Industrial Estate, Van Road, Caerphilly, Mid-Glamorgan

| *1899 | LSWR | 4-4-0 | BR 30120 | |

Location: Mid-Hants Railway, Alresford Station, Alresford, Hampshire

| *1903 | GWR | 4-4-0 | 3440 (3717) | City of Truro |

Location: Great Western Railway Museum, Swindon, Wiltshire

| 1907 | GWR | 4-6-0 | 4003 | Lode Star |

Location: Great Western Railway Museum, Swindon, Wiltshire

| *1909 | LTSR | 4-4-2T | 80 | Thundersley |

Location: Bressingham Steam Museum & Gardens, Bressingham Hall, Diss, Norfolk

| 1911 | GCR | 2-8-0 | 102 | |

Location: Dinting Railway Centre, Dinting Lane, Glossop, Derbyshire

| *1911 | Nord (France) | 4-6-0 | 3.628 | |

Location: Nene Valley Railway, Wansford Station, Stibbington, Nr Peterborough, Cambridgeshire

| *1919 | NER | 0-8-0 | 901 | |

Location: North Yorkshire Moors Railway, Pickering Station, Pickering, North Yorkshire

| *1920 | GCR | 4-4-0 | 506 | Butler Henderson |

Location: Great Central Railway, Loughborough Central Station, Great Central Road, Loughborough, Leicestershire

| 1922 | NSR | 0-6-2T | 2 | |

Location: Chatterly Whitfield Mining Museum, Nr Stoke-on-Trent

| 1923 | GWR | 4-6-0 | 4073 | Caerphilly Castle |

Location: Science Museum, South Kensington, London

| *1924 | LMS | 0-6-0 | 4027 | |

Location: Midland Railway Centre, Butterley Station, Nr Ripley, Derbyshire

| *1925 | SR | 4-6-0 | 777 | Sir Lamiel |

Location: Humberside Locomotive Preservation Group, BR Dairycoates Depot, Brighton Street, Hessle Road, Hull, Humberside (no public admittance)

| *1927 | GWR | 4-6-0 | 6000 | King George V |

Location: Bulmer Railway Centre, HP Bulmer Ltd, Whitecross Road, Hereford

| *1935 | LMS | 4-6-0 | 5000 | |

Location: Severn Valley Railway, The Railway Station, Bewdley, Worcestershire

| *1942 | SR | 0-6-0 | BR 33001 | |

Location: Bluebell Railway, Sheffield Park Station, Uckfield, West Sussex

| 1947 | GWR | 0-6-0PT | 9400 | |

Location: Great Western Railway Museum, Swindon, Wiltshire

| *1951 | BR | 4-6-2 | 70013 | Oliver Cromwell |

Location: Bressingham Steam Museum & Gardens, Bressingham Hall, Diss, Norfolk

Locomotives – Electric

| 1890 | C&SL | Bo (third rail) | No 1 | |

Location: Science Museum, South Kensington, London

Locomotives – Diesel

| 1955 | English Co-Co de | | Deltic Prototype |
| | Electric | | |

Location: Science Museum, South Kensington, London

| 1963 | BR | Co-Co dh | D1023 *Western Fusilier* |

Location: Torbay Steam Railway, Paignton Queens Park Station, Paignton, Devon

Rolling Stock – Powered Units

Electric

Date built	Company	Type	Number
1904	NER	Motor parcels van	3267

Location: Tyne & Wear County Council Museums, Museum Storage, Middle Engine Lane, Wallsend, North Tyneside (no public access except advertised Open Days)

| 1927 | LPTB | Driving motor car | 3327 |

Location: Science Museum, South Kensington, London

| *1937 | SR | 2-BIL Unit | 2090 |

Location: Southern Region Depot, BR Brighton (no public access)

| *1941 | LMS | Motor brake second | 28361 |
| | | Driving trailer composite | 29896 |

Location: Southport Locomotive & Transport Museum, Steamport Southport Ltd, Derby Road, Southport, Merseyside

Rolling Stock – Departmental

Date built	Company	Type	Number
1907	LNWR	Match truck	284235

Location: Steamtown Railway Museum, Warton Road, Carnforth, Lancashire

| 1908 | LNWR | Steam breakdown crane | 2987 |

Location: Steamtown Railway Museum, Warton Road, Carnforth, Lancashire

Rolling Stock – Passenger

Date	Company	Type	Number/Name
1846	S&DR	First and second composite	31

Location: Darlington Railway Museum, North Road Station, Darlington, Co. Durham

| 1850 | S&DR | Third | 179 |

Location: Timothy Hackworth Museum, Sedgefield District Council, Soho Street, Shildon, Co. Durham

| 1887 | GWR | Six-wheel tri-composite (in store) | 820 |

Location: Bristol Industrial Museum, Princes Wharf, Bristol, Avon

| 1925 | GWR | Third-class dining cars | 9653 & 9654 |

Location: Severn Valley Railway, The Railway Station, Bewdley, Worcestershire (one due to return to York in 1988)

| c.1926-7 | Nord (France) | Second corridor | 7122 |

Location: Nene Valley Railway, Wansford Station, Stibbington, Nr Peterborough, Cambridgeshire

| 1930 | GWR | Composite dining car | 9605 |

Location: In store (dismantled)

| 1930 | L&MR (Reproductions) | First Third | *Experience* |

Location: City of Liverpool Museum, Merseyside County Museum, Land Transport Gallery, William Brown Street, Liverpool

| 1934 | GWR | Buffet car | 9631 |

Location: Severn Valley Railway, The Railway Station, Bewdley, Worcestershire

| 1937 | SR | Buffet car | S12529S |

Location: Nene Valley Railway, Wansford Station, Stibbington, Nr Peterborough, Cambridgeshire

| 1939 | SR | Travelling Post Office | 4920 |

Location: Nene Valley Railway, Wansford Station, Stibbington, Nr Peterborough, Cambridgeshire

| 1941 | LMS | Royal Saloon | 798 |

Location: Glasgow Museums and Art Galleries, Kelvinhall, Glasgow

| 1947 | SR | Third open | 1456 |

Location: Bluebell Railway, Sheffield Park Station, Uckfield, West Sussex

| 1949 | BR | Travelling Post Office | M30272M |

Location: Birmingham Railway Museum, Warwick Road, Tyseley, Birmingham

Rolling Stock – Freight & Non-Passenger Carrying

Date built	Company	Type	Number
1917	GWR	Machine truck (Hydra D)	42193

Location: Great Western Railway Society Ltd, Didcot Railway Centre, Didcot, Oxfordshire

| 1922 | LBSCR | Cattle truck | 7116 |

Location: Isle of Wight Steam Railway, Haven Street Station, Nr Ryde, IoW

| 1947 | GWR | Motor Car Van (Mogo) | 65814 |

Location: Bristol Industrial Museum, Princes Wharf, Bristol, Avon

Appendix III – Museum Services

Opening Hours
Weekdays 1000 to 1800; Sundays 1100 to 1800
Closed all day: New Year's Day, Christmas Eve, Christmas Day, Boxing Day. For other Christmas/New Year arrangements please watch press for details.

Admission
An admission charge is levied; for details please contact the Museum.

Animals
No animals except guide dogs are allowed on the Museum premises.

Invalid Chairs
Facilities for invalid chairs are available but notice of arrival would be appreciated.

Museum Shop
The Museum Shop is open daily and sells guides, souvenirs, records, postcards and books. Non-fragile items may be purchased by post.

Catering
The restaurant is open daily from museum opening time until 1730.

Car Parking
The Museum car park is open from one hour before opening time until 1800. A charge is made. Parking for coaches must be reserved in advance by writing to the Museum.

Research Facilities
Library facilities, which include access to the photographic archive, are available in a small Reading Room by appointment and on production of a valid Reader's Ticket. Tickets may be obtained by written or telephoned application and include a brief guide to the library holdings, conditions of use and opening times. The Reading Room is available Tuesday to Friday only and admission is free.

Engineering drawings, paintings, engravings and railway posters are not held in the library. Enquiries concerning these items and possible arrangements to view them should be made in writing to the Curator of Pictorial and Related Collections.

Access to the small object collections held in reserve is only permitted at the discretion and convenience of the officers in charge of this material, subject to prior written agreement.

Education Facilities
These facilities take various forms and are fully explained in our 'Education Facilities' leaflet which can be obtained on application in writing or by telephone to the Educational Bookings Section. Our official booking form must be used and preferably at least three weeks' notice given where staff assistance is required. The service is free except for coach parking (single-decked only) which must be booked and paid for in advance.

Photography and Detailed Access to Exhibits
Photography is freely permitted but with hand-held equipment only and on the clear understanding that the results are not published without reference to the Museum. Use of stands with equipment may be permitted during the quieter times. However, at busy times, these facilities may be withdrawn should such equipment impede free visitor circulation. Any form of access to exhibits which cannot be obtained from the normal public areas requires a member of staff in attendance and in these circumstances a charge is made to cover the cost of staff time. Applications should be made in writing to the Museum Manager.

Functions/Receptions
The Museum is available for hire outside normal opening hours for private parties, social functions and receptions. Catering facilities can be provided in the form of buffet meals, formal dinners or snacks. Further details and quotations can be obtained from the Museum Manager.

Postal Address
National Railway Museum, Leeman Road, York YO2 4XJ.

Index

Note: Entries in **bold** type refer to captions